The Name on the List | Orly Krauss-Winer

Producer & International Distributor
eBookPro Publishing
www.ebook-pro.com

The Name on the List
Orly Krauss-Winer

Copyright © 2020 Orly Krauss Wiener

All rights reserved; No parts of this book may be reproduced or transmitted in any form or by any means, electronic or mechanical, including photocopying, recording, taping, or by any information retrieval system, without the permission, in writing, of the author.
Translation: Helene Hart

Contact: Orlykv59@gmail.com
ISBN

THE NAME ON THE LIST

ORLY KRAUSS-WINER

CHAPTER 1

They say that a person can sense when fate is knocking at their door. My father was sure he'd hear the heavy opening notes of Beethoven's Fifth Symphony. But on that bright winter morning on which darkness struck my family, he didn't hear a thing, other than the cheerful chirping of birds.

My younger sister Noa was a twenty-year-old soldier. She was the prettiest and most spoiled one in our family. Dad, who was in charge of driving her to her army base, was in the kitchen making coffee for them both and preparing himself mentally for the exhausting project of waking her up. All of a sudden, he was alarmed by her cries of distress, "I can't see! I can't see anything!" At first, he thought she was trying to wiggle out of going to the army and to stay at home, but she sounded terrified. He hurried to her room to find her lying on the bed, clutching her head and screaming hysterically. Her eyes were staring unfocused at the ceiling and she was shaking all over. He picked her up, rushed to the car, and drove to the nearest emergency room.

After extensive tests, we were given the bad news. The CT had shown a big lump in the neural area of the brain responsible for vision. It looked like a tumor to them.

And so, on a perfectly ordinary day in the month of March, our family fell apart. The doctors didn't want to operate on her. They were worried about complications. They said that there was only one doctor, in the United States, by the name of Professor Salzman, who could perform the operation successfully. But, they added, they were concerned that such a long flight would make her condition deteriorate, so we should ask the professor to come here. When we asked if he would agree to that, they told us to try to contact him directly. We contacted him. His assistant instructed us to send accurate medical reports. We sent them. For two nerve-racking days, we paced around the computer and fax like tigers in a cage. On the night of the second day, the professor himself called. Dad, who answered him, couldn't understand a word. He'd gone blank in all four languages he was fluent in, other than Hungarian. My mother grabbed the phone from him but immediately burst into tears and handed it to me. The professor sounded really kind and patient. He didn't usually leave the country to operate on patients, he said, but in this case, he would make a gesture of goodwill because our story had touched him. This gesture, however, would cost the symbolic sum of a quarter of a million dollars. I stammered my thanks, and after promising him we'd raise the money as fast as possible, I hung up, my hands trembling. Then I took Vered aside, and trying to control my voice, I asked, "Where on earth will we get two hundred and fifty thousand dollars?"

"We'll mortgage our parents' apartment," my older sister answered with the rationality of a computer programmer, and I hugged her enthusiastically. I could always count on her to be calm. She was the shock absorber and symbol of stability in my turbulent family, the only one of us three who was both happily married and had a normal job. The question of how we'd pay back the money didn't even occur to me. Clearly, we first had to save Noa.

But things soon became complicated. When we suggested to our parents that they mortgage the apartment, Mom remembered that they'd already mortgaged it for the big renovation they did last summer. And although she tried to persuade the bank's deputy manager, who she saw as her personal friend, her face had dropped by the time she put the phone down. "She can't do anything," she muttered and burst out crying. "Good God, who the heck needed that damn renovation?"

Dad, who had constantly threatened to leave home during the renovation, put his arms around her and said, "Enough, Yael…really. How could we have known this would happen? And what about our savings?"

"Savings?" Mom stared at him with glazed eyes and reached for the phone again, but just then, it rang. Alarmed, she picked it up. After a second, she handed me the phone with a confused look. "It's from abroad," she mumbled awkwardly. I answered. Professor Salzman's secretary was on the line. She explained that he was already speaking with the doctors in Israel and that we should set a date for surgery if that was okay with us. I couldn't tell her that we still had no idea how we'd raise the money, so I replied that it was absolutely fine and she booked the surgery for April 7th, three weeks later.

By the time I hung up, I was shaking from the pressure. Three weeks didn't seem long enough to get our hands on that kind of money. "There's no choice," I said to the desperate faces of my family, "we'll have to start raising funds from the entire family, all our friends, and anyone else you can think of."

"What about our savings, Yael?" Dad repeated nervously. He clearly didn't want to ask relatives and friends for donations. It was strange, but he of all people, who was loved by so many, cringed whenever he had to ask them for anything.

"Savings, yes," Mom quickly called her friend at the bank again. After a short conversation, she hung up and said, "We have about thirty thousand dollars, but if we withdraw the money now, we'll only get twenty-two."

"What are we going to do?" Dad buried his face in his hands.

"We'll call everyone," Vered answered, and went to the kitchen to get the family phone book. "Family, friends, close and distant, we mustn't skip over anyone, and hand over any particularly tough conversations to me."

We spent the night making marathon calls to every relative and friend. They were all shocked and shaken to hear what had happened to Noa, but none of them had great news when it came to the money we needed. One of my mother's uncles, a doctor by profession, offered to put us in touch with another neurologist he knew, who would certainly agree to perform the surgery for less. Another relative told us that his old paratrooper buddies had a special fund for such cases, and he'd try to solicit their help for our cause. One of the aunts, a religious woman, suggested we contact her rabbi, who she claimed could do wonders in identifying medical issues and in finding the right doctor to treat them. "Everyone calls him the CT. He's even better than that other rabbi they call the X-Ray," she told me enthusiastically, and I had to hold myself back from both laughing and crying. By the dim break of dawn, we were exhausted and desperate. If we'd received a thousand dollars for every suggestion we were given, we could have had Noa operated on twice. But unfortunately, that's not what happened. In our entire warm, noisy and sentimental family, there was no one willing to put their money where their mouth was.

CHAPTER 2

The next day, I decided to take action and go to the bank, to that remote, forgotten branch in the neighborhood I grew up in, where Mr. Klein was still the manager. Aaron Klein was a clerk at that bank back when I was a kid. He was a friend of my parents, and years ago, he suggested that my father and he buy a plot of land together on the main street of the town, a plot that was surely would have been worth millions today and that could have solved our problems in a flash. But back then, in a moment of childish recklessness that I found endearing, Dad decided to buy a motorbike instead of half a plot. A BSA motorbike with a sidecar. It took my mother years to forgive him, but Aaron Klein never could. They stopped being friends after that and settled for cool greetings until we left town and they lost contact altogether. But a few months ago, I bumped into him on a flight to Prague. Mr. Klein seemed genuinely happy to see me, and when he asked after my parents, he truly seemed to remember Dad fondly. Maybe he'd also reached the conclusion, as we all had, that his abundant charm, wonderful sense of humor, and unique view on the world far outweighed his practical shortcomings. It probably helped that Mr. Klein had spent most of his adult life in the company of people from the bank, who naturally were well versed in the world of finances but didn't know a thing about how life should be lived. Anyway, by the end of the flight, I was sure that Klein missed my father. He asked for my parents' phone number and I assured him that they'd be happy to include him in their Saturday card nights. Although Klein didn't call Dad, I clung to the memory of that encounter as if to a lifeline, hoping that at least for memory's sake he'd agree to give them a second mortgage on the apartment. I didn't tell anyone in the family about my plan, so they wouldn't try to dissuade me. In any case, no one was paying attention to me because they were going to the hospital to pick up Noiki, as we called her, to bring her home. The little one sensed, I guess thanks to the unique instinct she'd developed since losing her eyesight, that she could no longer trust the family to keep her morale up. Dad, who was in charge of that area, couldn't even complete a sentence, certainly not as sardonic and sharp as they usually were. Every time he opened his mouth, his eyes clouded over with a veil of tears, and then he'd immediately stop speaking, to prevent himself from crying.

"Well, I guess you'll finally be buying me a dog," Noiki said as soon as she walked through the door and felt her way along the wall to the sofa. Dad and Vered burst into tears, and only Mom restrained herself and said in a matter-of-fact tone, "You don't need a dog, you'll have surgery in a few days and you'll be fine." As she spoke, she made a face at Dad and Vered that left no room for doubt as to what she thought of their outburst. On the evening we heard the terrible news, she had already made it clear to us all that we were only allowed to cry when Noa wasn't around, and when she was, we were to be optimistic and confident that everything would work out very quickly, and that would be that.

Vered and Dad tried to suppress their tears, while I, who couldn't even handle easier situations, muttered something about errands to run and rushed out of the apartment.

Outside, a merciful winter sun was shining on the quiet, suburban street, the kind of sun that Noiki may never again see. I started the car and drove straight to the bank managed by Mr. Klein.

When I walked in, I saw him sitting behind a glass partition talking wearily on the phone. When he noticed me, his eyes lit up and he waved me over.

"How are you?" he asked warmly, and added in an apologetic tone, "Somehow, I never did get around to calling your Dad, you can see how busy I am here…"

I glanced around to see what he meant. In fact, the small branch looked pretty quiet. "I can see, I can see," I answered politely, "with all the new Bank of Israel regulations, you must be drowning in work."

"Yes," he muttered gloomily, wiping imaginary beads of sweat from his balding forehead. It was, in fact, freezing in there.

"May I offer you a drink?"

"No, thanks." I wanted to get this fateful conversation over as quickly as possible and preferably leave with a positive answer. "I'm here about a somewhat…urgent matter."

"I'm listening," Mr. Klein replied, focusing his gaze on me. I tried to sound businesslike as I told him about the tragedy that had shaken us, but I felt my throat slowly choking and small, stubborn tears squeezing from my eyes as I explained what I wanted.

"I see," Klein said eventually with a soft, compassionate look in his eyes, "so you're asking me to give you a mortgage on a property that's already mortgaged?"

"Just for a few months," I quickly wiped the tears away, trying to appear confident. "It would only be for a few months, maybe even less…until we can raise the money within the family. It's just that Noa…isn't doing too well. We can't take a chance and wait until then."

"Darya, Darya," he sighed, wiping his forehead again, which this time did look surprisingly shiny, "with all the goodwill in the world, I simply can't do it. After all, it's not my money, it's the bank's. I really would love to help; you know that your family is…was like my family once…"

"Then please, help us!" All my self-control evaporated and I forgot that I wanted to make a serious impression. The tears were choking me and I burst into sobs. I covered my face with my hands so I wouldn't draw the attention of the clerks. "This is our last hope," I cried, we have nothing other than the apartment."

"Darya," I heard his voice dropping to almost a whisper as gentle, dry hands gripped mine and lowered them from my face. "Listen, there's no need to cry. Maybe there is still something to be done. Calm down…relax. I can't talk to you like this."

The hope that his words sparked in me stopped my tears from flowing. Still choked up, I looked at him expectantly and wiped my eyes with the tissue he'd handed to me.

"Listen, kiddo," Klein looked around, as if wanting to share a secret with me, which gave me hope that he was going to say that he'd do it, despite the bank's regulations. But he said something completely different, which shocked me even more.

"Your family's wealthy, Darya," Klein continued, "somewhere in the world there are valuable assets that belong to you."

"What? Where?!" my body contracted with surprise, and maybe also from the suspicion that Mr. Klein was trying to get rid of me with some fabricated story.

"That I don't know," he answered, his eyes reflecting true sorrow, persuading me that he wasn't lying, "I heard about it by chance."

"From who?"

"From your grandparents," Klein shifted uncomfortably in his chair. "I was at your parents' once, playing cards, and I half-heard an argument between your grandparents, who were in the other room…"

"What did they say?" I asked. It was all becoming clear: Mr. Klein must have heard someone mention money and immediately pricked up his ears. That's why he felt uneasy, because he didn't feel comfortable admitting that he'd eavesdropped.

"They'd just arrived in Israel then, and your grandfather was upset that they couldn't afford to buy an apartment," Mr. Klein proved my suspicions right. "Your grandmother reminded him that they'd always rented in Hungary, but he insisted that it would be different in Israel and that everyone here was buying apartments, and for once in his life, he wanted to have a home of his own. And then your grandmother told him in no uncertain terms that he was not to even dare suggest she ask someone for the property back."

"Someone?! Who was it?" I urged him.

"Well, that's the thing, Daryakum, I didn't quite hear who they were talking about, your grandmother whispered his name. She seemed to found it hard to even mention him, you see?"

"Yes," I said, disappointed, and then I thought, "but hold on, didn't they continue the discussion?"

"They went on a little longer, but there was nothing in what they said that could help you now. Your grandfather told her she was terribly stubborn, and that at a certain age you can forgive, and that if he was prepared to forgive that someone, then she certainly should. But your grandmother shushed him by saying she would never forgive him, even after she died, and he had no right to interfere in the matter and that don't he dare even think of writing to him behind her back, because in the end she'd find out and she'd never forgive him either. Your grandfather tried to say that theoretically, part of it belonged to him too, but your grandmother kept insisting that she would never forgive him, and that's how it ended."

"And no one heard who they were talking about?"

"I don't think so," he answered, his eyes blatantly embarrassed. "Your father was very focused on the card game, and your mother didn't really understand Hungarian."

CHAPTER 3

My legs were shaking when I left the bank. Outside, the warm sun was still shining, and it helped my mental state a little. Instead of going back to my parents', I decided to go to my apartment in Tel Aviv. The strange story I'd heard from Mr. Klein required my turbulent mind to think clearly. I needed quiet in order to come up with a quick and effective plan. Somewhere in the world, my family had valuable property, his words floated around in my head. Where could it be, damn it, and why hadn't I ever heard about it? Not even a hint. Our family never seemed secretive to me. On the contrary. In loud and somewhat amused voices, they would discuss every detail of every conflict, old feuds, eternal loves, alliances, and infidelities, at least that's what the Hungarian side would do. Without a touch of embarrassment, they even discussed the future of my long romance with Oren, which had been going on for twelve years and didn't seem to be advancing as expected.

The brazen, Hungarian side said I would leave him in the end because I would get bored. The conservative Bukharan side claimed that he would leave me, because why should he marry a woman who agreed to live with him without a proper, Jewish wedding? They even made bets on the matter. Only my dad, who really liked Oren, bet on the possibility that we'd stay together and get married, but he refused to commit to when that would happen.uHuHun

I arrived home. The sound of running water coming from the bathroom indicated that Oren was back from a flight. So did the path of his uniform trailing through the living room. On any other day, it would have infuriated me and I would have greeted him with complaints when he came out of the bathroom. But today was different, completely different, and I picked up his clothes without even realizing it.

"What's up?" he said, bringing me back to the present as he emerged from the shower, tanned and tall and smelling wonderfully of soap. I stood facing him, mute, loosely gripping the pile of clothes. I didn't know what to say. Tips on how to tell your partner that your little sister has a fatal disease never appeared in the women's magazines I read on flights, nor in any other guide. The truth was, I was afraid of his reaction, which is why I didn't call the hotel he was staying at in Brussels to tell him what had happened. He had a way of reacting coolly to anything I saw as a national disaster.

"I meant to throw those in the wash after my bath," he said guiltily and pointed at the clothes I was holding. "Really, believe me, I didn't know you'd be home so early. Anyway, where were you?"

"Oren, we need to talk," I said.

He stared at me, puzzled. "What's the problem? It's just a few clothes, I'm just about to put them in the machine," he took his uniform from me and rushed with them to the laundry corner. Within seconds I heard the washing machine going. I didn't know whether to laugh or cry. In fact, I wanted to do both. I dived onto the sofa and stared at him when he returned. "You see," he said with his apologetic smile, the one he used to get me to forgive him for everything, "you don't have to make a fuss about everything. Can I make you something to eat? I brought escargot."

"Escargot. Of all things, that strange word is what released my tears again. Even as a kid, Noiki loved those big snails, which all her friends, boys and girls alike, were afraid to touch. She was thirteen when Oren became a pilot and she devoured those big "slimies" as she called them, when Oren brought her some from Paris. She was the first in the family willing to taste them, she and Grandpa Yoshka, who was always prepared to try new foods, especially if they looked like they would never appear on any observant Jewish menu.

"What happened?!" Oren was horrified and hurried over to me, wrapping his arms around me. The water dripping from his black hair blended with my tears.

"Noiki...she loves escargot...you know," I mumbled between gasps, "and now...she's sick."

"Sick? What's wrong with her? Indigestion? From the escargot?"

"No, Oren, she's really sick," I tried to steady my voice and stop crying. I knew I didn't have all the time in the world to waste on discussing food and having misunderstandings. Held in his arms, which for the first time since we'd been together couldn't make me feel safe, I told him the story.

Oren looked shocked by the time I finished, but not for long. "What are you going to do now?" he asked softly and stroked my hair. "Are you going to go on a detective adventure in search of your family's lost treasure?"

"Oren, it's not funny," I protested. It was precisely the reaction I'd feared.

"I'm not joking," he looked at me pensively and pulled slightly away, leaning his head on the back of the sofa. "We have to be practical now, and to me, your story sounds a little crazy. Shouldn't we first withdraw our savings from the bank?"

"Your savings," I quickly corrected him, studying his face with affection. How can anyone be angry at such a generous person? I thought and quickly continued, "I thought you were saving for an apartment."

"But this is an emergency," he spoke, as if to himself, "and we can also sell the car and motorbike, and then, together we'll have...let's see..."

I let him figure out the numbers while I focused on trying to control myself so I wouldn't burst out crying again. He wanted to sell the bike, his pride and joy. And I remembered, with regret, how I raged at him when he bought it, with his own savings.

"We can even get to about thirty thousand dollars," Oren muttered, "and then...how much more did you say we'll need?"

"Two hundred thousand dollars," I muttered despondently, after deducting my parents' savings too. "It's a lot, Oren, the amount we'd still need. No, I have to get my hands on that money...on the assets that Klein mentioned. We have to, we don't have much time!"

"I could ask my parents for a loan," Oren continued, trying to curtail the urge to act that had taken over me.

"Your parents aren't millionaires," I muttered, getting up from the sofa, "they'd probably have to mortgage their home themselves…and I won't allow it. No, it's not that I just want to go on some detective adventure, believe me. But it's vital we find that money." While I was speaking, I looked for the phone numbers of my relatives from the Hungarian side. I'd written them years ago, when Grandpa Yoshka died and I was put in charge of messaging all our relatives abroad.

"Here, I found them," I declared, "there's Dolly in Australia and Shandor Bachi in Florida, they're the only two still alive."

"Darya, you're crazy," Oren interrupted me with a sigh. "What will you achieve by talking to all the old folk? By the time they even remember who you are, they'll have died from old age. It's better to talk to my parents, see what they can contribute, maybe they have savings."

"Even if they do, I'm sure it's no more than my parents have," I said and started to dial Shandor Bachi's number. The family had a thousand and one stories about him. He'd never done a regular day's work in his life, and yet he lived like an English lord in an impressive and fancy villa in Florida.

Angela, his pretty, young live-in carer answered and told me he was resting. When I told her it was urgent, she said she'd pass on the message when he woke up. I tried insisting that she wake him up right then, but she refused, claiming he was an old, unhealthy man and the doctors had ordered him to sleep more. When I insisted, claiming that it was a matter of life and death, she promised he'd get back to me when he woke up.

I was so irritated by the end of the call, that I slammed the phone down. Ever since I'd found out about Angela's existence after visiting Shandor Bachi for the first time, we started to suspect that she was also his lover and was plotting to get her hands on his money. But no one, at least on the Hungarian side of the family, thought that there was anything wrong with that.

"If she's suffered my uncle for so many years without trying to poison him, then she deserves to benefit too," Dad said with a wink a few years ago and ended the argument he was having about it with my mother. She just rolled her eyes and snapped something about his Hungarian logic that would be the death of her.

To pass the time somehow until Shandor Bachi got back to me, I called Dad's cousin Dolly, but no one answered. I left a message to get back to me and tried to relax and hope for the best. The day crept endlessly on and Shandor Bachi didn't call back. Nor did Angela.

In the end, I broke and called him again. Angela, of course, answered immediately. She repeated that Shandor was resting, despite the fact that it was already two in the afternoon there.

"He had tests done today," she explained and her words rolled down the phone line like serrated gravel.

From what I knew of Shandor Bachi from the last two times I'd visited him, at Grandpa Yoshka's request, he didn't seem to be one to get tired from a few tests. Although he was old, almost a hundred by my reckoning, he was like Grandpa Yoshka, who didn't seem impressed with his chronological age.

"I see," I said as calmly as I could, trying to keep the sarcasm from seeping into my voice. Then I remembered that on my two previous visits to him, Angela had been of no help. The first time, she was simply surprised that someone she didn't know was calling and repeated my name loudly. Shandor, who naturally was by her side, heard the name Schwartz and quickly answered me. And the second time, she wasn't home and he answered the phone. After a quick analysis of the situation, I realized that if I wanted to see Shandor Bachi, I'd have to take a somewhat less acceptable path.

"Please give him my warm regards, and say that I hope he feels better," I ended the conversation. I didn't want her to suspect my next move, which I was already planning, down to the finest detail.

CHAPTER 4

My Grandpa Yoshka was the youngest of ten brothers. He and Shandor Bachi were the only ones to survive the Second World War. After the war, Shandor emigrated to the United States, where he lived an affluent life, how, no one knew. He didn't, however, seem to find happiness, as he remained on his own. He never married or had any children. Once, before I was even born, he arrived in Israel and said he wanted to adopt our family—to bring Grandma and Grandpa, Mom, Dad, and Vered to live near him in Florida. Mom was actually all for it, but Grandpa informed anyone who would listen that after seeing the lines to the gas chambers, he would never willingly leave the only country where a Jew could live with his head held high and without fear. My father was quick to agree with him, and so the offer was rejected.

Mom told me that she tried to convince Dad to at least go over to Florida to have a look, hoping that a closer glimpse of the good life would weaken his resolve, but Shandor Bachi was adamantly opposed. "If you come, it's to stay," he said stubbornly, proving he was a true Schwartz. And when Grandpa and Dad remained firm in their refusal, he returned to the United States and never invited any of us over again, even to visit. Only I had the guts, at Grandpa's insistence, to call him when I was in Florida and invite myself over. He didn't refuse and was even nice to me, both on the phone and even more so when we met. After that, I allowed myself to repeat the trick on the few occasions I was in Florida for work.

Today, when I remembered that old story, I thought a lot about why Shandor had wanted to take them under his wing. After all, he would have had to sponsor five people and sign a pledge to support and be responsible for them all until my parents could find work. Could he perhaps have felt bad because he'd kept the family treasure for himself, when apparently it belonged to us all?

I wonder how our lives would have turned out if Dad hadn't turned down that offer, I thought to myself and looked at Oren, who in his usual, practical way had begun to make arrangements for me to go immediately to the States to see Shandor in person. When I thought about the fact that I may never have met Oren, I felt a twinge of pain, which interrupted my train of thought.

***

Oren and I met in the Air Force. We were both cadets in the aviation course. My childhood dream was to be a pilot, and it all began in kindergarten, when I discovered that the huge, bright birds flying through the sky had drivers. When my father realized that it was an awesome way to make me work hard at the sciences, he encouraged my dream, even though Mom moaned that he was "ruining the child and making her live in an illusion that would one day blow up in her face." Mom was a literature teacher and was in the habit of using descriptive expressions, at least when she knew that she had a wider audience than just Dad.

"Why put ideas in her head?" I heard her say to him furiously one day, when I came home early from a model aircraft class that had been canceled, "You know that there are no women pilots in the Air Force! Do you think they'll open a special course for women, just for Peter Schwartz's daughter?!"

"Why not?" I heard Dad answer her, amused. "One word to Yigal and you'll see, they'll open an accelerated course for girls."

Yigal was Yigal Alon, the immortal commander of the Palmach. My father had been a fervent admirer of his ever since he'd arrived in Israel in 1949. Dad never forgave himself for arriving a year too late to join the Palmach in their fight against the British and for missing all the action that came with founding a new state. Dad being Dad, he simply concocted an imaginary life story that included being a brave member of the Palmach and friends with Yigal Alon himself. Since he had an incredible ability to laugh at himself, he also made fun of his imaginings. That's how he inadvertently taught the people around him an interesting way to deal with disappointment and dreams that had no chance of coming true— simply laugh at them.

When I reached conscription age, Yigal Alon was already among the dead, but so was the military law preventing women from being accepted to the Air Force's pilot school.

The truth was, by then my dream of being an Air Force pilot was also in the throes of death, especially after I realized that the process involved a grueling two-year course and an extra five years of military service. But Dad, who noticed my misgivings, told me that I had to at least try, if only so as not to disappoint Yigal, who'd gone to such lengths for me.

I got into pilot school, with a perfect score in my math and physics school finals and the concerned and piercing gaze of a father I adored and didn't want to disappoint. Obviously, that was not enough. I landed up with two stress fractures from the final, grueling cross-country march, wearing full army gear and carrying stretchers. The squadron's doctor told me unequivocally that if I didn't let my poor legs rest for at least a few months, the fractures would never heal. That was enough. Mom made it clear to Dad that she wouldn't allow his and Yigal's dream to cripple her child, and he didn't even try to argue. I could see in his eyes that his concern for my health overcame any other emotion.

So I said goodbye to my dream of flying, just like Dad in his time had set his Palmach dream aside. And I told anyone who wanted to know that the chief of staff decided I was too talented to go to waste in the cockpit, and that was why they made me a researcher for the Air Force's history department, which is where I landed up after I recovered.

I had only one memento from that year. Oren. On the second day of the course, he came up to me and my roommate and with true compassion, told us that although he thought the course was too hard for girls, we could count on him to help us through it. "It's because I'm a feminist," he continued, not noticing that we already hated him, "and I believe that girls can succeed in any field, with a little help and encouragement from the boys."

During the months of the course, I grew to like him and to understand that morons like him could be very sweet. But it was only after I was sent flying from the course and landed in the history department that we became a couple. Oren developed tremendously during that year. He was transformed from an overly tall and skinny kid who had no idea what to do with his hands into a hot, young man with loads of confidence. He also came with a warm and sappy Bulgarian family who reminded me of my own. He didn't try to stand in my way when I completed my army service and took a six-month trip to South America. He only said he hoped that when I returned, we'd move in together. And that, of course, is what we did. When I got back, he was waiting for me at the airport with my parents and two sisters, and after all the hugs and kisses, he placed a key in my hand. "Eighteen Yeshayahu Street, apartment three," he whispered in my ear, "and I've been waiting to decorate it with you."

Naturally, when I woke up at noon the next day, I took the bus over to see what the issue was with the decoration. And naturally, I stayed for dinner. I'd missed the pastelikos that his mom used to make for me.

Oren told me that he'd recently been transferred to the Air Force headquarters in Tel Aviv. He didn't say who initiated the transfer and why, even though he was considered one of the squadron's best. But I knew it was for me. Somehow, that act, which had never been discussed, melted me and opened my heart to him again, and to lay warm compresses on the scratches on my heart from the hormone-rich encounters I had during my travels through South America. After our meal of pastelikos and half a bottle of ouzo, I felt like it had always been my home. And we reached the same heights of passion and excitement when we had sex all night long. Oren was a sensitive guy and he knew my body almost as well as he knew my soul. He knew where to touch and precisely when to ease off.

The next day, I again woke up at noon, made myself a cup of strong, black coffee, and after a long time in the bathroom, which helped to drive the cobwebs from my mind, I went to the university to enroll in history.

Before we knew it, we'd slipped into a routine in our shared apartment.

Oren was an amazing partner. He added me to his bank account and told me I could spend money on whatever I wanted because he already had a monthly standing order for his savings account. I, of course, didn't want to live at his expense for even a second. Even as a child, Dad had always warned me about these situations. When I went to the movies with someone, he always gave me money for a ticket, half a serving of falafel, and a drink, even though Mom thought it was a waste.

I quickly found a job as a waiter at one of the restaurants on Yirmiyahu Street, and even though I worked most evenings and Oren stayed home alone, he didn't complain.

Our lives carried on smoothly for three years, until Oren was released from the Air Force and we experienced the first crack in our relationship.

Oren wanted to work as an El Al pilot. I, on the other hand, thought it was a waste of time for him. "You're so smart and talented," I grumbled, "so why don't you have greater ambitions in life than to be an airplane driver?"

"Because I don't," he gave me a puzzled look. "What's wrong with that?"

"I'm damned if I get it," I grumbled on, "people need ambitions, new interests, to expand their horizons a little, don't you think? Is there nothing you like doing apart from flying?"

"Yes, I like being with you," he silenced me in his usual, facetious way. It always sounded true when he said it, which made the situation even more problematic, because with him looking at me, his eyes filled with love, I couldn't go on complaining and sounding like an irritating, unbearable self-righteous pest.

"Okay, okay, go be a pilot, what can I tell you?" I complained in his arms, which were now wrapped around me. "But at least enroll at one the faculties, so you can say that you're studying something."

"Stop being so pretentious," he laughed and kissed me, "you sound like that woman in that sketch, who wanted everyone to know she was an engineer's wife."

I burst out laughing. He knew precisely which strings of my soul to pull, that was certain. We were always watching old Rivka Michaeli and Yossi Banai sketches. They were hilarious in the seventies, and they'd lost none of their punch. Miraculously, Oren could relate to my father's taste in almost everything, especially humor. That was another reason I loved him.

But in the depths of my conflicted soul, he now had a black mark against him, which had only grown bigger over the years. I simply couldn't understand how a person like him could live without food for thought, or at least be interested in more than a routine job and his life alongside the woman he loved.

When I finished my bachelor's degree and started my master's, he talked me into becoming an air attendant. "That way, you can get to all the research institutes abroad and get what you need for your thesis," he said casually, managing again to score points with me. So I went and became an air attendant, even though in my heart I knew I should accept the department's offer to be an undergraduate tutor. As usual, he managed to drag me into making easier choices that didn't require much effort.

When I finished my master's and began working on my thesis, I could no longer bring myself to accept the department head's offer to tutor. My thesis on Why did the Western Media Hide the Magnitude of the Jewish Holocaust in Europe was an excellent excuse. In order to obtain material and interview people, I really did have to run around the globe.

The obvious subject of marriage and children never came up. I thought that it was clear to Oren that it would just happen one day, so there was no need to elaborate on the matter. I also assumed it was the reason he saved such a considerable portion of his salary each month. But one day, when he dragged me down to the street with the enthusiasm of a child to show me the new, state-of-the-art motorbike he'd bought, for more than the annual salary of a production worker from an industrial town, all the informed assumptions I'd made about him became confused in my mind. At that frustrating moment, the seed of calamity was sewn, and it began gnawing at our relaxed relationship. Suddenly I saw a different Oren, one who was frighteningly similar to my father, who had also bought a motorbike once for a sum that he could have bought a quarter-acre plot with. My mother, as I've mentioned, never forgave him for that. As soon as I saw Oren's sparkling motorbike, I finally understood him for the first time in my life.

CHAPTER 5

We arrived in New York in the evening. Oren had arranged a flight with a five-day layover there for both of us, even though he still had his doubts about the plan succeeding.

"Are you sure it's the best thing to do?" he inquired again, when we were already in the hotel room, "In the end, you'll waste four days trying to break into the old man's house against his carer's wishes trying to squeeze a story out of him about some family treasure he may not even know about."

"If you have a better plan to get a hundred thousand dollars, you're free to suggest it," I snapped at him. When he put it that way, he made my idea sound far less wonderful to me than it had before.

"Perhaps we could rob a bank?" He looked out the window at the Citigroup Center towering over our hotel. "They won't judge us harshly when they hear why we did it."

"That's enough, Jean Valjean," I hugged him from behind, "the only illegal activity I'm asking you to do for me is to say I have a fever if they call me up for a flight."

"Too bad," he turned around and hugged me back, "but at least let me come with you and take Angela off your hands. I'll keep her too busy to bother you."

"Oh, you're too kind. A real martyr," I smiled wearily. I used to feel a stab of jealously when Oren talked like that, at least about women like Angela, who was incredibly sexy and had a startling resemblance to Catherine Zeta-Jones. The first time I saw her, I told Oren she was probably wasting Shandor Bachi's money on plastic surgery.

Oren quoted what my father had said about her and added that it was nice of her to make an effort and give the old man something to look at. "Why do you think he's reached such a ripe old age?" he asked, "If all he had to look at was some old witch, he would have died ages ago."

I had no answer for that since Shandor Bachi was already ninety-eight. I hoped with all my heart that he was still lucid and would remember everything I wanted to find out from him.

"You're really going, then?" Oren accompanied me to the door.

"Yes, I have to get there as early as possible, so that I can get to Shandor the moment Angela leaves the house," I explained. I was sure that if she was home, she would keep me away from him, tell me he was resting. If it was up to her, Shandor would probably rest for a long, long time. At least until she knew I'd disappeared into the horizon.

"And if she doesn't go out? What'll you do?" Oren asked.

"She'll go out, she has to. What can she do at home all day?" I said, trying to persuade myself that my plan made sense. Secretly, I wasn't at all sure that Angela would have to leave the house, but I decided there was no other option. I had to have a private conversation with Shandor, and I'd pay whatever price I had to when the time came. I was desperate enough to sleep in the neighbor's yard waiting for Angela to go out.

"When will you be back?" he kissed my forehead, his face glum.

"I don't know. I told you, after I hear the story."

"The story about your family's vanished treasure? Really, Darya, do you really think that your hedonistic, wasteful, gossipy family could not only safeguard the property and money for so long but also hide its very existence?"

"Oren, you really aren't helping," my heart contracted at his pure logic. But I could think of nothing better. It was my last grasp for a weak straw of hope, when all other options had yielded a total of nothing.

"Okay, okay, kishason, I'll be here waiting for you, fingers crossed," he kissed me again and released me from his grip to show me he had his fingers crossed on both hands. The word kishason (young maiden in Hungarian) brought tears to my eyes. Oren had done a perfect imitation of my grandfather's pet name for me and had unknowingly reminded me of what Mr. Klein had said. I hoped it was a sign from above that I was on the right track.

***

I arrived at noon in Boca Raton, where old Shandor Bachi lived. I stood on a corner from where I could watch his house without being seen, and waited, tense and ready. My heart pounded wildly as the hours passed. *What if Angela didn't leave the house today?* I tried to think of an alternative plan. Maybe I'd call and impersonate her bank manager and tell her she had to come in for an urgent meeting. It would have been a great plan if I'd known where she banked. I began to regret that I'd never tried to find out more about her in the past. My mother even thought I should befriend her, so I could sniff out her real intentions. Only now I was beginning to understand that her practical approach had its uses, even though it wasn't amusing and delightful, like Dad's impracticality. From now on, I'll listen to her more, I promised myself, right as I saw Angela slip out the front door and get into the car. Instead of calming down, my heart raced even faster, and I hoped that Angela wouldn't hear it.

I squirmed as she passed by, and when I saw her car disappear around the bend, I got up and edged toward the big, white house.

When I rang the doorbell, I heard Shandor Bachi's voice ask, "Who's there?" in a heavy, Hungarian accent.

"It's me, Darya Schwartz."

"Daryakum!" he sounded very surprised, but my heart overflowed at hearing the "kum" he added to my name. That's how old Hungarians express their affection. Then he slowly opened the door and hugged me. "Daryakum," his voice sang, "it's been so long since I've seen you! Do what do I owe the honor of your surprise visit? Why didn't you call first?"

"I was in New York and I wanted to see how you are," I explained. "I talked to Angela on the phone, and she said you didn't feel well so I was anxious…"

"I didn't feel well?" he mumbled in surprise and sighed, "I don't remember a thing. Angela worries too much."

"I guess," I replied a little cynically, noting to myself that, as I'd suspected, Angela didn't even bother to tell him I'd called, that's how worried she was.

"Come in, come in," Shandor Bachi said invitingly and started walking toward the spacious living room with big French windows overlooking the blue ocean. "Would you like something to drink?"

"No, thanks," I sank into a wide leather armchair. I assumed that Shandor barely knew where the water was kept, he certainly didn't know where the glasses were. Angela had him relying on her for everything.

"How are you?" he sank into a matching armchair, facing me. "Is everything all right at home? Is Dad in good health?"

"Dad's fine, everyone's fine, except for Noiki, she's very sick."

"Noiki's your younger sister, right?"

"Yes, Bachi, I'm sorry to have to give you such terrible news, but it can't be avoided. Noiki's very sick, she suddenly went blind."

"Blind?" he sounded alarmed, "How does a little girl suddenly go blind?"

"That's what we're also asking. The doctors say that it's..." my voice trembled but I immediately regained my control. I had to finish the sad story before Angela returned. "The doctors say that it's a growth, probably benign," I quickly continued as I saw the old man's face drop, "but it's pressing on her optic nerve and...it has to be operated on as soon as possible. There's just one professor who can do a good job, Professor Salzman from Mount Sinai, and he...he wants an enormous amount of money. We don't have much, so yesterday we called everyone, the whole family in fact, and you, too. We spoke to Angela and..." again I choked back the tears. It was becoming very embarrassing. I was unable to string two sentences together without turning on the waterworks, damn it.

"Drágám," I heard Shandor Bachi mutter, his voice choking. I raised my tearful eyes and saw him holding his arms out to me. Without much thought, I got up and knelt before him, resting my head in his hands and wetting his light trousers with my uncontrollable sobs.

"Drágám, drágám..." he continued muttering the word darling in

Hungarian, "I'm so sorry, I…how can I help? How much money do you need?"

"A lot," I mumbled, "but—"

"How much is a lot, kishason? I'll ask Angela to find out tomorrow how much I can withdraw from my pension fund, because, you see, some of it is invested in a long-term savings account and—"

"There may be no need, really, thanks, Bachi." The mention of Angela's name helped me to muster self-control. It was vital I finish my investigation before she returned.

"I'm fine," I continued, and sat cross-legged at his feet, on the carpet, "it's just I try not to cry when I'm with the family, you understand. As it is, they're at wits' end, so it all came bursting out here."

"I see," he nodded and I could tell from his expression that he was trying really hard not to show me how shocked he was at the disrespectful way I had chosen to sit.

"Is it okay that I'm sitting on the floor?" The truth was, that's how I felt the most comfortable.

"It's perfectly fine, feel right at home. You are in a bad mental state, after all."

"Thanks," I said, relieved. He originated from the Austro-Hungarian Empire, where people were ostracized for less than sitting cross-legged on the floor. Dad always had something to say when I dared to chew gum or eat sunflower seeds from the shell, behavior that only cows were permitted in Hungary, and even then, not the cows of the aristocracy.

"Listen, Shandor Bachi," I hurried on, "we may have a way of obtaining the money we need, without anyone having to take out his pension. That's why I came to you. I wanted to ask if you know about any considerable sums of money or property that may belong to the family, somewhere in the world?"

As I spoke, I studied his expression, trying to detect any suspicious reactions that could reveal that the treasure, or what was left of it, was in his possession.

"What are you talking about?" he looked so puzzled that my suspicions almost vanished entirely. I took a deep breath and told him in a few, short sentences what Mr. Klein had told me. By the time I'd finished, the old man's mouth had dropped open, and wide-eyed, he said, "I have no idea, Daryakum, I have no idea what you're talking about."

"I thought that's what you'd say," I sighed, but I was still far from discouraged. "I think it's something we'll have to uncover slowly. We'll need to read between the lines of all the family stories to find out who had a lot of money and property back in Hungary in those days and look for him."

The old man laughed dryly, "Are you telling me that you'll listen now to all the stories about the family? Not that I have any objections, of course, I'd love to tell you, but don't forget that your grandfather and I had another eight brothers."

"And which of them were wealthy?" I attacked immediately, before he'd have time to make up stories.

"Oy, Darya, Daryakum, some of them were wealthy for certain periods, before the war, but I find it hard to believe that anything remains. Don't forget that seven of our brothers were murdered in Auschwitz.

"And Grandpa? Was he also wealthy?"

"Your grandfather? My brother?" The old man smiled suddenly, his eyes seeming to look through me into another, bright, green, and carefree world.

"Your Grandpa Yoshka was rich in many ways," he began with a sigh. "He was my younger brother, and I loved him very much. And not only I did. Everyone found him a delight. In Baja, the small town we were born and grew up in, people said he was as handsome as a Greek god. And he was also very charming. That's why he did so well in his work as a traveling salesman, selling construction products. He had hands of gold and a brilliant mind, and he was an outstanding athlete and a wonderful dancer," the old man smiled as if envisioning Grandpa in his youth, spinning around with a beautiful girl on the dance floor. Fascinated, I leaned my head on the armrest of the armchair behind me and listened. I'd almost forgotten my suspicions. I even forgot that Angela might get back soon. Enthralled, I was carried away by the old man's voice into another, entirely different world. A world in which I naively assumed had only one concern: Which tune, which waltz would they dance to that evening, in the club on the banks of the blue Danube?

CHAPTER 6

Grandpa was the most handsome man in Baja, perhaps in the whole of Hungary, that's what Sandor Bachi said. Even as a youth, he managed to evoke the envy of his father and nine older brothers. Worse still, he aroused the resentment of their brutish neighbor, Paul Molnar, who was in love with Martha, the most beautiful girl in Baja and who later became my grandmother. Molnar wasn't Jewish, but he didn't particularly hate the Jews, not until he fell in love with my grandmother, that is. Some claimed that even afterward, he didn't hate the Jews, because basically Grandma was also Jewish. According to gossip, Paul Molnar, who was a member of the fascist Hungarian Arrow Cross Party, was behind Grandpa's expulsion to the Mauthausen Concentration Camp. Apparently, he hoped that Grandpa would quickly die there. Grandpa Yoshka, however, was in no hurry to die. In fact, he lived much longer than even Molnar's sons. When he heard that both boys were no longer alive, and only Molnar's grandson still lived in Baja, he wrote to Shandor, gratified that "It is God's way of rewarding the wicked," even though he was usually the perfect infidel and "God" was not a word he used.

Grandpa stopped believing in God even before the war broke out. He came from a devoutly religious family, and for no particular reason, chose heresy when he was very young. Presumably, this choice stemmed from his rebellious, subversive character, which he passed on to both Dad and me, and which was behind the annoying tendency I still have to argue about things I'm not even certain I believe in.

Grandpa was huge and formidable as a youth, some would say a bully, and he would ambush his younger cousins on their way back from Cheder, as they called Jewish school, and force them to eat ham. There were those who said that he was sent to Mauthausen as punishment from God, but they couldn't explain why he survived that terrible camp, whereas some of his older brothers, who were true to the Jewish traditions, were sent to Auschwitz in the summer of '44, never to return.

In fact, aside from the fact that He forced a few, tough months on him in Mauthausen, it would be easy to believe that God had a soft spot for Grandpa Yoshka, just as parents or teachers sometimes prefer the naughtiest and most reckless children of all. challenged the norms.

Yoshka, the baby of the Schwartz family, was born in 1900. His mother insisted on calling him Yosef, after Joseph the dreamer, even though his father wanted to call him Franz, after his own father. From the start, it was clear to everyone that he was going to be special, for better or for worse. His mother, who melted the very first time his cheeky blue eyes peered at her from the diapers he was swaddled in, decided that this baby would grow up right by her side so that people's evil eyes wouldn't be able to hurt him, heaven forbid. She also found a way to keep her husband away from their bed, so she wouldn't get pregnant again and bring more babies into the world to distract her attention from her enchanting baby.

Yoshka grew up to be a very spoiled child, and as such children believe, he felt he deserved all that life had to offer. And indeed, he managed to get anything he wanted in a tenth of the time it would take anyone else. Although his father secretly envied him for stealing all of his mother's attention, he also found it difficult to resist him and forgave him for the pranks he played and even the damage he caused.

Young Yoshka soon found himself at the head of a town gang that called themselves the Terribly Secret Gang. Since he came from a family that was proud of its deep roots in Hungary and of one of its ancestors who was a judge in the court for Jewish cases back in the fourteenth century, the adults didn't see him as one of the ruffians. And even though he loved playing hooky from Jewish school, his teachers didn't see fit to expel him and settled for loving lip clucking, saying that he was probably just bored because of his sharp mind and quick comprehension. When one of the unruly town goys tried to harass a Jewish child, Yoshka would lead his gang of ruffians and make sure that the goy regretted the day he was born. This didn't stop him from harassing Jewish kids himself, especially his devout relatives. Even his older brothers, who were supposed to discipline him, treated him with amused affection. None of them could resist his charm, and Shandor, who was closest to him in age, adored him blindly, tagging along behind him wherever he went.

One day, when Yoshka was twelve, he came home alone after dark. Somehow, his sharp senses told him that someone was following him. He bent over as if to tie his shoelaces, and as he felt his stalker approaching, he abruptly turned around, grabbed the person by his two, muscular shoulders, and pinned him to the ground. "What do you want?!" he demanded threateningly in the boy's ear. He thought it was one of the goys who were jealous of him. The term "antisemitism" was foreign to him, because it wasn't used by the Jews of Baja. They considered themselves the respected subjects of Emperor Franz Joseph and were very proud of it. They never tried to use their religion to blame the gentiles of discrimination.

"I just wanted to…meet you…" the stunned boy stammered. His voice was that of a child's, and Yoshka suddenly noticed how young his face was. Despite the size of his well-built body, his stalker was merely eight years old. He introduced himself as Shani Goldberger, the son of one of the most distinguished Jewish families in the region, a wealthy textile merchant family that had branches all over Hungary. His family lived in an enormous house by the Danube River, which even the members of Yoshka's Terribly Secret Gang were afraid to go near.

"I want to join your gang," the young boy said fiercely, after the surprised Yoshka let go of him.

"You don't say?" Yoshka scoffed. "And how, dear sir, did you think we'd agree to accept you into our ranks? You're no more than a spoiled child who has grown up in a castle full of servants. What good would you be to us?"

"We don't have servants, just one housemaid who cooks," the boy dared to argue with him, "and I'm not a child, and I'm not at all spoiled. If you want, sir, you can test me in any field of your choosing."

The next day, Yoshka and his friends put young Shani to every test they could come up with. To their surprise, they discovered that the boy was good with a bow and arrow, at fencing, and could even swim the Danube across and back. Yes, he was a proper thug, Yoshka decided after the tests, and even forewent the last test, of wrestling with him himself, after he pinned down two Secret Gang members.

Shani became an honorary member of Yoshka's secret cell, and the two boy's souls were bound to each other. They were yet to discover the tests their deep friendship would undergo.

***

When Yoshka was fourteen, Archduke Franz Ferdinand was shot, and his death led to the outbreak of the First World War, which everyone called the Great War. The best of Baja's boys were called up by the Hungarian army and marched to the front and beyond in order to protect the benevolent rule of Emperor Franz Joseph. Many Jews were among them, a few from the Schwartz family too. Yoshka wandered around town for days, frustrated at the three, stupid and worthless years preventing him from enlisting and experiencing the adventure for himself. His immense frustration was eased only by the fact that there were so many single women, grass widows, and fiancées with their eye on the beautiful and well-developed boy. Many romantic and dubious legends were associated with his name. Some said that the widow Farkash, the thirty-year-old beauty who one day jumped into the Danube and drowned herself, didn't do it because her husband died in battle, but because of Yoshka, who preferred to run around with her younger sister and didn't respond to her overtures. Yoshka never bothered to counter those stories with more than an indifferent shrug. His buddies from his gang claimed that their hero was a knight, and it was unimaginable that he could do such a thing. They even threatened to defile the slanderers' homes with the heads of slaughtered, wild geese, but the stories flew constantly through the air, as fast as those geese could fly.

The Molnars had a good, neighborly relationship with the Schwartzs.

Ida Schwartz and Margot Molnar would do all the housework together, except for cooking (for obvious reasons). The Molnar's younger son, Paul, was older than Yoshka by a year, but they were never friends because Yoshka firmly refused Paul's just demand to be admitted into his gang. Paul had every right to be included, as he was just as much a thug as any of them. He clearly could have passed the admission tests if he'd been given the opportunity. But Yoshka dug his heels in and refused to explain. Shani naively reasoned that it was because Paul wasn't Jewish, but Yoshka curtly explained to him that he didn't discriminate on religious grounds. Only a year after the war broke out, Shani finally understood the true reason behind Yoshka's refusal: It was Martha, his very own sister.

Shani had three sisters, each pretty in her own way, but Martha, or Fekete, the black one, as they called her, was the most beautiful of all. It took only one look into her dark, intelligent eyes to be immediately captivated. Her gaze seemed to challenge people, as if asking, "Who can resist me?" Few could. Martha was no wallflower. She was tall and shapely and kept her hair in a fashionable style. Every time it grew a little and her mother would urge her to put it up, Martha would insist on having it cut so that her hair was precisely shoulder length and dangerously becoming. She also had a sweet smile, perfectly straight, white teeth, and high cheekbones she would pinch before she left the house to give them a crimson blush. She was breathtaking in her fluttering chiffon dresses that would whirl around her calves whenever the wind from the Danube took hold of them.

One day, as she walked past her brother, who was sitting under the lime tree with Yoshka, she said hello with a dismissive glance. Yoshka couldn't control his feelings for her and astonished Shani by confessing them. Despite his youth, Shani immediately understood what lay behind the ongoing hostility between Yoshka and Paul Molnar: Martha and Molnar were close friends, and he would often wait for her after school and offer to carry her books. The Goldberger family didn't disapprove of their friendship. They had grown very distant from their religion, and non kosher delicacies were often served at their table.

That day, Shani decided to matchmake his sister with his good friend.

It would be the gift that he'd always wanted to give him, a token of his appreciation for agreeing to let him join the glorious gang, he thought to himself. That evening, he tried as nonchalantly as possible to find out what Martha thought of Yoshka. When she answered scornfully that she didn't waste her time thinking about unbridled ruffians, he didn't react, but he did begin to devise a plan.

One evening, about two months later, when Martha and Paul were crossing the thicket by the Danube on their way home, they were ambushed by bandits, who had their faces hidden behind black masks. Two of them held the terrified girl's arms, while the others went for Paul, hooting excitedly like Indians in Karl May's books. Petrified, Paul shouted to Martha that he would go for help and ran off. Two of his assailants ran after him, but they stopped when he disappeared through the trees. A second later, Yoshka and Shani attacked the assailants and beat them until they ran away shrieking. Martha was overwhelmed with gratitude for her saviors. Yoshka walked her and her brother to their huge house, where he bowed to Martha and said earnestly that it had been his honor to save her, and off he went. That was the night that he captured her heart. She even apologized to Shani for calling his good friend a hooligan and made him promise to never tell Yoshka. From then on, she and Yoshka became close friends, and under her influence, he even left the gang. Since he was a responsible boy, he made Shani his official replacement and would wait himself for Martha after school and carry her books home. She was also responsible for Yoshka going back to school, and he even read the books she recommended. The hearts of all the townsfolk, except for Paul Molnar's, expanded in admiration as they watched the stunning boy and girl walking by, the way the heart expands when looking at a magnificent work of art. Everyone said they were a match made in heaven, because those two beautiful creatures fit together like two parts of a puzzle.

In 1918, after the war, some of the town's young men returned home, a few more intact than others. Only one of them, Yoshka's older brother Mark, returned with more than all his parts—he came back with a young Polish woman by the name of Gizella. Rumor had it that she wasn't Jewish. Not only that, they claimed that she was also married to a Polish man and was the mother of a young daughter whom she abandoned to follow Mark. Yoshka, although he was no longer a thug, was still curious and adventurous at heart, and one day, he stole into Mark and Gizella's room to see if the rumors were true. He didn't find what he was looking for, proof that Gizella was married and a mother, instead he found a medal of honor from the Hungarian army in the name of someone called Thomas Ferenczi. Yoshka was shocked. His imagination raced with images of his brother killing Ferenczi and robbing him of his medal and girl. He didn't dare to confront Mark, so instead, he became friends with Gizella, who he called Gizi. Gizi longed for a close and true friend. The Schwartz family only seemingly accepted her, but they were really giving her the cold shoulder. They were willing to forget her Polish origins, despite the fact that they considered the Poles the most inferior of Eastern Europeans, but abandoning her child was unforgivable.

Gizella and Yoshka had many heart-to-hearts, especially when Mark began traveling frequently to Budapest in search of work. He also realized that it was a matter of time before his family lost their patience and the restraint of the Habsburg aristocracy in which they all shrouded themselves would be shed to reveal the stormy temper of the Magyars, who were thought to be descendants of the Huns. By then, Mark was passionately in love with Gizi and felt a desperate need to compensate her for all the sacrifices she'd made for him.

Yoshka soon learned all about Gizella's life. She was a simple country girl, she told him, and her family, who wished for a better future for her, were quick to marry her off to a wealthy grain merchant from Warsaw twenty-five years her senior. Gizella took pity on Yoshka, who seemed delicate to her, and she didn't describe the acts of rape and abuse she suffered at the hands of her husband. She only told him that she had never loved him. After the war broke out, there was a demand for women to wash the officers' uniforms for a small fee. She decided to become a washerwoman so she could save a few pennies for herself and finally fulfill her dream of leaving her husband. She never dreamed she would also leave her daughter, Sophie, who was the love of her life, but when her husband found out that she was taking in laundry behind his back, he banished her in disgrace and refused to let her see her daughter. Looking at Yoshka's compassionate face, she didn't have the heart to tell him about the beating her cruel husband gave her before banishing her or how she had met Mark when she returned battered and beaten to the camp. Gizella was so afraid and confused, she didn't notice that Warsaw had been occupied by the Austro-Hungarian army and that the officers in charge of the camp were now Hungarian. Mark fell in love with her in that stormy way Hungarian men reserved for women of tiny proportions with sweet, bruised faces. Gizella had to stop him from chasing down her husband with his pistol drawn, as she knew it could cost him a military trial and imprisonment—the Austro-Hungarian army was known for its civil and polite conquests and did not allow any bullying or looting, certainly not against the civilian population. Worse still, associating with the local girls was also strictly forbidden, so Mark and Gizella had to hide their love for months. This constraint only served to intensify their love. The problem became fully apparent at the end of the war, when the Austro-Hungarian army began to withdraw from Polish territory. On the advice of one of Mark's closest friends, Gizella disguised herself as a Hungarian soldier, called herself Thomas Ferenczi, and became Mark Schwartz's personal servant. Then, on the battalion's march back to Hungary, they were attacked by defecting soldiers on horseback who refused to obey their commanders and surrender. Instead, they hid in the forests and waited for an opportunity to attack. Gizella, who had walked most of the way beside Mark's horse, was the first to detect them. She tried to warn Mark by shouting, but the din of the retreating battalion was so great that he didn't hear her. Armed with a knife, she charged the riders and attacked the first horse. She stabbed him straight in his soft stomach, forcing him onto his hind legs. Stunned, his rider fell off and Gizella watched him being trampled under his horse's hooves before she too, fell to the ground in a faint. She woke up to Mark's troubled face. "Shh, shh, not a word, Thomas," he heard him murmur in her ear, "you were a hero…from now on you'll ride the horse, and I'll walk."

Gizella received the medal of honor for her actions in a short and dignified ceremony at the headquarters in Budapest. They were then both released from the army, and only on the train to Baja, Mark allowed her to take off her uniform, abandon the name Thomas Ferenczi, and become his beloved woman once again.

Yoshka and Gizella's friendship grew stronger after she shared her stories with him. He had only admiration for her fortitude and courage, and they spent more and more time together. As far as Martha was concerned, there was nothing wrong with it, and she befriended the little woman with the scarred soul herself. The wagging tongues, however, wouldn't let them be, and when Gizella's stomach began to swell, the town gossips claimed that Yoshka was the father. Luckily for all concerned, Mark found a job in Budapest, and he moved there with his wife. When Martha asked Yoshka if he'd heard the rumors, he reacted so badly that she never spoke of it again.

***

The 1920s arrived with the message of socialism. All across Europe and even beyond, young and enthusiastic intellectuals were reading Marx's Capital. In Hungary, an avid socialist by the name of Béla Kun, a Jew, came into power.

According to Shandor Bachi, Shani was the first in Baja to become enraptured by the new theory. With all the fervor of his youth, he also tried to convince his good friend Yoshka of the righteousness of his new path, but Yoshka was in no rush to be enticed. "Are all people really born equal?" he argued, despite Shani's flushed cheeks and enthusiastic reading of select chapters. "If so, of what use were the admission tests for our gang? If all people are born equal, there is no point in tests. From now on, you can accept everyone just on the basis of what's written in this book."

"Maybe they aren't entirely equal in their abilities," the boy mumbled after careful consideration, "but they are equal in their human rights."

"If so, everyone has the basic human right to be accepted into your gang," Yoshka snarled with deliberate contempt, for he knew very well how important the Secret Gang was to Shani, so much that he'd even asked to include it and all its members in the secular socialist-Zionist Jewish youth movement that was being founded in Baja at the time.

Shani became a little flustered and stopped preaching the principles of socialism to his friend. He secretly suspected that Yoshka was an elitist and that he didn't want to share the privileges that his charisma and good looks awarded him. Those disagreeable thoughts about his good friend, whom he still admired, startled him and he rejected them. Yoshka's idea—that he should reexamine the conditions for admission to the gang—weighed heavily on him. Under Shani's leadership, the gang had become the official defender of the Bajan Jews, when the buds of hatred began flourishing after Béla Kun came to power. Although anti-Semitic statements were being whispered only behind doors, Shani, a very sensitive boy, could sense the shift in attitude, but because no one dared to articulate their fear, he attributed it to his gang's activities rather than to their religion.

Salvation, which according to Shani would be achieved by convincing Yoshka to adopt the socialist idea, eventually came from an unexpected source—his sister, Martha. Her relationship with Yoshka was full of ups and downs because of his need to flirt, but her influence on him was constant and unshakable. One fine day, when she said she was interested in starting a communal club in Baja, Yoshka was immediately won over by the socialist idea.

Martha, who had begun to study art and philosophy at the most prestigious higher gymnasium in Baja, wanted to establish a group of artists that would live and create together, and although Yoshka was not interested in the artistic aspect of the idea, two others captured his imagination. One was the fact that men and women, married or not, could live together in the club. The second was an important principle taken from Capital, according to which the members of the commune would devote two hours of their day to the general good and would be free for the rest of their time to engage in their hobbies. To Yoshka, that sounded very tempting. His hobbies were mainly flirting, swimming in the river, and playing cards and soccer. He immediately expressed his enthusiastic agreement to join the commune.

From that moment on, no obstacle stood in the way of the socialist, artistic initiative. She and her friend Shari put all their energy into looking for a large house to accommodate the needs of the club, which included twelve members before it was even founded, but then they encountered the first obstacle, in the form of Martha's father, who caused quite a stir when he heard about it. He was an educated man who secretly called himself an intellectual, he could even be considered an art enthusiast, especially when it came to the wonderful paintings he bought on his travels in Europe for his collection. However, the thought of his daughter belonging to a group of socialist bohemians that called themselves artists, and of living with them in the same house to boot, shocked him to the tips of his manicured fingers.

"That will not be happening!" he slammed his fist on the table in uncharacteristic rage. Martha's mother and sisters scurried around, removing the porcelain and crystal dishes before he could shatter them. Martha remained seated, erect and defiant, but the tears welled in her eyes. She was her father's favorite daughter. He was so proud of her, too, and he never raised his voice at her.

"I'm already twenty," she said to her father, her voice trembling, "you can't stop me from fulfilling my aspirations."

Then she got up from the table and fled to her room so she wouldn't burst into tears in front of him.

"Over my dead body will you fulfill them!" her father shouted furiously.

That evening, Yoshka was the one to deal with her raging tears. Not wanting to show how desperate she was, she did her best to calm down, but the moment she began to tell him about her father's reaction, she burst into uncontrollable tears.

"Martha, my Marthakum," Yoshka murmured, stroking her hair gently. He wasn't used to such outbursts from her; she always showed perfect self-control. Even when she was mad at him, like when wicked tongues were wagging around town, gossiping about him and other women, she would casually deliver her polished stings. For him, her self-control was part of her appeal. She never cried bitterly as she threw herself at his feet, like many of his women did when he'd had enough of them. It also hurt him more easily when she did say something. Sometimes he would even persuade himself that he was the injured party, because Martha never minced her words, which were much more painful than the odd fist in the face he would receive from a betrayed husband. Later, he would even tell Shani about it, his tone hurt, his shoulders hunched. He would look so terribly hurt that the boy would take his gang to defend Yoshka's good name and they'd beat the hell out of any man who dared to raise a hand against Yoshka. As a result, Martha would land up having to apologize to Yoshka for hurting him, and Shani would say that he didn't understand why she believed the gossips instead of trusting her beloved knight, who had saved her from those nasty bandits.

Yoshka was astonished by how different he felt about Martha. Her tears didn't arouse a response of disgust and contempt like the tears of those other women he firmly denied having any connection with. He grew even more astonished when he noticed that his heart was overflowing with compassion and love. He promised to do whatever necessary to help her fulfill her plans. That very night, he told his father that he needed money for a just and worthy cause. Surprised, Ignetz asked him where he thought the money would come from since their hardware and construction materials store could barely manage to support his six older brothers' families. The young man made a quick decision and told his father that he wanted to be the store's traveling salesman. That way, they would increase the number of their customers, who he would offer to assemble the equipment for, if they weren't blessed with his hands of gold. Despite his conservative nature, Ignetz thought it was a wonderful idea, and a few weeks later, he used the business's savings to buy a sputtering car. They stuffed the car with building materials, and Yoshka became a traveling salesman for Schwartz Ignetz and Sons.

Martha continued making plans and recruiting members for her commune. After twenty members had signed up, she decided to put on shows with their help, so they could raise the funds they needed for rent. As many of them were musicians and actors eager to be on stage, they didn't foresee any problems. In those days, Baja was a remote city in southern Hungary. Its residents longed for cultural initiatives so they could feel like they were living in Budapest, or even Vienna.

The two soon managed to make enough money to rent a spacious building on Janusz Hus Street, and that's where all the members of Baja's first artistic commune lived.

As it happened, Yutzi, Martha's older sister, had started having an affair with a married man. In light of that scandal, the fact that Martha was living with a man in a bohemian commune was considered nothing but an unfortunate incident.

CHAPTER 7

The insistent ring of the phone snapped us away from the green lawns on the banks of the Danube. Shandor Bachi sighed and picked up the receiver. "Hello, Angela," he said. I tensed. The old man noticed and gave me a quick wink. "Yes, yes, drágám, I need a lot more stuff from the drugstore, yes, yes, didn't you notice that I've run out of vitamins? Yes, Pharmaton supplements too. Come on, Angela, at that place across town. Okay? Good, yes, I'm fine. Bye."

"Good, we now have another two hours or so before she gets back," he answered my silent question, proving that his senses hadn't been dulled by age.

"So where were we, drágám?"

"At Grandma's commune," I responded admiringly. The fact that my grandmother, whom I knew as a kindly old lady with white hair, was a bold and modern revolutionary, had my imagination running wild.

"Oh, yes, the commune," he smiled nostalgically. "Martha Schwartz's commune lasted only a year. But the same year, things happened that decided peoples' fates for many years."

***

In Szeged, a city close to Baja, Admiral Nicholas Horthy was leading an army comprised of what remained of the Hungarian senior officers and had founded a right-wing government that opposed Bela Kon's government. Horthy's army carried out atrocities against supporters of

Kon's regime and against the Jews, and when the Rumanian and Czech Republic's armies invaded Hungary, they helped Horthy establish a fascist dictatorship in all parts of Hungary.

Despite these events, Martha didn't for a moment consider giving up her commune, and Yoshka supported her. He was doing very well selling construction materials across the divided country, which had been ravaged by the wounds of the civil war before it was done licking its wounds from the First World War. Yoshka didn't see his travels as life-threatening. On the contrary. He enjoyed traveling as much as any good adventure. Shandor, however, who was sent by their father to accompany him and keep him out of trouble, often felt afraid, even petrified by the adventures that Yoshka welcomed wholeheartedly. That was how his younger brother landed up succumbing to the frequent overtures of Johanna Keleti, the coquettish wife of one of Admiral Horthy's senior officers.

Johanna lived in the family's summer home, which had partly been destroyed by the bombings and was in urgent need of repair. She insisted that Yoshka personally oversee the renovations and was willing to pay him very generously to do so. Yoshka had no choice but to agree. The payment he would receive could support the commune for a month. Shandor smelled trouble. As it was, they were Jews and socialists who belonged to a commune, and as such, they could expect to have problems with Horthy's army. But Yoshka didn't listen to him, and in no time, they found themselves in trouble. Naturally, Mrs. Keleti wasn't satisfied with only renovations, she also wanted to play around with Yoshka. As usual, especially with customers as beautiful as Johanna, he couldn't bring himself to refuse, even though he realized how risky it was, because of her husband Erik Keleti's high status and temperamental nature. In the end, he decided to give in to the woman, but also complete the renovations as quickly as possible.

The renovations took about a month, during which he spent a lot of time in the Szeged area and rarely saw Martha. As such, she had no way of consulting with him when her father had a heart attack. It was two years after the Great War had ended. The Austro-Hungarian Empire had collapsed and become a thing of the past. Trade in upscale fabrics, which the ladies needed to sew elegant dresses, was down. Silk, velvet, satin, and rustling taffeta were no longer in demand. Mr. Goldberger's business was dying, and it broke her father's heart, giving him a serious heart attack that left him a wreck. Martha, his favorite daughter, was the only one in the family who rushed to his aid. Her two sisters were too busy taking care of their families. Yutzi had managed to convince her married man to get divorced and marry her and was far along in her pregnancy. Anio, her other sister, had twins to take care of. Shani was preoccupied with socialist dogmas and wanted nothing to do with their capitalistic business. He was proud of his productive craft. He was doing beautiful woodwork for the commune and was in great demand as a carpenter.

Martha considered her options for a week, and after understanding from the doctors that her father would never be the same again, she decided to take over the management of the dying establishment. She did an excellent job, using the same, well-developed commercial sense she applied to running the commune. She stopped ordering luxury fabrics altogether and ordered only plain, everyday fabrics such as cotton and synthetic organdy.

And so, while her darling Yoshka was trapped in Johanna Keleti's manicured nails, Martha was flourishing. She did a wonderful job of saving her father's business, which helped to relieve her guilt over rebelling against him and boosted her self-confidence in her ability to make money and be resourceful.

Her neighbor Paul Molnar had just completed his studies at the gymnasium and become a certified bookkeeper. He offered to help her and she hired him as an accountant for the Goldberger's business. This helped Yoshka realize that he was losing control over the situation. Mrs. Keleti kept finding reasons and pretexts to call him in to do more repairs, and after a few months, he began to suspect that she damaging the house herself. He was at a loss, and for the first time in his life, he realized that he had to act with determination and courage to escape the swamp he was sinking in as a result of his reckless behavior.

One fine day in early September, after Admiral Horthy's forces had begun to clean up the country, he stood before Martha and proposed to her. Martha was stunned. Although she loved Yoshka with all her heart, reason told her that it wasn't a good time for her to marry. Yoshka, who could see the doubt in her face, misunderstood her and immediately said he was willing to stop traveling and to live with her in Baja, to be her supportive and protective husband and take care of her and their soon-to-be-born children. Martha became even more alarmed by the word "children," for that was the main reason she didn't want to get married. She actually loved children but believed that parents should devote themselves to raising them, at least in their early years. When she said this to Yoshka, he quickly promised that he would put himself at the disposal of their future children and raise them himself, and she'd be free to run the business as she wished. Martha burst out laughing, but not from joy. Despite all her love for Yoshka, she couldn't imagine him raising children, an occupation that required immense patience, a trait she had found him entirely lacking in. Yoshka, upset by her laughter, rushed out of the house and slammed the door in fury. Now he had a reason to seek solace in Mrs. Keleti's arms.

***

Martha, who was almost entirely preoccupied with rebuilding her father's business, didn't place much importance on the slamming door, and she assumed that he'd think it over and realize she was right. When two weeks went by and she hadn't heard a word from him, she began to fear that she'd hurt his feelings. She then ran to Shani and asked him to help her appease the man she loved.

Shani, long tired of his role of mediating between the stormy couple, said, "I'll be your messenger just this time, on condition that you meet each other halfway. You have to give me real power to do what you're asking for."

"What do you mean?" she wondered.

"That you agree to marry him."

"But, Shani, don't you understand, I would have to let all of our father's work fall apart."

"Let it! Who cares? In any case, exploitative enterprises that only make the merchants and middlemen rich are coming to an end—"

"Excuse me, but our exploitative enterprise is the family's only source of income."

"When will you start thinking in broader terms than the family?"

"I do, Shani. In case you didn't notice, I'm also supporting the commune. Who do you think buys most of the fine paintings from the artists who live there? And who organizes plays in the summer for the company of actors? You and your socialist friends, who have meetings every evening and argue about unrealistic theories?"

"Our meetings are just the beginning," Shani tried not to get angry, "and they will lead to a great revolution."

"But until then, people need to live on something."

"Fine," Shani sighed, secretly admiring his sister's practicality and hoping that one day she'd help his cell of socialists too. "I'm prepared to talk to Yoshka and say that you're willing to get married but you'll have to postpone having children until times are easier."

"Why, then, should we get married?"

"Martha, really, I've already told you that you both have to take steps."

"But why that step in particular?"

"Do you have any other ideas?"

"Yes," Martha quickly answered as she thought, and since no brilliant idea came to mind, she eventually stammered, "I'm…prepared…to get engaged."

Shani left for Szeged to try to appease Yoshka with Martha's suggestion.

The heavy rain that day forced Yoshka to leave the renovation work on the front of Mrs. Keleti's house for another time, and instead he stayed with the lady of the house in her warm bed. When Shani arrived at her house, he found Shandor staring passively at the rain, drinking coffee, and waiting in the barn that had been renovated and converted into a visitors' wing.

"Where's Yoshka?" Shani asked briskly, shaking the rain off his coat. He wanted to get the job over and done with.

"Taking care of business," Shandor replied cautiously. He knew that Shani was the second-most important person in Baja who must never know about his brother's affairs.

"And where is he doing that?"

"Where did you come from? You look exhausted. Will you join me for morning coffee?"

"I don't have time for idle chatter, I have an important message for Yoshka. Where is he?"

"And what is the message, if I may ask?"

"An important message from my sister."

"Which sister?"

"Shandor, what are you going on about? Which sister can it be?"

"How would I know? You have three sisters, as far as I know."

"What are you trying to hide, Shandor?" Shani suddenly feared the worst, "Did something happen to Yoshka?"

"Yoshka is safe and sound, but—"

While Shandor was trying to come up with an excuse to tell Shani, he suddenly heard the sound of horses' hooves approaching from the woods surrounding the Keleti summer home. His body tensed. Could it be Johanna's husband and his companions? After all, that was why he was waiting in front of the estate—to warn Yoshka if necessary.

"But what?" Shani demanded as Shandor jumped up and muttered in a commanding voice, "Where is your wagon?"

"Outside, on the other side…I had to circle the wall to reach the entrance…"

"Run and wait for us there, in the wagon!" Shandor thundered sharply, "And take care not to be spotted by the horsemen!"

Shani had no idea why, but the fear in Shandor's eyes made him follow orders without question. He slipped out the side door and crept to his wagon, which he'd left in the bushes by the woods. His experience as the gang's leader was very helpful.

Shandor, who lacked his experience, tried to go unnoticed by the horsemen, but unfortunately, he ran into one of them as he was hurrying to the main house to warn Johanna and Yoshka. He stared for a moment at the huge mustache decorating the rider's face, and only when he heard the two lashes of a whip burning the flesh of his back and leaving him with a big, cross-shaped scar did he snap out of his shock and run. By the time the riders had dismounted, he'd made it to Mrs. Keleti's bedroom and shouted loudly, trying not to look at what was going on there, "Yoshka, Ishtenem—God—run, fast! Mr. Keleti…he's outside!"

By the time they arrived dripping wet in Baja, even innocent Shani had figured out what activity Yoshka was up to that morning. The anger burning in him must have somehow kept him warm because he was the only one of the three who didn't get ill that day. Yoshka and Shandor, perhaps as punishment from God, both came down with severe pneumonia. Shani was at a loss. He felt obliged to tell his sister exactly where he'd found Yoshka, but when he saw him lying helpless in his bed, burning up with fever and coughing incessantly, he chose to believe that he'd been punished enough. Martha's devoted care gave him hope that their differences would be resolved without his intervention.

Martha, on her part, didn't tell anyone that she had sent Shani there, and in the meantime, Paul Molnar proposed to her with an expensive engagement ring. Naturally she turned down his proposal, but not in the way she'd turned down Yoshka's. She now had experience with the humorlessness with which men can take laughter on such occasions. Fearing she would lose his excellent and devoted bookkeeping services, she applied all of her skills in pleasantry and tact. Still, Molnar took her refusal to heart, and his anger and indignation at Yoshka, whom he blamed for all his grief, only grew stronger. The fact that the woman he loved had immediately focused her attention on caring for his long-time rival certainly didn't help to alleviate his resentment.

It took Yoshka a few months to recover and regain his strength, while Shandor continued to cough and feel frail for quite some time, but his life was out of danger. Shani willingly relinquished his role as mediator between his sister and his friend, when he discovered to his relief that Yoshka's illness had fanned the flames of their love and it was stronger than ever. None of them knew or wanted to know what Joanna Keleti's betrayed husband thought of the incident at his home. After a few months passed and there was no sign of danger from Szeged, they all breathed a sigh of relief and moved on with their lives. Yoshka started traveling for work again, but without the faithful Shandor by his side. This time, he avoided Szeged. Martha was doing an amazing job running the business and opened a sewing workshop, where seamstresses worked diligently to design a line of bohemian and artsy dresses for the women to wear to the commune's theatre. The income from Mr. Schwartz's combined store and workshop flourished.

It turned out, however, that Mr. Field Marshal Erik Keleti was indeed planning his revenge. His wrath at his wife's act of betrayal had stuck in his throat like a bone, though he hadn't had time to find out all the details. It was enough for him to see the terrified Shandor scurrying into his house and the look on his wife's face when he saw her lying sobbing in bed. He couldn't extract a confession from her and he was home for only one day, not enough time to find out all the details. Like the good, unconquerable Magyar and hot-tempered husband that he was, he preferred to spend the day with his wife, whose tormented conscience made her ten times nicer to him than usual. His men, on the other hand, were sent into town to find out more about the rascal who had sneaked into his wife's bed in his absence. When his men returned with reports regarding the two Schwartz men who for months had been renovating his summer house, he preferred to keep the story to himself and wait for the right opportunity to take action. He had seen one of them, and he figured that the whiplashed scars on his back would remain there for quite some time.

Despite Martha's efforts, the events of the late 1920s in Hungary eventually led to the end of the commune. Admiral Horthy's reign of terror hung like a shadow over her future, and her people, although bohemians, wanted a calm and peaceful life. Shandor and Imre went back to living with their parents, and Yoshka stopped his travels through the empire of which nothing was left but Hungary, which had greatly shrunk. These were the circumstances when Yoshka and Martha got married in a modest ceremony at the Goldberger home. Their wedding was soon followed by the birth of their son Peter, the sweetest, most beautiful baby that Baja had ever seen.

Shani, Martha's brother, was the only one who wasn't swept away with euphoria by the birth. Although he loved his little nephew with all his heart and soul and would carve special toys for him that no other toddler in the city had, he could sense that storm clouds were developing on the horizon.

***

Until 1933, the life of the small Schwartz family went smoothly. Little Peter was his parents' pride and joy and made his father lose his interest in women who weren't his wife. Even people with no inkling of the details of his adventures noticed that his behavior had changed beyond recognition. He stopped taking long trips out of town and would go home early in the evening to join his wife and son playing. Martha would leave Peter with him and go to work, and he would teach him to play with a ball and roll on the soft grass he planted in their yard. The day the toddler started standing on his own two feet, Yoshka opened up a small soccer school, and he taught his son and a few of the neighbors' younger children to kick and butt the ball. People were truly astonished…was this the same Yoshka Schwartz who never showed any interest in children other than to silence them on the street?

That year, when the dark forces came into power in Germany, the storm clouds thickened over the Schwartz family's heads, too, but none of them could detect them, just like the other Jews of Baja—not until they heard a rumor that Field Marshal Erik Keleti, Johanna's husband, was to be made mayor by Admiral Horthy's party. Yoshka sensed the danger before Keleti came to town and implored Martha to move to Budapest. They would join his brother Mark, who had set up a hotdog stand at the train station, and his business was doing well. Martha wouldn't hear of it. She had no idea of the enormous danger hanging over her husband's and Shandor's heads, especially since Shandor still bore Mr. Keleti's scar on his back.

The field marshal soon arrived in town, and word that he was looking for a man with whiplashed scars on his back spread like wildfire. Shandor's heart was gripped by icy terror, but ever since that incident, he had refrained from swimming in the river like the others, so that he wouldn't have to take his shirt off in public. Still, he was terrified, and he couldn't sleep at night. Yoshka suggested that he move to Budapest until the danger passed and Keleti gave up his search. But then salvation arrived from an entirely different source. A Gypsy circus arrived in town, and of all people, Imre the painter, their quiet, brooding brother, fell for Julia, the Gypsy rubber girl. In the beginning, he would visit the big top and stand on his feet for hours on end, mesmerized by her act, but he didn't dare talk to her. Yoshka, who had never been one to behave that way, went with him one day to the circus, started chatting with the girl, and even suggested with a laugh to the troupe that Imre, a gifted painter, could join them on their travels and paint the backdrops for their acts in exchange for the beautiful girl's hand in marriage. The circus folk, headed by Igor the magician who was blind in one eye and who happened to be Julia's father, weighed his suggestion seriously and told Imre that he could join them, but he'd have to wait patiently until Julia reached marrying age, as she was just fifteen years old.

Imre was bewildered and unsure, as he had never planned to go beyond Baja's borders, but then the terrified Shandor came running, after he heard that Field Marshal Keleti had sent his men from door to door in search of the man with the cross embossed on his back.

"We accept your proposal," he told Igor, speaking for Imre, and that's how the two of them found themselves in a trailer with a brown bear by the name of Adrianus the Great. They set out, never to return to Baja.

***

"And so, Daryakum," Shandor Bachi sighed, looking at me, "because of your grandfather's little stunt, I left Hungary with Imre and never returned to see my family or home."

"And that's it?" It would be an understatement to say I was disappointed. I felt like a person shaken from a dream just as it was getting interesting. "What happened to Yoshka and Martha, who stayed in Baja, and where did you, Imre, and the circus end up?"

"Darya, Darya, those are stories that could take at least another night," he smiled indulgently, "and they won't get you further on your quest to find the family treasure."

As if to prove it, I heard a key turning in the lock and Angela appeared in the doorway. She was holding paper carrier bags, and an expression of disapproval spread across her face. "Hello," she nodded at me.

"Darya is on a mission," Shandor said before I could mutter an apology. "She's interested in documenting my war stories. She has connections with a producer who wants to make a movie about them, right, Darya?"

"Uhm...right," I mumbled, even more embarrassed than I'd expected. I had no idea what movie he was talking about, and more than that, how, with him being so protective of me, could I still suspect him of hiding information regarding the family's treasure?

"Really?!" Angela immediately looked impressed, "And will I have a role in the movie?"

"Of course," Shandor Bachi winked at me, "a leading role, I believe."

"That's awesome!" Angela looked pleased and smiled at me. I stared after her as she disappeared into the kitchen with the bags in her arms.

"So, then, we have the night too," Shandor noted with a mischievous grin. "Angela would do anything to be in a movie, but the question, my child, is if you're interested in hearing the stories of a silly old fool just for curiosity's sake. As you see, they don't hold any hint of family treasure."

"Gosh, I almost forgot what I came for," I staged a sigh. "Do you have any idea where I could find a lead?"

"Look," he closed his eyes for a moment and thought, "Imre's paintings were worth a lot of money in those days, especially the paintings of Angelika, the nun from San Sebastian."

"Who was she?" I was intrigued.

"The only woman I ever loved," Shandor Bachi said, staring out into the darkness.

CHAPTER 8

Shani, who was passionately campaigning to leave for Palestine, was the one who finally told Martha why Shandor and Imre were forced to run away with the Gypsy circus.

For months on end, Shani had kept Yoshka's secret to himself because it could clearly have come between his sister and her husband. As a matter of fact, he didn't really care if that happened, because he'd been feeling very angry and resentful toward Yoshka ever since the incident. Meanwhile, however, he had become deeply attached to his nephew Peter. Whenever he thought about Yoshka and Martha separating, heaven forbid, he would be overcome with grief at how miserable it would make Peter feel. Shani worked clandestinely to obtain immigration certificates for the three of them and for himself, border pass documents all the way to Italy, and tickets for the sea voyage.

After obtaining all the paperwork, he came to Yoshka and told him it was time to leave Baja and even Hungary and go to a new land where their lives wouldn't be oppressed by antisemitism in general and Field Marshal Keleti in particular.

Yoshka roared with laughter. He was no longer afraid of anything, not since Shandor had left Baja. In fact, he could barely recall his affair with the mayor's wife. As far as he was concerned, that story was over and done with.

"To Palestine? To the desert, with camels?" he looked at Shani as though he were suggesting they go to Mars. "Have you lost your mind?"

"The situation here in Europe is deteriorating," Shani insisted, "especially ours, the socialist Jews. You yourself have read Shandor and Imre's letters. They write explicitly that Jews and Gypsies are being persecuted all over Europe. That is why they had to go as far as the border between France and Spain, you know."

"Nonsense," Yoshka said dismissively, "they went all that way because there's more money there and people are prepared to waste it on nonsense such as circuses. It is no indication that the Gypsies are being treated badly, and, in any case, they've never exactly been welcomed by the Europeans."

"And what about the Jews, Yoshka? The Numerus Clausus edicts? That's why my sister was forced to hire Paul Molnar, a goy, as the official manager of Papa's business."

"You know it's temporary," a cloud passed over Yoshka's chiseled face at the mention of his long-time rival. "You know that Martha did it mainly because she wanted to spend more time with Peter."

"It's no temporary matter. You're delusional, Yoshka, the situation is only getting worse. The fascists are being backed by the Nazis in Germany, and soon we won't be able to work in any respectable profession."

"You can always be a carpenter," Yoshka hissed angrily. He didn't like being at the mercy of Paul Molnar. Although he was still traveling for work and selling building materials, he could no longer charm his customers as he could in the past. Many of them were feeling the ramifications of the economic crisis, and perhaps there were those who didn't want to buy from him because he was Jewish.

Shani didn't give up. He believed it was vital and urgent to go to Palestine. Only there, could he and his family live their lives with their heads held high. He was also excited to hear how socialism was flourishing in the Land of Israel—in small and strange groups, but nevertheless with great success.

Troubled, he went to his sister, and when even she teased him, he blurted out the story about Yoshka and Johanna Keleti. All he wanted was for Martha to understand why it was so urgent and imperative that they leave for Palestine, but she'd already worked out the rest for herself. She'd always been very smart.

***

Apart from Shani, Shandor was the only one who knew that the secret was out. Three years after he and Imre left Baja, he received a surprising letter from Martha, demanding to know if the story that Shani had told her was true. "My dear Martha," he replied evasively, "all that I can attest to is that I was drinking coffee on my own in the barn nearby a certain estate, while Yoshka negotiated with the lady of the estate regarding an additional fee. As far as I am aware, there were no complaints about the work we did at that estate, and we received payment in full, including the extra payment."

Shandor didn't know what Martha understood from that letter. All she answered was, "Thank you." Only he and Imre understood what he meant when he wrote that payment was received in full. Paradoxically, and even amusingly, the scar from the field marshal's whip had helped them during the three years they had been wandering across Europe. One day, when the cross on Shandor's back happened to be discovered, in a moment of brilliance, Igor the magician decided to announce to the public that Shandor was a special human being who, thanks to the benevolence of Jesus Christ the son of God himself, was born with the cross tattooed on his back and without a foreskin, already circumcised, just as Jesus himself was. Since for obvious reasons they couldn't display the second fact on stage, the first became the highlight of the circus show, and Shandor, who was shy by nature, had to go onto the main stage every night and expose his back to one and all. This required him to take care of his famous back, as countless people would gather every evening just to see it, and Shandor started lifting weights for hours every day. Eventually, he became an attraction and the target of hordes of women who scrutinized him yearningly. This wouldn't have bothered anyone from the circus, except that Julia, the rubber girl, also developed an eye for him. Shandor noticed how often she'd perform tantalizing tricks with her body whenever he happened to be in the vicinity. He started to feel uncomfortable, a feeling that grew stronger when she started to sneak into the trailer that he shared with Adrianus.

The love story between Shandor and that enormous bear began when they were forced to live together, because there was no free trailer to house him and Imre. A few days later, Imre asked them to find an alternative solution, because he couldn't stand Adrianus's snoring and smell, and they quickly cleared a corner in the kitchen trailer for him. Shandor, however, couldn't take the odors in the kitchen, which made it hard for him to fall asleep. He was a little apprehensive about sleeping alone with the bear, but he solved that by watching his trainer and copying the methods he used to calm Adrianus whenever he lost his good temper and growled with impatience. Shandor soon realized that calming Adrianus was quite simple. All it took were a few cheap sweets, such as candy-coated apples, and he would become as happy as a kitten. He started collecting the half-eaten overly sweet candy that the children would throw away. He would give them to Adrianus whenever he had trouble falling asleep, especially when the moon was full. Adrianus would lick them quickly, stretch out in his bed, and cuddle Shandor's head to show his thanks.

One frozen night in mid-December, Shandor discovered that Adrianus's lap kept his body warmer than a stove. From then on, the two friends slept like that throughout the winter. Shandor developed an inner clock that woke him fifteen minutes before the other circus folk, so it wouldn't become widely known that he was sleeping curled up in the bear's lap. But Julia's intrusions didn't occur at predetermined times, and he was forced to be on his guard to greet her and send her away. Julia didn't say exactly what the purpose of her visits was, but he could smell trouble. Her eighteenth birthday, the day she was to become Imre's wife, was three months away, and Imre was waiting longingly for her. Shandor felt that the situation required immediate action. He was sorry to leave the circus, but most of all, he regretted having to say goodbye to his friend, Adrianus, so he secretly tried to come up with ploys to stop Julia from pursuing him. One day, however, before he could find a solution, she was seen by one of her friends slipping out of his trailer. That friend wasted no time and told everyone that Shandor wanted Julia.

Known to be sweet-tempered and amiable, Imre was livid. He screamed at Shandor, swearing and cursing, and Shandor was afraid he would also use his fists. This would leave him with no choice but to protect himself, and as the weights he lifted every day had made him much stronger, he was afraid he'd inflict serious bodily harm on Imre.

"Aren't you ashamed?!" Imre's shrieks rang in his ears. "All my life, I've wanted only one girl, and you want to steal her from me?"

"Imre, Imre," Shandor stammered and stepped back quickly, his heart not allowing him to humiliate his brother by telling him the truth. All he could come up with in those few moments before a fight broke out was an even more humiliating lie, "I didn't…it wasn't me who wanted her…it was she who wanted…Adrianus."

"What did you say?!" Imre froze, his fists falling to his sides.

"I said that…Julia…desires…the…bear."

"I don't believe you," Imre growled, staring at him in confusion and disgust. "How could a delicate girl like Julia be attracted to…such a gross beast?"

"Adrianus isn't a gross beast," Shandor fumed. "He's gentle and good-natured, whereas Julia's not a real girl, she's a rubber woman; with a body that behaves in such a twisted way, who knows how her heart works?"

"But I love her," Imre mumbled, his eyes shimmering with tears.

"You love an illusion, my dear brother," Shandor said as he cautiously moved closer. He felt sorry for his tormented brother, but it was clear that nothing good would come of his love for a temptress like Julia, a true Jezebel, "She's an illusion that you created in your imagination. Imre, she's not for you."

"And what will I tell Igor?" Imre murmured desperately, "I promised to marry her in a few months."

Disconcerted, Shandor knew it was one thing to tell his brother tales about Julia and the bear, but it was an entirely different matter telling her father, Igor, whose explosive temper and extreme love for his daughter were common knowledge.

"Then we have to get out of here," he answered eventually, his voice weak now, "you're right about Igor, he wouldn't believe us, and even worse, he would try to destroy us."

"Where will we go?" Imre wondered apprehensively.

"Wherever our feet take us," Shandor replied, adding that even if they had to walk back to Hungary, it was better than staying with the circus, where they were at the mercy of a volatile father and his rubber girl with a passion for bears.

Under the cover of darkness, after everyone had fallen asleep, they sneaked off with just a bag of clothes and food. They walked for two hours across the hills and mountains before hunger struck and they sat down to eat. There, under the light of the full moon that had emerged from behind a big cloud, they saw a huge, thick, and hairy shadow coming toward them. Imre screeched and almost fainted, but Shandor realized instantly that it was no robber, just his friend Adrianus. He jumped to his feet and fell into his arms. Imre had no choice but to agree to the bear's joining them, even though he was still angry with him for seducing the woman he loved. Shandor, noticing the turmoil he was in, quickly reassured him that he'd seen Julia seducing the bear, not the other way around.

***

They decided to keep walking until the break of day and then look for someone to point them in the direction of Hungary. As fate would have it, they'd been walking in the opposite direction. At dawn, they heard battle cries and gunshots approaching. They tried to find a place to hide until the danger passed, but the noise confused Adrianus and, instead of hiding, he dashed frantically in their direction. Shandor didn't know what to do. His instincts told him to stay hidden, but his concern for his friend overcame him and he found himself running after him. Before he could realize what was happening around him, a bullet hit him in the arm and he cried out with pain as he plummeted to the ground. He was quickly surrounded by people as dark-skinned as Gypsies, who were talking and shouting in confusion. Their language sounded like Latin to him but he didn't understand it.

Shandor looked at their murderous faces surrounding them and his heart froze in terror. One of them held a knife up to his face and a loud cry escaped his parched lips. "Help!"

The man leaned toward him with a quizzical look, his knife still drawn. Shandor closed his eyes and prayed until, suddenly, he heard familiar growls. He opened his eyes again and saw Adrianus coming toward him, surrounded by men cheering in their strange language. He tried to shout to his friend to run away and save himself, but he was unable to utter a sound. The human ring around him opened, allowing Adrianus to reach him and kneel by his side, snarling fiercely at the man holding the knife.

Adrianus picked up Shandor and started walking with him toward the large, earth-colored citadel. The group of men walked behind him. By the tones of their voices, Shandor could tell they were arguing, but as hard as he tried to remember his Latin from school, he couldn't understand a word they said. Their voices slowly faded, and he lost consciousness.

When he woke up, he was lying on a crisp, clean bed such as he hadn't slept on in years. Adrianus growled fondly at him, whereas Imre sat on a chair by the bed and looked at him with concern. "We're in Spain," he informed Shandor, when he noticed that he was awake and looking at him inquisitively. "We've been caught up in a civil war, and it seems we've joined the Republican side."

***

It took Shandor a whole month to regain his strength, during which he managed to gain a good grip of the Spanish language, which was a little similar to Latin, as he'd thought. He'd also befriended his Republican hosts, who worshiped him and Imre for bringing Adrianus along. Already during the battle they'd found themselves in, the latter turned out to be a highly efficient secret weapon since the fascists believed in a lot of strange superstitions. The fact that the bear had joined the fighting forces made them believe that God himself was standing with their enemies.

As long as he didn't have to fight himself, Shandor was proud that his friend had chosen the oppressed side, at least from Shani's point of view. Although Shani couldn't see where they'd ended up, Shandor imagined that if he had known, he would have been very proud of him.

The Republican fighters seemed to be dependable. In their spare time, when they weren't being attacked by the Fascist army, they would spend their time playing soccer in the day. At night, they would drink and sing melancholy songs to a heart-wrenching guitar. Even Adrianus would leave his candy and sway to the rhythm of the music, his eyes misting over with a thin film.

The commander of the fort was Antonio Luspares, a handsome, hot-blooded young man. Shandor was dazzled by him from the moment they met. He reminded him of his brother Yoshka, whom he missed terribly, despite him being the source of all his troubles. Antonio, too, had a pair of bright blue eyes and a long, thin face that hinted at an iron will and a particularly capricious temperament when it came to women. Antonio loved his women with the same ideological zeal with which he regarded the socialist ideal, and they rewarded him generously. Most of the women who lived in the fort or its vicinity loved him right back, even though they gave themselves to the other fighters too. They were all socialists at heart, and as such, none of them were the private property of any other.

There was a convent near the San Sebastián port, and the nuns who lived there supported the Republican faction, contrary to the position taken by most of the Spanish clergy. Although they expressed their support through food and medical care alone, Shandor suspected that they were also secretly in love with the fort commander and that's why they supported his men. Only the eyes of Angelika, a young nun from the French Basque, didn't shine with the same revealing glint of lust when they rested on Antonio. On the contrary, she seemed to be hostile and angry. Shandor didn't know why, but it was enough for him to know that she wasn't keen on his commander, as he had fallen deeply in love with her the first time that he saw her.

Angelika had enormous, brown eyes that exuded tenderness and kindness, as long as she wasn't looking at Antonio. Her lips were also soft and formed the shape of a heart of crimson velvet. Her skin was pale and delicate, and her cheeks were stained a natural peach. She didn't use makeup, and she would cover her hair with a wimple, the way nuns do. Her modesty was what made her one of the most beautiful women Shandor had ever seen. She also took care of him most of the time, mainly when Adrianus had to go into battle. The Republicans had enlisted Imre, despite his fear. "No healthy man can sit idly while our republic is in danger," Antonio declared, when Shandor tried to explain to him that Imre wasn't cut from fighter cloth.

This meant that Imre had to be with Adrianus, despite the resentment he still felt toward him. He knew that only under cover of his terrifying shadow, which had made the fascist nationalists flee, could he survive, safe and sound.

Once he no longer had to be concerned for Imre, Shandor could allow himself to lay back in bed and enjoy Angelika's devoted care. If he'd been allowed to, he would have continued that way until the end of the war, but after a month, Antonio and his friends began claiming that he should have recovered completely by then and added that if he continued to complain about the pain in his injured arm, they'd have to operate on it. In light of the threat and the fact that there was no qualified doctor in the fort, Shandor realized that he had no choice but to join the war. He wasn't keen on the idea. He hated everything about war. He had thanked God for his good luck when the Great War ended just when he reached conscription age. He was certain, like so many others, that it would be the last war in Europe. He would never have imagined that a wrong turn and a confused bear would lead him directly to the heart of another equally cruel and bloody war.

And so, given no choice, Shandor Schwartz joined the Spanish Civil War, making sure to stay near Adrianus and Imre so he could return to the fort and his Angelika at the end of each day. One rainy evening, to his dismay, he discovered that she wasn't his alone.

***

That evening, which as previously mentioned was particularly stormy, Angelika was trying to decide if she should go to the convent or to stay at the fort until the rain stopped. Antonio told her that he would be happy to give her a room to herself, where she could sleep alone, instead of risking her health by running around in the rain. That month, many of the nuns from the convent had come down with pneumonia.

Angelika still seemed hesitant when Imre went and pleaded with her not to go out into the storm. Shandor noticed his strained and eager expression and needed no more proof to understand the magnitude of the tragedy: Imre was also in love with the woman so dear to his heart.

Shandor was beside himself with despair and pain. Angelika was the only woman he'd ever fallen in love with. At night, half-asleep in bed, he would imagine her coming to him with tears in her eyes and confessing her love for him as she struggled with her vow to love only God in heaven. He didn't dream of carnal desire for Angelika, she was pure and that was how he wanted her to remain, but he did want her to love him and be by his side. As far as he was concerned, that damn war could have lasted forever, if it would make the woman he loved stay with him.

And now he was forced to share that pure but overwhelming love with his brother, who he had sworn to himself to protect.

Imre had no idea of the war raging in Shandor's mind. When it came to emotion, and in many other ways, he was like an innocent child. Just a few days after the night Angelika stayed at the fort, he started pleading with her to let him paint her, just her face. The Nun from San Sebastián, he wanted to call the collection of paintings portraying Angelika's beautiful and pure face, always wrapped in her wimple, the background and color of each painting of a different form. There was The Nun at Sunset, The Nun Smiling on a pale background, The Silent Nun had a purple background, The Sad Nun was a dull blue, and so on and so forth. The paintings were to be displayed all over the world and sold for a substantial sum. They also made the daring Republican fighters catch their breath, but it was only Shandor who knew what made them react that way: He realized that Imre, just like him, had looked into Angelika's soul and fallen in love with what he'd seen.

The last painting in that series was called The Nun and the Bear, and naturally, it portrayed Angelika and Adrianus. That painting was the most beautiful in the series and received enthusiastic responses from anyone who had the good fortune of seeing it.

After a year of civil war, the Republicans had the upper hand. The

San Sebastián fort was the standard-bearer of that fierce struggle, for its fighters had never been defeated. In the other towns and villages in Spain, victory and defeat were in competition. Every time the freedom fighters, as the Republicans called themselves, were defeated, they would flee the scene of the battle and somehow find their way to San Sebastián, whose fighters were known near and far for their courage and for their two good luck charms who made sure that their courage didn't fade away—the nun and the bear.

That year, ten nuns from the San Sebastián convent had died of pneumonia. Angelika survived along with two elderly nuns who hadn't left the convent since the disaster. Naturally, she spent a lot of time afterward in the company of the fighters at the fort, fussing about them as if trying to draw life from them. The atmosphere at the convent was somber, and she felt that if she spent too much time there, she'd get sucked into the darkness and gloom and never ever leave.

The Republican fighters accepted Angelika's constant presence with enormous enthusiasm, for she was different from the other women who spent time at the fort. She made them feel like she really and truly cared about them and that she believed that their just socialistic goals were in line with the Son of God Jesus's true intentions. She was also not interested in Antonio, their commander, a fact that increased her standing in everyone's eyes. In no time, she became the fort's good luck charm, a title she shared proudly with Adrianus. No one could have imagined that, in the end, her welcome presence would lead to tragedy.

***

One night, when most of the fort fighters were singing mournful ballads around a bonfire, they suddenly heard gunshots. Shandor and Imre were talking quietly about their favorite subject—news from their hometown Baja—when they got the fright of their lives. The gunshots were coming from Angelika's room. They both dashed over and stopped, stunned by the horrifying sight they were met with. Angelika, her clothes ripped, was kneeling by Adrianus, who was lying on the floor with his chest bleeding.

"Adrianus! What happened?!" Shandor cried out, his heart pounding as he knelt beside his gurgling friend.

"It was Antonio..." Angelika whispered in tears as she tried to stop the blood flowing from the bear's chest, "he tried to...attack me...and Adrianus...came to help me..."

"Help! Quickly! Call for help!" Shandor shrieked in terror, as Adrianus convulsed, leaving little room for hope.

Imre, whose desire for revenge had been ignited by Angelika's words, dashed out.

"Antonio! You coward! Where are you hiding?!" he screamed as he raced around the courtyard, "Come, come out of your hiding place and face me in a duel!"

The fighters quickly surrounded Imre, who was like a man possessed. "What happened?" they tried to ask him and calm him down, but Imre snatched a pistol from one of them and raced into the darkness, shouting out Antonio's name. Antonio eventually staggered out of a corner in the yard, his eyes staring blankly. "Antonio! You miserable bastard! How dare you rape Angelika?!" Imre shouted, aiming the pistol, and before anyone could stop him, they heard a shot. Antonio was hit in the shoulder, and he faltered and fell to the ground. Shocked, a few of his comrades ran to help him while others grabbed Imre and beat him to a pulp.

The turmoil in the courtyard didn't penetrate Shandor and Angelika's consciousness. They were still crouched over Adrianus, trying to revive him. Angelika held his head and Shandor wiped the wounds from Antonio's bullets, crying uncontrollably. "Help! We need help! Adrianus is dying!" he kept shouting, his voice hoarse, but no one could hear him. The noble bear, his good friend and the only one to come to Angelika's aid, rattled a few more breathes, blood foaming from his mouth, and then rested his paw in Angelika's hand, as if to comfort her, and closed his eyes for the last time.

Angelika buried her head in his chest and burst into bitter tears. Shandor was beside himself with grief. He grabbed the bear's paws and shook them, as if he believed it could bring his friend back to life. "Adrianus, you are my best friend, don't leave me," he murmured in Hungarian. "What will I do without you?"

Suddenly a number of enraged fighters burst into the room. "Your brother has lost his mind!" they told the stunned Shandor, "He shot our commander, Antonio, and he will be executed at dawn!"

"And all because of that 'saint' who was about to be tempted by the bear," one of them said, grimacing in disgust. "Look how she's clinging to him now!"

"Have you all gone insane?! What are you thinking?!" Shandor shouted, the panic and surprise forcing him to come to his senses, "Do you not see that Adrianus is dead? Antonio is the one who tried to rape Angelika, and the poor bear only wanted to save her from him!"

"Oh, did he?" Antonio's voice cut the air as he walked into the room, his arm now bandaged, an expression of condescending contempt on his face, "Were you in the room when it happened?"

"No, but that's what…Angelika…she told me…" Shandor stammered, looking at Angelika, whose head was still buried in the dead bear's lap.

"Angelika is lying, she's just trying to defend herself!" Antonio declared, "She's a corrupt woman who is merely pretending to be a nun. Deep down, she longs to sleep with bears, regular human beings cannot satisfy her twisted desires."

"How dare you? Angelika raised her teary eyes and glared at him. Antonio didn't lower his eyes. Instead, he turned to Shandor and said, "Tomorrow your brother will be executed at dawn, unless you take him and this imposter away—and don't you ever return!"

CHAPTER 9

I, too, felt shock and grief as I listened to the story of the poor bear who died a hero's death defending Angelika's innocence, when suddenly I realized it sounded familiar. A moment later, I remembered how I'd cried when reading the same story in an old book about the Spanish Civil War.

"But…Shandor Bachi," I mumbled awkwardly, "I know that story, I read it in a book called The Charm of San Sebastián, by Hugo Scott…"

"Yes, my child, that's right," he smiled, "and do you think I read the same story and told it to you as though it were my own, hoping you don't read such old books?"

"Uhm, no…not really, I didn't mean…" I stammered.

"No, no, don't be embarrassed, Daryakum, that's what everyone thinks, the stories are incredibly similar, aren't they?"

"They are."

"That's because I told it to Hugo Scott. Without me he would have remained an anonymous journalist. He was such a coward, he never set foot on the battlefield."

"Really?"

"Really and truly," Shandor Bachi grinned, reaching out to the dresser beside him and pulling a thick album from the drawer.

"Look, here's Hugo Scott and me in Paris, in a café," he pointed at a faded picture. I studied it carefully. Shandor Bachi was an incredibly handsome man in those days, almost as handsome as Grandpa Yoshka was in the old pictures. Hugo Scott had one hand on his shoulder and was holding his famous pipe in the other. It was clearly him. But the picture wasn't proof that Hugo Scott hadn't got his material for his famous book by visiting San Sebastián himself.

"Here's what you're looking for," Shandor said quickly, as if sensing my doubt, and pointed at an old yellowing document. "This is the contract we drew up, read it, kisashon."

I read it. The document said in English that Mr. Shandor Schwartz hereby transfers the rights to publish his stories from the Spanish Civil War to Mr. Hugo Scott, for forty percent of the royalties that Scott receives on his book. Shandor agreed not to reveal to the world that the book was basically based on his experiences, and in exchange, he would receive the same percentage until the day he died. Thereafter, the rights would pass to his heirs.

Confused, I said nothing. My expression must have reflected what was going through my mind, because Shandor Bachi looked at me and roared with laughter.

"I'm sorry, my child," he said at last, when he saw the frustration in my eyes, "I've never had the opportunity to tell this story, because I made a commitment in the contract not to, and you seemed so stunned, that…I couldn't help myself."

That was an understatement…saying I was stunned. Suddenly I understood how Shandor Bachi could afford such a high standard of living without working a single day in his life. The Charm of San Sebastián had been one of the world's most famous bestsellers for the two decades following the Second World War, and it was still selling well.

"His other books about the Spanish Civil War were also based on stories I told him," Shandor added with a modest glance, "and they were all a huge success. I received forty percent from those too, while he got sixty, and all the glory too, of course."

"I understand," I gulped in sour frustration. Shandor Bachi hadn't hidden any family treasure.

"I'm sorry, Daryakum, I've wasted your time in vain. I was just swept away with nostalgia. I've never told that story to anyone before, except Angela."

"Not at all, Shandor Bachi, you really haven't wasted my time," I quickly protested to hide my disappointment. Despite the frustration of knowing that he wasn't hiding the family treasure, I still really wanted to hear the rest of the story.

"Well then, should I continue the story? Do you feel like listening?" he asked hopefully, and I nodded vigorously before settling back in the armchair.

***

Shandor, Imre, and Angelika wandered for days after fleeing from the San Sebastián fort. Shandor, saddened and stunned by Adrianus's death, was interested in nothing and disappeared into a cloud of grief. That's why he didn't notice that Angelika had led them into France. Just a week after the cursed day he had lost his good friend, he noticed that they were in the heart of a picturesque little town at the foot of the mountains and that he didn't understand the language the locals were speaking. Angelika led them to a small convent on the outskirts of the town. "The mother superior is my spiritual mother," she explained. "She took me in after my family was struck by tragedy, and she suggested I join the San Sebastián convent when I could no longer bear the memories of the terrible events that occurred in this village."

Imre wondered why Angelika had never told them about it before. On their way to the convent, he tried to encourage her to tell them about her life, but Angelika sunk into sullen silence. Shandor, who was still consumed with grief, didn't say anything, thinking that it was the beautiful nun's right to keep her secrets to herself.

The mother superior, a tall, meticulous woman, was delighted to see Angelika, and even agreed to assign a room at the convent for Shandor and Imre, provided they followed the rules of the convent, which included praying three times a day. Naturally, she also forbade them to stare at the young nuns. Shandor and Imre agreed without argument. In any case, they didn't have eyes for anyone but Angelika, and even that they hid unless they were certain she wouldn't notice.

Two days later, Angelika appeared in their room and informed them that they had to move on. "The bad memories are upsetting me again," she explained tiredly and helplessly. "It's too much for me, and it would be best to decide where to go now."

Shandor, who was beginning to recover from losing the bear, thought it was a good time to change direction and go east. "I think that we should head home," he said to Imre in Hungarian. "I understood from Yoshka's last letters that Field Marshal Keleti has given up and stopped looking for me, and I miss everyone terribly."

"I really want to get to Paris," Imre said, much to Shandor's surprise. "It's the only place where I can work on my painting technique and develop artistically."

"Angelika, what do you think?" Shandor asked, sure she wouldn't be eager to settle in Paris, such a dangerously bohemian and sinful city.

"Let me weigh the idea until evening," the nun replied, already deep in thought.

The two brothers, happy she hadn't decided to join another convent or suggested parting ways, nodded and promised to wait for her answer and do whatever she wanted.

After she left their room, Shandor put his hand in his pocket and pulled out the last letter he'd received from Yoshka, on the terrible day that Adrianus had been killed. He'd felt so numb that, until now, he hadn't found the energy to open it.

Yoshka gave an amusing description of his last argument with Martha, who without pausing for breath, expressed her desire to bring another child into the world and to leave Hungary for a place where they could live more freely. He thought she was overly influenced by Shani, who was still dreaming of establishing a socialist society in Palestine. "I still don't understand," Yoshka wrote, "how the concepts of socialism and freedom got mixed up in my beautiful wife's delusional mind. Most people, if you let them live as they wish, certainly wouldn't be happy working to support others. And besides, I'm not interested in bringing more children into a world in which they'll have to live as refugees." He was convinced that the evil winds blowing through Hungary would pass. "We, the Hungarians, are hedonists, and we love life," he wrote. "We have never allowed political worldviews to force us to forego a good bottle of wine or a generous portion of chicken in paprika sauce with dumplings on the side. I believe that soon the winds will die down here, the economic situation will improve, and everyone will come to their senses. The Germans have a slight advantage over us when it comes to classical music, but other than that, they don't have much understanding of the true pleasures of life. That lack of understanding, of the important nuances in our lives, is what makes them restless and wild and drives them to conquer the world. However, they, too, will understand soon enough that no matter where their feet, guns, and bombers take them, the emptiness inside them will never be filled."

Shandor smiled to himself as he finished reading his brother's letter. Life according to Yoshka Schwartz was remarkably simple, yet his letter contained a philosophical note. He wondered what Yoshka knew about having a void in his gut that couldn't be filled, when suddenly another page dropped out of the envelope, written in a child's handwriting. It was a letter from Peter, and when he started reading it, his eyes filled with tears.

"Shandor Bachi," Peter wrote in a round, meticulous hand, "How are you? Papa told me that you live in a circus and that your best friend is a big bear. I do not go to the circus anymore, because Tibor Salushi, my best friend, told me that they hurt the animals so they can train them to perform all the tricks. Tibor also said that it can't be that you have a bear for a friend, because for him to agree to be your friend, you would have to hit him first. I also hit Tibor, because he accused you of hitting the bear. I am sure that you never hit anyone, but I'm still very curious to know how you managed to train him to be your friend. Maybe you gave him honey? I read in a book that Mami gave me, that bears love honey, but the bees don't like them stealing it. I know that you wouldn't steal honey from the bees. So how did you find honey? Please write to me about it. I am very curious to know. And please, when you come back to Baja, bring me a bear too, to be my friend, but a small bear, so we can grow up together. I love you and miss you very much, your nephew, Peter Schwartz."

Shandor felt his heart bursting with longing and love for his little nephew. What a moral decision he'd made, to not go to the circus anymore, only because he'd heard that they abuse the animals there. He made a firm decision, that no matter what Angelika's decided, he was going home to Baja.

***

Angelika surprised them in the middle of the night when she came into their room and woke them up. She urged them to set out under the cover of darkness, for she didn't want to run into any of the townsfolk.

"The mother superior told me that word is out that I'm back in the village, and people want to see me," she said in a choked voice, "but I don't want to see any of them. I will never forget how they all behaved after our tragedy."

"How did they behave?" Imre wondered, buttoning his shirt. He was embarrassed to be seen by her in only his undergarments, but she didn't seem to mind. All she cared about was leaving.

"Imre, I still can't cope with the memories," she said, her voice frail and urgent. "Please, I'm asking you, don't bother me with questions about my past. As soon as the time is right for me, I will tell both of you about it."

"Where are we going?" Shandor asked, his voice faint with sleep. Right then, all he wanted to do was hold Angelika in his arms to ward off the bad memories.

"To Paris," she replied softly and looked directly at him, using the light of the oil lamp she was holding, "I'm sorry, Shandor, I know what you're forfeiting, but I don't think we have a choice. Eastern Europe is heating up, that's what the mother superior told me. If we want to save ourselves, we must go west."

"I didn't know the mother superior was such a great strategist," Shandor said, being difficult, as they stepped through the convent gates. "Where did she develop such a deep understanding of the direction fire takes? Just this evening, I finished reading my brother Yoshka's letter, and he insists that the evil winds would blow over soon, at least in our homeland. He doesn't mention fires at all."

"Shandor, my dear," Angelika answered and stroked his forehead with her hand. Her rare and sudden touch lit a flame inside him he had never before felt, "I'm asking you to come with us. We need you. I promise, when we reach Paris, I'll tell you all about myself, even about the bad things that fill my memories."

It took just those three sentences and a light touch to make Shandor forget his vow to return to Hungary and that he'd never asked to hear about Angelika's bad memories.

***

They wandered through the South of France for a month, until they reached Paris. With Shandor's wonderful ability to tell stories and Imre's artistic talent, they would stop when their money was running low in whichever town square that they were near, (they stayed away from large cities), and Imre would paint Angelika there. As soon as the people noticed his talent, they would gather around, asking him to paint them too. Imre was willing to do so for the sums that Angelika determined, making everyone happy.

One day, a local woman from one of the villages began talking to Angelika. The woman wondered what the odd trio was doing together. Angelika told her nothing, but the woman quickly offered her a tempting wad of banknotes to tell her. Shandor urged Angelika to tell the woman whatever she wanted, as long as she gave them the money. Angelika had no idea what to say, so Shandor promised to concoct a few stories for her, and all she'd have to do was translate them for the woman. Angelika agreed and the two of them started telling his and Imre's stories, beginning with the day they joined the circus. People slowly started gathering around, and the wimple that Angelika was holding filled up with notes and coins, enough for them to live on for the week. From then on, Shandor told stories, and by the time they arrived in Paris, he had learned exactly what interested his audience. He also discovered, to his surprise, that he had a fantastic talent for languages and that he thoroughly enjoyed it when people listened eagerly to what he had to say. Once in Paris, he even dared to go on his own to bars and cafés to tell his tales, even when he wasn't paid for it. That was how Hugo Scott, the American journalist sent to cover the Spanish Civil War, heard about him. But Scott, who had been stuck in a

Fascist army base near Madrid during a week-long siege, escaped to Paris and never had the guts to return to Spain. He promised his newspaper's editor that he would build up his strength in Paris and return quickly to the battlefield, but in fact, all he did was look for a celebrated fighter like Shandor to tell him his battle stories, and then find an underhanded way to mail them off in envelopes bearing the right stamps.

∗∗∗

Immediately after arriving in Paris, they began looking for a suitable apartment to rent. Naturally, Angelika wanted a room to herself. Shandor and Imre didn't argue, they didn't even think about the nature of their relationship with her. They understood without discussing it that they would have no physical relationship with her. That was fine by Imre. Her mere presence in his life was more than he could have asked for. Imre was not a man devoid of desire, but he used it to give his paintings a stormy and thrilling air, and this enabled him to live in peace and harmony alongside his beloved nun.

Shandor was different. When he was younger and trailing behind his passionate brother Yoshka, he would sometimes think that although he'd been born last, Yoshka had received the lion's share of passion and zest for life. With the years, however, he realized that he hadn't calculated it accurately. He, too, had his urges, but they were suppressed by his temperate disposition and tendency to look at himself objectively and with a generous dose of mocking cynicism. During his circus years, after his muscles began to swell and he'd displayed the cross on his back, women would flock to wait for him at the foot of the stage. A few of them did so with reverence and only asked to touch the cross. The others would ask to touch other parts of his body too. Sometimes Shandor would agree and give in to their desires. These women served no purpose for him, other than as a release for his urges, and on their part, the women didn't seem to want more than that. Sometimes, they would drag him to the bushes at the edge of the circus and sweep him up in a whirl of fleeting passion, after which none of them would even bother to tell him their full name.

Shandor didn't take it to heart, on the contrary. He supposed they were married, and the memory of the price he'd paid for the married woman who fell in love with Yoshka had been well engraved in his flesh.

Angelika evoked very different feelings in him. He couldn't imagine her being swept away with him in a storm of passion like the provincial women he met on the road. Whenever the thought occurred to him, he would immediately feel the weight of sacrilege and feel disgusted with himself. The only intimacy he allowed himself to imagine was a protective embrace. Shandor longed to protect Angelika, and he could sense in the way she moved how vulnerable and fragile she was. He was terrified of hearing about what had happened to her, because he was afraid it involved carnal lust in some way. As a result, he was horrified when he realized that their constantly empty pockets wouldn't enable them to pay the rent for an apartment large enough to have a room just for Angelika.

The days they'd spent in hotels had left them just about penniless, and they knew they had to find an apartment to live in. When Angelika heard that they'd have to share a studio apartment with no separating walls, she reacted with apparent calmness. But the evening they moved their few possessions into the apartment, she sat down, and without warning, started to tell them about the terrible circumstances and events that had led to her becoming a nun. Shandor, who thought that he'd seen and heard it all while traveling with his wayward brother Yoshka, found himself rigid and shaking with rage at the horrific story of her father, who first raped her when she turned ten, and about her mother who was afraid to stand up to him and who ran away from home. When Angelika was fifteen, her mother came home during the dead of night. Her drunk father had passed out, and she woke Angelika and told her to run away to the convent. Then she set fire to the house and disappeared, never to return. Angelika's expression was frozen as she told the story, even when she added that after the fire in which her father perished, a rumor spread through the village that she had started the fire. The mother superior lied for her and told the police that Angelika had come to her at dusk and spent the night confessing the terrible things that her father had done to her. This did nothing to end the juicy gossip spreading through the village, and

Angelika fell victim to the repeated harassment of brash young men and threats from her father's family.

One day, she was sent with another nun to the market to buy supplies for the convent, and they were attacked by the same, young men. Fortunately, her friend managed to get away and call the mother superior, who saved Angelika, but she had already been stripped and tied to a tree. That night, Angelika realized that she had to get away from the village. The mother superior gave her enough supplies for the trip and sent her to the San Sebastián convent with a letter for the nuns.

Angelika finished her story with the same, blank expression. "There is no way I will ever feel the need to share physical closeness with a man. I truly love you both, but my love does not involve physical desire. I am incapable of such feelings, because they only cause suffering and pain for me. The positive side of the situation is that you will never have to worry about me betraying you."

***

Life in Paris was good for Imre, at least until 1940, when the city was conquered by the Nazis. He spent a lot of time with famous painters who admired his talent, and an established gallery owner started displaying and selling his paintings. Shandor, however, was still restless, even after they managed to escape that tiny, crowded apartment with the money that Imre was making. He was constantly trying to find a way to rescue the family in Hungary. Unlike Yoshka, he didn't view fascism and the hatred of Jews that had spread across Europe as a passing fad. He was constantly apprehensive, because even after the dark wave passed it would leave behind very grim residue. He wrote about his fears to Yoshka, but Yoshka responded with his characteristic tone that bordered on amusement and so angered Shandor. "We are construction professionals," he read in one of his more irritating letters, "and wars don't have to concern us. On the contrary, wars always bring destruction and devastation, and we have to rebuild it all, and that's how we earn our bread and butter, with honesty and generosity. I think that your fears and concerns stem from the fact that you are far away from here and from the paradox of your own life. I can't imagine a man being capable of living with a nun who both he and his brother are in love with, who wouldn't go quite insane as a result."

Annoyed, Shandor jotted a quick letter to Yoshka reminding him that Imre was living the same way and wasn't concerned about a thing. But Yoshka was unimpressed and, in the margin of his next letter, he noted that in his opinion, Imre had always lived in a delusional bubble.

Every now and then, Shandor would decide to stop worrying about his irritating younger brother, especially after receiving a particularly infuriating letter in which Yoshka would insinuate that he worried so much about others because he couldn't cope with the complications of his own life. But then he'd find another letter in the envelope, from his nephew Peter, and that always made him even more adamant to have Yoshka's family moved to a safer place.

When his friendship with Hugo Scott began to grow stronger, following the publication of selected chapters of his upcoming book about the civil war in a widely-read American newspaper, Shandor pinned all his hopes on the journalist. And Scott led him to believe that he could organize American visas, at least for Yoshka, Martha, and little Peter. They even agreed it would be in lieu of payment for material that Shandor had already provided, yet Yoshka firmly refused to emigrate to the United States without being ensured a job. Again, he claimed that you don't bring a child into the world just to raise him as a penniless refugee. "If you're serious about how you feel, why don't you go to America ahead of us and see if you can find any contracting jobs for me?"

Shandor was furious but he got the hint. If he was finding it hard to leave Paris, only because he was bound by his love for a nun who would never be his, how could he ask his brother to leave his homeland, family, property, and work and emigrate to a foreign country when he didn't even know the language?

Still, he continued to see Scott, share his stories with him, and devise plans to make the Schwartz family from Hungary emigrate against their will.

Meanwhile, The Charm of San Sebastián was published and became an overnight bestseller in the United States. Thrilled, Hugo Scott told Shandor that the publishing house had already given him a generous advance to write a second book. Naturally, he asked Shandor to supply him with more stories and to sign an agreement promising never to tell anyone. Shandor was prepared to agree, but only in return for half of Scott's profits from the books. After lengthy negotiations, they decided that Shandor would make do with forty percent, of the advances, too. Satisfied, Shandor was convinced that he would now be able to provide his unwilling brother with the financial support he needed until things worked out for him in America. He would learn the language and find a good livelihood for himself and his family. His fears were allayed and he continued putting his own life in order, which was not an easy task. His daily routine consisted mainly of sitting in cafés with his friend Scott and telling him stories. In the early evening, around eight o'clock, Shandor would hurry home to eat dinner with Imre and Angelika, who insisted on the two of them spending the evenings with her. She claimed that their way of life, which was different from that of ordinary people, wouldn't last if they didn't maintain it by spending intimate time together in the evenings, which they devoted to discussing their issues.

At first, to Shandor's immense surprise, they found that they had none, other than economic survival. Angelika collected the little money that the two men earned, Imre from his paintings, Shandor from his stories. She kept a meager sum aside to pay the rent at the beginning of each week and bought cheap groceries in the market with however much remained. In the evening, she would prepare a big, nutritious meal for them, though not very tasty. Then they would reminisce about the fort of San Sebastián and Adrianus, whom they missed terribly, and agree that if it hadn't been for the evil Antonio, the Republicans wouldn't have been defeated. They would end the evening with a prayer for Adrianus's soul, may he rest in peace. Angelika would go to bed with a book in hand, and Shandor and Imre would write letters to the family. They didn't discuss their relationship much. They believed that their arrangement could bother people only because they were accustomed to loving couples, not trios, but they were happy and content with their lot.

Only after their financial situation improved did Shandor begin to feel a little restless, which bothered him mostly at night, of all times. He found this very strange. Each of them had their own room, and every evening they would out, eat like kings. But then he'd find himself thinking about Angelika and have trouble sleeping.

When they first arrived in Paris, Angelika had three black nun habits and three nightgowns. The only difference between them was the fabric they were sewn from. While her habits were made of rough cotton, the nightgowns were made of soft, pliable wool, which made them comfortable to sleep in. Before going to bed for the night, Angelika would wash in a small tub that she placed in the kitchenette and then put on a nightgown. Shandor, who was either talking to his brother or writing letters, didn't dream of entering the room, unless she spoke to them, which she rarely did.

After their financial situation improved, they both started pampering her with gifts, buying her chocolate or flowers every day. One day, on his way home, Shandor happened to glance into a store window, and he noticed a beautiful, long white nightgown with lace trim on the collar and sleeves. He marched right in and bought it as a gift for Angelika. When Imre saw how pleased Angelika was with it, he appeared the next day with another lace-trimmed nightgown for her, this time in blue. By the end of the week, Angelika had received four new nightgowns. That Friday evening, she said thank you and asked them to stop spoiling her so extravagantly, because they didn't know what fate would bring and they should save the money for a rainy day. She would be happy with just one bouquet of flowers a week, she said, and when she saw the disappointment in their faces, she added that a small bar of chocolate with the bouquet was also an option.

That night, for the first time ever, Shandor found it impossible to sleep. He couldn't focus on his weekly letter to Yoshka, and he kept trying to guess which nightgown Angelika would wear that night. No matter how hard he tried to stop thinking about it, the more his mind developed a will of its own and kept badgering him. Worse still, he kept imagining her removing her black rough nun's habit, standing naked in front of the mirror, shaking her braid loose, and brushing her long hair, her determined and sober expression slowly becoming reflective and hazy: With her long, delicate fingers, she gathers her dark hair and lets it fall over her ripe breasts, with only her nipples peeping through. She looks at her image in the mirror, smiles pensively to herself, picks up the white nightgown and pulls it over her head and down over her narrow hips, flat stomach, and long legs, until it covers her body. She is beautiful, as glowing and expectant as a bride on her wedding day. *Who is she waiting for*? Shandor wondered, shaking, feeling ashamed, humiliated, and furious. Stop thinking about her! he thought to himself angrily and hurled the inkwell at the wall. The stains looked like an hourglass, and Shandor saw it as a mute prophecy of their happy times beginning to run out.

***

Shandor managed to make it through the following three nights by arriving drunk to dinner so he could immediately fall into a dreamless sleep. However, on the fourth night, he awoke in horror from a dream that was even more lustful and wilder than his daydreams. This time, there wasn't even an inkwell to slam against the wall, and he felt that if he didn't do something, he would end up bashing his head against the wall until he killed himself. He stood up, dressed, and left the house. His feet led him back to the bar where he'd left Hugo Scott.

Scott gave him an understanding and inviting smile. He was sitting at the bar with two French women. Shandor knew them. Jean Marie was a wealthy heiress studying philosophy at the Sorbonne, but she really wanted to be an erotic poet. Nicole wrote a social column in a small Parisian fashion magazine. They both had aspirations to write for the American newspaper that published Hugo Scott's articles. They wanted him to teach them English, and when the time was right, to help them get work with the paper.

Meanwhile, between one English lesson and another, they were also enjoying their time as lovers. Scott liked to needle Shandor and tell him that they're the complementary triangle to his with Angelika and Imre. That night, they became a foursome, and Shandor stopped dreaming about Angelika at night.

At first, Angelika and Imre didn't notice Shandor's frequent nights out. He came home every night and got up at the same time as always. He naively believed that the new arrangement could last forever. He still believed that Angelika was the only woman deserving of his love, whereas Jean Marie and Nicole were there only for fun.

About two weeks after his nocturnal pleasures began, he came home one night to find Angelika sitting in her blue nightgown by the table in the entrance hall with a bottle of red wine and a half-empty glass to keep her company.

"Shandor," she said softly as he entered the room. She looked so magnificent, so beautiful, that he couldn't breathe. Her hair lay loose on her shoulders, a perfect dark frame for her pale, sad face. "Where have you been?" she asked, "I was worried about you."

Overwhelmed with emotion, Shandor's heart tremored. How did she know he was out, he wondered. To know that, she would have had to go into his room.

"I was with Hugo Scott at the bar," he tried to sound as casual as possible. "How did you know I was out? Did you go into my room?"

"Yes," she admitted. Her cheeks were a little flushed, for she herself had set the strict rules that forbade both men from entering her room after bedtime unless a fire broke out or the Germans invaded Paris. The chances of both were slim. "I thought I heard the door. I got up to see what was happening and I noticed that your coat was gone, so…I went into your room…after I knocked a few times on the door and there was no answer."

"Angelika, don't worry about me," he replied tenderly, after taking a few good swigs of wine from the bottle. "I'm a big boy, I know the streets of Paris, and I couldn't possibly get lost."

"I'm not worried about you getting physically lost in the streets of Paris but that you'll lose your spiritual path."

"What do you mean?"

"Shandor, don't play games with me," her face suddenly darkened, "I know what men do at night outside their homes, especially men like Hugo Scott."

"Most of them actually do it at home, that's the normal way to live,"

Shandor objected and immediately regretted it. The wine must be talking, he thought and tried to take her hand.

"It's hard for you," Angelika said matter-of-factly, and to his relief, she didn't try to pull her hand away, "I thought this would happen. I thought that a man like you wouldn't be able to bear an arrangement such as ours for very long."

"Are you angry?" he felt as frightened as a little boy.

"No, I'm just sad."

"Why?"

"Because I love you, Shandor, and it hurts me that you're going to be leaving us soon."

"Angelika, who said anything about leaving?!" The fear in his chest was growing, and he felt it was about to explode.

"You don't know it yet, but that's precisely what's going to happen. I'm willing to do anything, except what you want me to do."

"Angelika, my love, I don't want you to do a thing. I've learned to live the way we do without any of us getting hurt."

"It won't last long, Shandor, the nature of physical desire doesn't dissipate if it comes with the true love of the soul. That's what is written in all the books that I've read. And eventually, your desire for me will grow stronger. You'll start dreaming about holding me in your arms, even when you're with another woman, and your frustration will only grow deeper. You'll have to do something, and in the end, it will push you away from us."

Angelika was now sobbing, and Shandor, who couldn't control himself, stood up and took her in his arms, trying to stop her tears. But after a few seconds, he realized he was doing exactly what Angelika had said he would and what would eventually force him to leave.

***

That night, Shandor and Angelika knew the intense excitement known only to lovers when they realize their love for the first time. Shandor felt a joy more exhilarating than he had believed possible, even though

Angelika was bashful and timid, not like the daring women he'd known before her. He compared her taste to that of a tropical fruit he would never ever have. Juicy and sweet and wild. The touch of her pale skin felt like a wonderful blend of velvet and silk. Her groans, muffled for fear of waking Imre, were like the notes of a wonderful composition that no musician, however ingenious, could ever have written.

But then, as she lay quivering like a placated kitten curled up in his arms while he stroked her, he realized that they felt entirely differently about it. Shandor was certain that everything could return to normal, whereas Angelika felt that nothing would be the same.

"But why?" Shandor demanded to understand, "I promise you, I'll never come near you again if you don't want me to. Everything will be exactly as you wish. To me, what happened tonight in this room is better than being with a thousand women. Always, even when I feel that carnal urge to take another woman, this night will appear in my mind, and that foolish desire will pass, I assure you."

"Men always think only of themselves," Angelika said, moving away from him as she looked at him, her eyes filled with compassion.

"What do you mean? Didn't you enjoy it as much as I did? Did I force myself on you?" Shandor fell anxiously to his knees at the foot of Angelika's bed, "I am so sorry, my love, but if only you had said something, even a single word of refusal…"

"No, you silly thing, that's not what I said or will say, because I would be lying to you, and more so to myself. And that's what scares me most, Shandor, my love. I did enjoy it, even though it never occurred to me that I could, after what happened with that twisted soul who called itself my father."

"What's frightening about that?" Shandor asked, "You should be happy that you're a normal woman. Your soul wasn't damaged beyond repair by your damned father's actions."

"You may be right. If things had worked out otherwise, perhaps I, too, could have been happy. But Imre, you, and I all vowed to stay together, to have a certain arrangement, and we cannot and must not change it."

"Oh, that's what you mean," Shandor said awkwardly and looked in the direction of Imre's room, praying with all his heart that he hadn't woken up and heard something of the magical act that had just taken place in their home.

"Yes, our Imre, whom we both love so deeply. How do you think he'll respond to the fact that we broke the agreement?"

"Imre…he's…not a normal person. He may not mind."

"And if he does?"

"Then we'll decide what to do," Shandor mumbled wearily. He knew that only after a good night's sleep, he'd be able to think clearly about matters. "Come, let's go to sleep. Tomorrow we'll decide what to tell Imre."

"Tomorrow won't change anything. The sun will only shed more light on the problems and make them more apparent."

"Angelika, I don't know what to tell you. Decide how you want things to be, and we'll make it happen."

"And what if my options are to sleep only with you behind Imre's back or suggest he join the party?"

Shandor couldn't help himself and burst out laughing, but he stopped immediately at the look of reproach on Angelika's face.

"You know, Shandor," she continued, "I don't blame you for this any more than I blame myself. And that's why I know that things can't go on as before. I don't trust myself not to lust after you again. And it's not fair to Imre."

Then leave him and come with me, the words were on the tip of Shandor's tongue, almost choking him, but he managed not to speak them.

"We have no other way out," Angelika continued, her eyes soft with compassion, "I thought that I knew myself. I was challenging God when I thought I could live with two men whom I love without physical desire becoming involved. But he proved that I have committed the sin of pride. I believed I was better than other people, and for that I must be punished. Tomorrow, you talk to Imre, tell him that you've fallen in love with another woman and that you're leaving home for her. And I'll talk to God…I will beg him to forgive me for my sins against Him. I hope that He'll forgive me and us all. Difficult times await us, and we'll be needing His help."

The next day, Shandor left the home he'd shared with his brother and the woman he loved. And he would never fall in love again.

CHAPTER 10

"And what happened meanwhile to your grandparents and your father?" Oren asked the next day, when I got back to New York told and told him Shandor Bachi's stories.

"They stayed in Hungary until the end of the war," I replied absentmindedly. Somehow, despite my other concerns, I couldn't focus on anything but Shandor Bachi's eternal love for Angelika. I kept asking myself if I was capable of falling so deeply in love.

"Why didn't Shandor bring them to the United States in the end?" Oren asked inquisitively.

"Because when they could still go, they didn't want to, and after they realized their mistake, it was no longer possible. The Hungarians wouldn't let them leave."

"Well, I see that these stories didn't bring you any closer to your family treasure."

"Yeh," I mumbled, "I didn't really make much progress."

"Maybe he's just messing with your head, using tales about bears and nuns to keep you away from the treasure."

"I don't think so, Oren, I really don't. He showed me his contract with Hugo Scott, and it seems reasonable that with the forty percent in royalties he received for Scott's three books he'd be able to live comfortably without having to work."

"Okay, but it's always nice to have a few more dollars."

"Stop it, Oren, he wouldn't lie to me in such a situation. In fact, he said he would check his bank account today, and if he could, he'd send us a little money."

"A little money," Oren muttered, "I think that you should end your treasure hunt and agree to let me ask my parents about lending your family the money."

"No," I insisted, "you know perfectly well that they aren't millionaires, and I'm not going to let them also mortgage their home. Not before I at least do all I can to find any money that's rightfully ours."

"Darya, you do understand that it's not a game, right? This is your sister's life we're talking about. How long are you prepared to let her be blind?!"

"Stop it!" I burst out crying, "Stop making me feel guilty, I'm doing all I can!"

"I know, I know," he quickly hugged me, "it's just driving me crazy that I can't do anything to help."

"You're an enormous help, Oren," I reassured him quickly, trying to stop crying. Deep in my heart, I knew that if I loved him the way that Shandor loved Angelika, I would have no issue with accepting his parents' help.

***

In the evening, I called home. Vered answered. "Noiki's condition hasn't changed," she kept her report short, "but I think Dad's on the verge of a nervous breakdown. He's listening to Albinoni's *Adagio* all the time and crying."

"Why specifically Albinoni's *Adagio*?"

"Because it's sad."

"Then hide the cd from him. And what about Mom?"

"She's already consulted with a few other doctors, and they all say the same thing, that Noa has to have surgery, but only the professor should perform it. There's no one in Israel anywhere near his level. They also say that there's no immediate danger of her condition deteriorating, so we have a little time to raise the money."

"How much is a little?" I wondered.

"I don't know, a few weeks, perhaps, that's what Mom understood. Meanwhile, she's also been to a few rabbis and witches, and they all say that Noiki will be fine in the end, they just didn't say when the end would be."

"And how's the kid behaving?"

"Like a queen, or maybe tyrant's the word I'm looking for. That's why I've started sleeping at their place. Mom and Dad would collapse without me. What's news with you? Are you getting anywhere with him?"

"Not really. Do you want me to take time off work to come and help you?" I asked, hoping for a refusal, and Vered didn't disappoint me.

"No, it's okay, keep trying to raise the money, that's more important. Did you make any progress with Shandor Bachi?"

"No," I sighed, "he promised to check out his pension fund and see if there is any money available to give us, but we can't count on it. Oren also offered to ask his parents for a loan. What do you think?"

"Me? It's up to you. You realize that they'll expect you to get married afterward, at the very least."

"I do," I answered, thinking that Vered had all the luck. Her husband Gilad's parents were kibbutzniks and no one expected them to have money. "So then, you say we have a couple of weeks?"

"That's what the doctors say."

"All right," I sighed again, "see you tomorrow."

✳✳✳

Afterward, Oren and I went to a Mexican restaurant on Third Avenue, drank margaritas, ate nachos, and then sat in silence. That's when we noticed three young flight attendants who had been on our flight walk in.

"Hey, there's Oren!" one of them called out, and they waved in our direction.

"They're waving to you," I told him, and he shifted uncomfortably in his chair.

"I can see that."

"Can we join you?" They were already at our table. Oren looked like he wanted the ground to swallow him up.

"Why not?" I answered for him, expecting a kick under the table. I couldn't remember the names of any of them, but I couldn't be expected to remember the names of everyone who ever worked with me on flights, no matter how pretty they are.

One of them sat down beside Oren and whispered something in his ear. He blushed.

"I don't think that's a good idea," he said at last, "Darya and I are in the middle of a discussion."

"Okay," she got up and pulled her two friends to the bar, "if you change your minds, we're here, at the bar."

"What did she want?" I demanded to know.

"She wanted us to go with them to some club."

"Why do you think she had to whisper the invitation in your ear?"

"Because…" Oren squirmed under my piercing gaze, "because…yesterday, I met them here, I had a bit to drink, and—"

"You went with them to a club?" I stared at him in amazement, "I can't believe it!"

"No, are you kidding? I went back to the room to sleep and I promised them that maybe another day…"

"Oh, that sounds more like you," I said, a little disappointed, especially since I hadn't felt even a hint of jealousy. "Why didn't you go with them to the club?"

"Darya, come on. Do you really think it would have been right for me to go with three bimbos, especially when you're going through such a difficult time?"

"But I wasn't here yesterday, Oren, nothing would have happened if you'd gone out to dance, released some tension."

"I didn't feel like it. I was worried about you, and…. What's with all these questions? Are you trying to pick a fight with me because I didn't do anything wrong?"

"No, sorry. Oren, I'm just trying to explain to you that despite the difficult situation, you can enjoy yourself a bit."

"All right, all right, I've always thought that you were too sophisticated for me," he growled. "Let's go back to the hotel, pick up is at six tomorrow morning."

I walked behind him, looking miserably at his stiff back. He didn't make my imagination run wild, and that's what I really wanted. A crazy thought crossed my mind and I couldn't get rid of it: If I knew that he'd gone out with those three silly flight attendants, like Shandor Bachi had with his Parisian women, would it have excited me as it did Angelika back then?

That night, I found it hard to fall asleep. Something we ate was giving me indigestion, or maybe the incessant thoughts racing around my brain were the problem. That made more sense. I was trying to decide whether I could allow myself to continue searching for clues that would lead me to the enormous family treasure, which may exist only in Mr. Klein the bank manager's imagination. And yet, Shandor Bachi had also said that there could very well have been money involved in Dad and his parents' surviving the war.

"Your grandmother Martha saved them, at least that's the official story," he explained to me, his face blank. "For years I corresponded by letter with your Grandpa Yoshka, but he wouldn't discuss it. Only when I visited him in Israel did he agree to say a few words, but he gave me no details. He said that Martha had been very brave and had disguised herself as a Christian, with fake documents she received from someone from the Zionist Relief and Rescue Committee, possibly from Kasztner himself, who was later murdered in Israel. She stayed in Budapest, not far from the ghetto, near to where the workcamp that your father and Peter were, so she could visit them every day and bring them food. She also managed to keep them off the transport lists to Auschwitz, although how she did that, exactly, he didn't want to tell me. I believe she bribed a member of the Arrow Cross Party. They were responsible for the camp, with money or something else."

"Something else?" I was intrigued. To my defense, I will say that it was late, and I was finding it hard to concentrate.

Shandor Bachi smiled. "Yes, Daryakum, something else, something else that your grandfather's honor won't allow me to speak of."

Grandpa's honor, I wondered, who thought about honor in that hellhole?

Suddenly I remembered the subject of my dissertation: Why the Western Media Hid the Magnitude of the Holocaust of European Jewry.

"Shandor Bachi," I said uneasily," what year did you emigrate to the States?"

"At the end of 1940," he replied, his face a mask.

"And…well, you had connections with a seasoned journalist there. Couldn't you have asked him to shake up the world? To use his newspaper to share what was happening in the death camps?"

"Oh, Daryakum," a heavy sigh escaped Shandor Bachi's lips and his eyes filled with tears. "I…even I didn't know what was going on. I didn't believe it. Your grandfather was the only one who sent me letters. And he…in his letters, everything sounded optimistic…so optimistic…"

***

I was present only in body on the flight back to Israel. I did what I had to automatically, while basically, all I could think about was where I would go next. *Should I play detective and fly off to Hungary, to Budapest, where I had no idea what to do and try to find clues that would lead me to my family's money?*

"Tell me, you're Oren's girlfriend, right?" one of the flight attendants asked, snapping me back to reality. I looked up: It was the one who'd invited him to the club the night before.

"Yes."

"You're so lucky," she continued, unabashed, "but tell me, why aren't you his wife?"

"What's it to you?"

"Nothing, I just wanted to know if you're serious about him or not."

"That really doesn't matter," I snapped angrily, "even if I wasn't serious about him, no way would he look at an idiot like you!"

"Maybe I'm an idiot, but if I had a boyfriend like Oren, I wouldn't make him chase after me for twelve years."

I was so angry and frustrated that for a moment I couldn't speak, which made it easier for the stupid little fool to scurry to the kitchen without having a pitcher thrown at her.

∗∗∗

I was too furious to speak to Oren the whole way home. Only after we were in our apartment, did I ask him, my voice tense, "Why did you gossip about us with those three idiotic flight attendants we ran into at the restaurant?"

"Me? When did I gossip about us?"

"You told them that for twelve years I've been refusing to marry you!"

"First of all, I never said that, and secondly, isn't that true?"

"Then what did you say?"

"Nothing, I just said that we've been together for twelve years. I didn't say anything about you not wanting to get married. I guess that even idiots like them can work it out themselves."

"Oren, if you have any complaints, tell me, don't go pouring your heart out to idiots at the bar!"

"Okay, then I'm telling you—I want us to get married. I want us to have a family, and I don't understand why you're behaving as if you've heard this only from other people…As if I haven't been specific enough these twelve years!"

"Because I don't like you telling the whole world about it, like I'm wronging you in some way. Don't you understand, I don't have the energy to deal with it right now?"

"As far as I remember," he replied, unbuttoning his shirt, "you're the one who brought the subject up this time."

"And you made me bring it up!"

"I didn't make you do anything. Those girls were openly flirting with me, so I took the wind out of their sails in the best way I knew how. I told them we've been together for a long time and that I really love you. What's wrong with that?"

Almost naked now, he walked toward the bathroom in his underwear. I looked at his brown muscular back and tried to understand why the spectacular sight made me feel nothing but anger; who my anger was directed at, myself or him, I had no idea. The sound of running water coming from the bathroom couldn't cool me down. I was fuming. I knocked on the door and declared, "I'm going to my parents!"

"Don't you want me to come with you?" I heard him ask through the door.

"Not really," I said, "I don't feel like arguing with you there, too. Bye!"

***

Vered opened the door for me, and a cheerful, sandy-colored golden retriever puppy jumped on me. "Quick, come in," she urged me, "all I need now is for him to run away."

"What's this?" I asked and patted the bouncy puppy, "Have we already bought her a guide dog?"

"Just a dog," Vered retorted, "she's getting everything she asks for, and on a silver platter, too. Soon we won't have any money left for even half the operation."

"Well, what do you expect? They're heartbroken," I mumbled.

When I saw Dad coming out of Noa's room, my heart broke too. He looked like he'd aged overnight. Before the tragedy happened, we were proud of how young he looked. He was seventy-five years old, but he looked no more than fifty. We believed it resulted from the combination of his fine genes and his love of life. Now his joy had been taken away, and his eyes looked desperate and pensive, as though asking himself or God (whom he had never believed in) if he and his family hadn't suffered enough in the Holocaust that he should be punished again.

"Dad," I called out to him—he didn't seem to have noticed me. He focused his eyes on me and tried to smile.

"Daryakum, how are you?" he hugged me warmly. The puppy jumped on us, barking happily.

"Mickey, sit," Dad scolded him, and the puppy immediately sat down.

"Why Mickey?" I asked curiously, "What kind of name is that for a dog?"

"It's short for *mikor alszik,* Dad explained, "it's a Hungarian expression, it means 'when he sleeps.' It's what we say when someone is good only when they're asleep."

"Yes, I remember," I muttered to myself. We each had our turn at being called that. "Where's Noa?"

"Sleeping," he said and collapsed onto the sofa. "She asked me to read her the book The Paul Street Boys. She loved it as a child."

Tears came to my eyes as I sat down beside him. The puppy howled and walked to the door.

"I'll take him," Vered volunteered quickly and attached the blue leash to his collar.

"Where's Mom?"

"She went to the health food store, some witchdoctor said that we must give Noa vitamins to make her stronger."

"Dad, it's going to be all right," I put my arm over his shoulder, "they'll do the surgery and she'll be healthy again."

"Yes, yes," he muttered, "of course she will…but when?"

"Soon, very soon," I said, trying to cheer him up, "I was at Shandor Bachi in Florida, and he promised to send as much money as he can."

"As much as he can doesn't sound like much," Dad grumbled sourly, "he always was a miser."

"Tell me, do you still have relatives in Hungary?"

"Maybe, why?"

"Because I want to appeal to anyone I can, to ask them for money."

"Daryakum, sweetie, do you think that there are millionaires living in Hungary? The country only recently renounced communism. It's just a mess there right now."

"I still think it's worth finding out."

"I don't know, Daryakum, if it makes you feel better, go. In any case your flights are at the airline's expense. But I wouldn't pin your hopes on it."

"Dad…"

"Okay, I know that Grandpa used to correspond with someone in Hungary, possibly a relative. I kept the letters. Do you want me to check the address?"

"Yes, please," a wave of excitement washed through me—maybe I would find a lead.

Dad heaved himself up and opened one of the heavy drawers in the chest of drawers in the corner.

"Here, these are letters from Hungary," he said and looked at one of the envelopes. "The address is 35 Andrassy Avenue, Budapest. Well, I'll be!"

"What is it?"

"That was where we lived after the war," he said excitedly, "how did I not notice that before?"

"Really, how?"

"How do I know? I guess I had a lot on my mind," he sighed, and the sadness settled in his eyes again, "but it really is interesting, your grandfather corresponding with someone who stayed behind and was living in our house in Budapest. He never mentioned it to me."

"Look and see who it is," I suggested, "so I know who I'm going to visit."

"Darya, I don't think you'll discover that they're wealthy, no matter who it is," he sighed but opened the envelope. The page was covered in small, cramped handwriting. Dad put on his glasses and started to read. I waited patiently. "I don't believe it," he mumbled to himself, "it's from her, from Gizi, his sister-in-law. It never occurred to me that she may be alive after all these years."

"Gizi, the Polish woman? Who disguised herself as a Hungarian soldier and was awarded a medal of honor?" I inadvertently revealed that I knew plenty about the family, more than he knew I'd been told. But Dad wasn't focused enough to notice.

"Yes, it's that's Gizi, definitely," he smiled as if watching the story unfold before his eyes, "the little hero. Apparently, she continued to live in our house after my parents immigrated to Israel."

"When was the last letter sent?" I urged him.

Dad took out all the letters and looked for dates. "The last one is from October 1995. About ten years ago."

"That makes sense, because that's when he died."

"Yes," Dad sighed. Everyone in the family believed that Grandpa Yoshka would live forever. Twenty years after he and Grandma immigrated to

Israel, during the Hungarian Revolution of 1956, he buried his beloved wife and stayed in their small, rent-controlled apartment in Ramat Hasharon. When we suggested he move into a retirement home, he adamantly refused. He was independent, he would cook a hot, Hungarian three-course meal for his lunch every day, after which he would treat himself to two cigarettes and a beer. Then he would read until evening, before going out to play cards with friends. He didn't want to change his routine, he loved it too much. That is until his friends began to drop like flies. That's when he bought a bicycle with an auxiliary motor, so he could go visit his friends who lived further away. In the end, that bike led indirectly to his death. One day, he came out of the bank and got on his bike. A reckless truck driver reversed without checking the mirror and hit him. Grandpa wasn't killed, he only broke his hip. After he underwent surgery and recovered from the injury, he was put into a retirement home, where he didn't like the food and wasn't allowed to smoke. And so, one night, he apparently decided to show his dissent by not waking up in the morning. He passed away quietly and without any problems, probably after he realized that he'd lost that war.

I was very attached to him, and after noticing on my frequent visits how he was fading away, I pestered Dad to get him out of there. But Dad claimed that it was the best place for him and that he even had friends to play cards with again. The fact that he decided to forgo that pleasure and die proved that I was right. And I was, even though I never said it to Dad's face after Grandpa died. I was pretty sure that that was what Dad meant when he said he had a lot on his mind. I was convinced he felt guilty.

"I wonder if Gizi's still alive," I muttered to myself.

"I doubt it," Dad said, searching through the letters again, maybe for a phone number. "She would have to be almost a hundred years old, and she's not a Schwartz, so she may not have the longevity gene."

"Still," I said, "it's worth finding out."

"Daryakum, even if she is alive, I'm sure she won't be able to give us the money we need."

Instead of answering him, I picked up the phone to the flight crew schedulers and asked for leave, for family reasons. To my relief, Dana picked up. She had also been an attendant, and we'd been friends ever since. She said I would have to come in and fill out forms, but when I told her what had happened to Noiki, she immediately said not to worry, she would fill out the forms for me. I asked when the next flight to Hungary was. The following morning, she said.

"Is it full?"

"No, there are loads of available seats. Do you want me to book for you?"

"Yes," I said, thanking her inside for not asking too many questions, "and Dana, thanks. For everything."

"My pleasure," she answered and hung up.

Meanwhile, Noiki had woken up and Dad ran off to her room to see if she needed anything.

"Yes," I heard her reply, "could you make me a cup of coffee before Mom comes home?"

I went into her room and stood there for a moment, astounded. It was filled with balloons, flowers, and baskets of candy, as if she were having a party. The cheerful spectacle was in stark contrast with my little sister's small and unhappy face as she fumbled around and asked, "Where's Mickey?"

"Vered took him for a walk," I responded, sat down beside her and took her cold hands in mine.

"Darya?"

"Yes," I squeezed them, "how are you, sweetie?"

"Fine, fine, I…" Noiki threw herself on me and burst into tears, "I just don't understand why these eyes of mine are choosing to do only what they shouldn't damn it. if I can't see with them, why can I cry?"

"Go ahead and cry, it helps," I whispered to her, hugging her tight. My heart went out to her.

Suddenly I remembered all the times I'd been horrible to her, and I broke out crying as well.

"Enough, stop it," she sniffled and tried to smile. "It also has its advantages, being blind. For example, I can't see the awful clothes that you're probably wearing."

"True," I whispered and tried to smile, but then I remembered that she couldn't see me anyway, so there was no point in trying.

"You don't have to act all brave with me," I whispered to her. "Talk to me. Let it all out."

"Darya, I'm scared," her head was resting on my shoulder and her tears were wetting me. "What if I'm like this forever?"

"You won't, you'll have the surgery and then you'll be fine. I promise you that in two weeks' time, three tops, you'll be able to be the family witch again and tell everyone exactly how terrible they look."

The noise from the front door indicated that visitors had arrived. Before I knew what was happening, the room was filled with Noiki's friends, and Mickey was running from one to the other, barking at them all. I jumped to my feet. This was precisely the kind of atmosphere that I couldn't cope with. I felt very uncomfortable with the carnival in the room.

"It'll be all right," I whispered to my little sister, who looked even smaller and more pitiful surrounded by all the commotion. "I'll make sure of it."

***

I got home to find Oren fast asleep. I decided not to wake him so we wouldn't get into another unnecessary argument, and I hoped to get away with leaving him a note on the dresser telling him I was going to Hungary, instead of telling him face to face.

I climbed into bed and tried to fall asleep. I couldn't, of course. I kept thinking about Shandor Bachi's stories and the surprise with which Dad had reacted when he realized that his father had been corresponding with Gizi until the day he died. What does it mean? I tried to make sense of all the facts, but it didn't lead to the results I'd been hoping for. I momentarily regretted not questioning Dad more explicitly. But I assumed that if he knew about any money any of our relatives may have, he would have certainly tried to get his hands on it.

***

I woke up with a start from the phone, which was ringing insistently. I answered as quickly as I could, hoping that Oren wouldn't wake up. But he turned onto his back and looked at me, his eyes troubled.

"Who is it?" he asked.

"I don't know," I muttered as I heard Dana's voice in my ear.

"Darya, are you still asleep? Your flight's in two and a half hours. I have your ticket here."

"Wow, thanks, Dana," I replied, "I'll be right there."

"What's up?" Oren wondered.

"I have a flight in two and a half hours, to Budapest," and got dressed as fast as I could.

"What? Are you on standby?"

"No, I took a few days off and booked a flight to Hungary," I avoided his eyes.

"Why didn't you tell me?" he got out of bed and ran after me. It was precisely the kind of scene I'd been hoping to avoid.

"I didn't think it was important enough to wake you. You were fast asleep."

"Darya," he grabbed me by the door and held me tight, "you're running away from me!"

"I'm not, Oren, this is all about Noiki! Why are you making such a big deal out of it?"

"Because I feel it's not just that, something between us doesn't feel right."

"It's nothing. You're feeling that way because I'm stressed out. I'm sorry, Oren. When it's all over, I promise to put more into our relationship."

"How long will you be away?" he put his hands on his hips, his tone harsh, his expression cold, just like a housewife being left at home with the kids while her husband ran about town. I suppressed a smile.

"Oren, I swear, I have no intention of staying any longer than necessary, really!" I hugged him again and swore to myself that I really would apply myself more when it was over and Noiki was better. But then again, I would have made a vow of silence and become a Carmelite nun, if it assured me it would make her better.

***

I made all the arrangements on the ground at lightning speed. That way, I also didn't have much time to think. Only when I was leaning back in my seat on the plane, did I suddenly realize that I was facing a three-hour flight and I hadn't even brought a book along to read. I asked for a newspaper, but it occupied my mind for exactly thirty-two seconds. Even the headlines were boring. It made sense, in a way. After all, everything was dwarfed by our family tragedy.

I only hope that Dad won't get sick now from all the worry. By trying to forget my fears, I was developing new ones. But he hadn't been well for a while, even before this happened. No one has said anything explicit to me, but from the way Mom spoke to him sometimes, I realized that he'd had a heart attack twenty-five years ago. I was five at the time. But thanks to his infectious love of life and optimism, he'd managed to avoid another attack. He even challenged fate, and at the age of forty-five, he solemnly announced that from his next birthday on, he would be losing a year every birthday, so that when he reached ninety, he'd be even and ready to die. We all cooperated happily with him. On his last birthday, we wrote "Sixteen" on his cake, in white cream letters.

CHAPTER 11

The freezing cold European spring welcomed me as I walked out of the terminal in Budapest. I stood in the long line for cabs and planned my next steps. I planned to go directly to 35 Andrassy Avenue, on the Pest side, hoping that Gizi was still alive and well and living there.

I have no idea what I'll do if she's not there, I thought despondently and pressed my nose to the cab window. The soft light of the sun was illuminating the sleepy quarter on our drive down the main avenue. "There's the Duna," the driver told me, like an old, experienced tour guide, pointing at the spectacular river reflecting the light back so proudly. The Duna was the Danube River, of course, and although I certainly admired it, I couldn't help thinking of all the Jewish bodies that were probably buried in its bed. Even when people walked by, huddled in gray coats and in their own worlds, I found it hard to see them as just innocent people walking to work. To me, they all looked like executioners, or at least like the children or grandchildren of executioners.

"This is Andrassy Avenue," the driver said, looking at me in relief. He probably expected more enthusiasm from a tourist and a tip to match. I left him twenty forints, so he wouldn't think I had some issue and also so he'd explain to me where number 35 was. He pointed to the right side of the street and said in broken English, "That house, it's number 35."

It was a red brick building, like all the buildings on the street. Below it was a café, which was still closed. I stood there and looked at it, trying to imagine Dad's family living there. I took a deep breath, and, holding my breath, I entered the stairwell. "Gizella Schwartz" was written on a door on the first floor. I took another deep breath and knocked on the door, first hesitantly, and then resolutely. *After the fourth knock, I heard a woman's squeaky voice on the other side of the door, "Who's there?" she asked in Hungarian.*

"Darya Schwartz," I replied, hoping that the name "Schwartz" would make her open the door. And it did.

"Darya Schwartz?" the old woman who opened the door was skinny and wore glasses. Her hair was completely white, and she wore it tied tightly back. Her blue-gray eyes stared suspiciously at me for a long moment but then lit up with a radiant smile that made her face beautiful. "Darya Schwartz," she repeated my name and continued in a rush of Hungarian, most of which I couldn't understand. My grasp of Hungarian was so minimal that all I managed to catch was that the similarity between me and my grandmother Martha was amazingly unmistakable.

"Do you speak English?" I asked hesitantly, "I understand almost no Hungarian."

"That's a shame, a real shame," she replied, but much to my relief, in English that wasn't at all bad. "Come in, I'm sure you'd like something to drink."

"Yes, please," I mumbled awkwardly, "maybe coffee."

Coffee is excellent," she said, and to my surprise, immediately led me out again. "We have a lovely café outside."

"It's closed," I said and stayed rooted in the middle of the hall, not knowing what to say. I couldn't figure out if she was inviting me to the café because she didn't have coffee at home, or if she just felt like going out.

"Then we'll have a drink here," she answered cheerfully, closed the door and walked briskly to the kitchen. I followed her.

"Don't worry, I have delicious Dobos torte here," she said, as if wanting to compensate me for the closed café.

"That's okay, thanks, I don't eat cake in the morning."

"Well what do you eat?" she sounded surprised, "You know, there is nothing like cake in the morning, it gives you energy for the whole day."

"And makes you fat for life."

"Darya, Darya, you have nothing to worry about, our family doesn't have a tendency to gain weight."

I smiled in response, although I wondered which family she meant exactly. After all, she wasn't a blood relation of the Schwartz family.

"And what brings you to me?" she asked after we sat down in her small living room. "In truth, I no longer dared to hope I'd ever see anyone from the family again before I died."

"Why?"

"There were a few disputes between your grandparents and me," she replied without explaining.

"Oh."

"Daryakum, my dear, I don't want to fill your young head with silly arguments from the past. You must be visiting to see the sights, find your roots, as people say these days."

"Not really," I replied weakly, "I actually came to hear about the past."

"You came all the way from Israel to meet me and to hear about the past? From me?" the old woman seemed taken aback, and I thought I could see suspicion in her eyes, so I quickly explained myself.

"I'm a flight attendant, so the ticket didn't cost me much, and…my younger sister is very sick, we need a lot of money for an operation, and I heard from someone who used to be close to the family that there is property of significant value somewhere in the world, and maybe even a lot of money. It could help us a lot, so I wanted to ask you if you know anything."

"Property and money?" Gizi frowned, wondering what I could be referring to, and stood up to search through the dark chest of drawers beside her. "Property and money, you say…if so, maybe it's time to open the parcel."

"What parcel?" I said, intrigued. Gizi didn't answer, she just opened a drawer as I held my breath.

"This one, here, that old Molnar gave me forty years ago," she turned to me, holding a parcel wrapped in brown paper. "Oh, my young darling, you probably don't even know who old Molnar was."

"Actually, I do," I looked away from the package. "He was a friend of Grandma's and worked as a bookkeeper at her father's textile factory."

"That's right," she said and sat down beside me, "although I don't think the word friend is quite accurate. Molnar, the poor man, was in love with

Martha, your grandmother his entire life." On second thought, Gizi added that Paul Molnar had undoubtedly been in love with Martha, but opinions about the title "poor man" were divided. Back then, as well, during those disastrous years.

***

Yoshka would certainly not have agreed with that description, since Molnar had received ownership of the family's business from Martha and then forced his way through a small crack into her heart.

Yoshka and his questionable love affair with Johanna Keleti were responsible for that crack, but he was in no hurry to take responsibility for it. His only claim against himself was for not paying heed to Shandor's pleas and not leaving Hungary with his family quickly, while he still could.

"But what could I have done?" he asked himself and Gizi when he was in Budapest one time. "I looked at Peter, and I saw how happy he was at home with his playmates, and I just couldn't bear to take him away to a strange land, where everyone spoke a foreign language."

Peter was four when he learned to read. Within a few months, he already knew the stories from *The Paul Street Boys* by heart, and by playing the part of Nemecsek the small blond private, who amazes everyone with his heroism and pays for it with his life, he taught the storyline of the book to the children he played with on the street, even those older than him.

Yoshka and Martha would look through the window of their home and watch the children having fun, and their hearts would go out to their young son, who had chosen such a noble and tragic part. Martha would allow the tears to well in her eyes, as did Yoshka, but only in secret.

After Yoshka's affair was discovered, it was the only thread connecting them—the thrill of being the parents of such a wonderful child.

***

When Peter began school, Martha began an open affair with Paul Molnar. That was after Shani told her about Mrs. Keleti.

Martha was furious, especially when she realized that Yoshka had proposed to her while he was still having the affair. The day the letter arrived from Shandor, finally confirming it, she put on her most beautiful dress, pinched her cheeks lightly like she used to as a girl, and stormed off to the fabric store. Molnar looked at her in surprise as she walked into his office. He had never seen her so agitated, or so beautiful.

"Come," she said to him and pointed to the next room, which used to be her office. It had a small sofa. Without uttering a sound, Molnar stood up and followed her. He thought she wanted to share a secret with him.

"I want to be your lover," she said in the same, mechanical, commanding tone, "if you're interested, of course."

"What?!" Molnar's confused gaze became horrified. For years he'd dreamed of this moment, but now that it had come, he didn't know how to respond.

"You heard me," she smiled sardonically, without an ounce of joy.

"But Martha, why? Why now?"

"Paul, I don't have time for questions. Perhaps you could loosen your tie and sit here beside me?" she suggested, then patted the crimson velvet-covered sofa.

"I…I don't understand, Martha," he stammered as he sat down beside her. "What do you want to do?"

"What people do when they're in love," she told him and undid his tie for him, "and don't say that you don't know what I mean. I know you've had plenty of such relationships with my seamstresses."

"There were…. Maybe," he blushed, "but you're married to Yoshka, and I…I proposed marriage to you, and you turned me down. You preferred him."

"I made a mistake," Martha admitted as she unbuttoned his white shirt. When she saw his pale, exposed chest she felt momentarily distraught: It couldn't match the tanned and well-built chest of her handsome husband. But then she told herself that beneath that chest beat a loyal and loving heart and that was what mattered.

Molnar flinched and moved away from her. "If you think you've made a mistake," he began, his voice thick with emotion, "then you can't correct it with a reckless act of love. Divorce Yoshka and marry me. My proposal still stands."

"Paul, I can't do that, at least not right now," she answered weakly, realizing that even though Yoshka had humiliated her, she was still in love with him. "Maybe with time, but now this is all I can offer you—an affair, as so many of our married acquaintances have, including my dear husband."

"Then it's revenge that you're looking for," he replied and began rebuttoning his shirt.

"Revenge or not, what does it matter? I'm prepared to give myself to you, so why concern yourself with definitions?"

"I can't do this," he said as he stood up, his face expressionless "With anyone else, yes, but not with you, Martha, I love you too much."

"This is all I can offer you for now," her face flushed from the humiliation. *Damn you Yoshka Schwartz, she thought furiously to herself, I can't even get my revenge on you!*

***

Weeks had passed since her romantic proposition and subsequent rejection. Martha Schwartz and Paul Molnar continue to see each other for business purposes and did not speak a word about what had happened. Inside, however, they were both reeling inside.

At first Martha was angry, but as time passed, her feelings of humiliation faded as other emotions began to develop; feelings of self-worth and of respect for him and his noble behavior.

Molnar, on the other hand, felt like an idiot: The only woman he had ever loved had offered herself to him on a silver platter, only without the formal seal, and of all the things he could have done, he chose to reject her. What was he thinking, he wondered at night as he tossed and turned in bed. Had he really believed that Martha—the most beautiful woman in town, her magnificence merely a reflection of her noble soul—would ever agree to leave her husband, the father of her son and marry him? After all, her love and devotion to Peter were common knowledge in Baja. There was no chance at all that she would ever hurt her child, even if it meant giving up everything she desired.

And it so happened, that one day, when Martha came to collect the money she had owing to her, Molnar jumped to his feet as she entered and declared passionately, "I'm willing!"

***

From that day forward, Martha was filled with energy. She walked around town with two red patches permanently adorning her cheeks, with no need to pinch them at all, like neon signs proclaiming, "I am a woman who is loved!"

Everyone in town could see what was happening; everyone, that is, but Yoshka. He finally began to realize what was going on only months later, yet he blamed the difficult times, at least in part. The financial situation of Schwartz Ignetz & Sons was deteriorating rapidly. He no longer returned from his trips around the country with money stuffed in his pockets and his cheeks puffed out with pride.

He began to weigh the benefits of moving to Budapest and joining his brother Mark, who was doing well in the sausage industry, which still had businesses that worked with the Jews. Martha, however, thought differently. She was still making a good profit from her father's business, under Paul Molnar's excellent management. Peter was ten years old, a gifted student and outstanding athlete, and she didn't want to uproot him and move him to the big city, where she thought he may be ruined.

Shani, who usually took her side, took Yoshka's this time. Although he was still angry with him for refusing to join his band of socialist Jews, he knew that what was done was done, and they now had to save whatever they could.

One day, he appeared on Martha's doorstep, just as she was about to leave for work.

"Martha, I think you're making a mistake," he told her, somber as usual. "The situation is deteriorating, and I plan on going underground before the Arrow Cross comes to drag me off to a labor camp. And I want you to put my mind at ease, I want to know that you and Peter are safe."

"Then rest assured, we are," Martha replied calmly, "and about going underground, to me it seems unnecessary. No one from Baja has been taken off to the labor camps."

"I don't intend on sitting around waiting for it to happen."

"You've always been impatient," she said sullenly. "You've never thought that the best way to help your family is to just stick around and help. You don't even help me take care of Papa."

"What point is there in taking care of him? Just to draw out his life so they can kill him in a death camp?"

"Shani, what are you talking about?"

"I'm talking about camps for Jews, my dear, blind Martha. Open your eyes! You hear about these camps everywhere, in Poland, and in Czechoslovakia; camps where they kill Jews with gas and then burn them!"

"Shani, Shani, those are just rumors designed to scare us. I'm not as naïve as you believe. I know that the Germans hate us, so they are spreading these rumors to make us flee from our homeland and from all of Europe."

"Perhaps, but those who don't can expect to suffer and be tortured to death."

"Well, then, run away if you're so afraid. Why are you still here?"

"Because I want to fight the Germans, I'm not one to avoid battle."

"Shani, really," she burst out laughing, which made him even angrier, "there are no Germans here, don't you see?"

"They will come, Martha, don't delude yourself."

"They will not. Even though our government is acting like it's under their rule, which really does make our lives more difficult, it's their way of protecting us from a German invasion."

"You're either naïve, or the time you're spending with your goy lover is making you temporarily blind. Do you not see what is going to happen? When the Germans give even the slightest hint that they want to eradicate the Jews in their terror camps, your wonderful Hungarians will turn against us. As it is, they aren't particularly fond of us, especially the Arrow Cross people."

"They are doing what they see as the lesser of two evils."

"Martha, you are living in a fool's paradise! Each day brings us closer to our end. You made a mistake not listening to me and leaving when you still could! And now, you're making another! Leave that goy! He may be in love with you, but as soon as he is ordered to kill you and your family he won't think twice!"

"He wouldn't do that!"

"And how he would! Don't you understand? You are married to his greatest enemy. Ever since we were children, and deep inside, he resents that you chose Yoshka and then brought a son into the world with him. Do you think he'll forgive you for that, because the two of you are having an affair? Yes, you are a beautiful woman, Martha, and a very smart one at that, but you have no understanding of what is in a man's heart. Even ten affairs wouldn't be enough to cure Paul Molnar's resentment! As soon as he has the opportunity, he will settle the bill between you, using the entire Schwartz family!"

"You're wrong, Shani," her voice trembled, but he didn't know whether it was because of what he'd said, or because she suddenly noticed Yoshka leaning against the doorway. They could see from his expression that he'd heard their whole conversation.

***

That evening, Peter was sent to sleep at Martha's sister, Yutzi's. Martha was afraid that things might spiral into a loud argument, and she preferred to keep Peter away from the eye of the storm. Peter was delighted. His cousin Tibby was a year older than him and quite the hooligan. Whenever Peter stayed over, he would come up with adventures, which was precisely why Martha didn't send him there too often.

That night, after they went up to bed, Tibby surprised him with a plan to sneak back into Peter's house.

"Why?" Peter wondered disappointedly, "I thought we'd do something more interesting, like swim to the island and catch rabbits."

"Forget about rabbits," Tibby said dismissively, "I heard my mother whispering to my father that fireworks are going to go off at your house today, and I want to go and see what she means."

"What? My parents are probably having a party or playing cards with their friends, nothing all that interesting, certainly not fireworks."

"Peter, you don't understand anything. When your parents throw parties or play cards, do they send you to sleep here?"

"No," Peter admitted thoughtfully, "and they haven't had a party for a very long time."

"Well, then, my mother must have meant something else, so let's go see what it's all about. If it's boring, we'll swim to the island, all right?"

"Fine," Peter agreed, his curiosity piqued. Were there really going to be fireworks?

They waited until Tibby's parents fell asleep, listening for his father's snores to saw through the air, then climbed out of bed and sneaked out.

When they arrived at Peter's house, they crouched under the big living room window and peered in over the sill. It took once glance to see that they weren't having a party. Yoshka and Martha were sitting facing each other, the coffee table between them, and talking.

"It doesn't look at all like fun," Peter said very rightly. His parents didn't seem happy at all.

"Shh…" Tibby hushed him, "let me hear what they're saying."

"What could be so interesting?" Peter said, puzzled, just as his father said something strange to his mother—

"I don't care if you have an affair with another man, but not with Paul Molnar!"

"Really?" Martha seethed, "I don't remember you asking me who I prefer you to have affairs with!"

"It's not the same for me, I don't do it with women who've been in love with me since we were children."

"Yoshka, the main reason I stayed with you, despite your affairs, is because I thought you were a decent human being. I beg of you, don't prove me wrong about that too!"

"What's indecent about what I said?"

"Everything! You're just trying to outsmart me! If I'm not making a fuss over your affairs, fairness requires you to act in the same way. Without digging around for excuses."

"But…" Yoshka started to say something when suddenly they heard a knock at the door. It could not be a sign of good news, especially not at such times.

They both rushed to the door, nervous. They opened it to find Peter standing there, staring at his father. "Mami's right," he said confidently, even though he wasn't quite sure what the word affair meant.

***

Martha was beginning to pay more attention to the war in Europe. Her feelings were split between her love for her son and her anger at Yoshka and passion for Molnar.

After Peter took her side in the argument that night, he began to cling stubbornly to her, not enabling her to spend time with her lover.

Molnar wondered why she couldn't come to him in the mornings when Peter was at school. Martha's grim reply was that she wasn't in the right mood in the mornings. Deep down, however, she knew that wasn't quite the truth. In fact, by innocently jumping to her defense, Peter had created a kind of barrier in her heart. She could no longer let herself be carried away by her lover without wondering if her actions were justifiable. Constantly brooding over it, she lost any enjoyment she got out of the relationship before it could die a more natural death.

She sometimes went to work in the morning, but only to collect the money. Molnar would make her coffee and discuss only business matters with her. Until one day, in 1942, he surprised her with a question unrelated to the business.

"I've been seeing a girl for a few weeks now, and I would like to propose to her. Will you give me your consent?"

Martha was shocked, but she didn't let it show. She was sitting straight in the armchair, her cup of coffee in her hand. "Paul, I'm not your mother or your sister. Why are you asking for my permission?"

"My mother and sister have both consented. In fact, they were the ones who suggested I approach her."

"If so, it would be nice of you to do as they wish."

"I can't do this without your blessing. You know full well that you were and will remain my only true love."

"People should get married because they love each other," Martha said, her face frozen.

"I am well aware of that," Molnar replied, but at the sight of his beloved Martha's face, he didn't continue. He was going to remind her again that he proposed to her before Yoshka.

"Then don't rush into marriage, wait until you fall in love."

"Martha," Molnar went down on his knees and took her hand, "there is no doubt in my heart that I will never love anyone else as long as you're around. Promise me, my love, that when Peter grows up, you'll leave your husband and marry me. I'll wait for you until it happens!"

"I can't promise you anything, certainly not at such a turbulent time. As you know, tomorrow we may all be sent away on trains." Martha revealed her secret fears, planted there by Shani before he left town.

"I won't allow that to happen, Martha, for without you, I have no life."

"I will go wherever my son goes."

"I know, and I will make sure that nothing bad happens to you," Molnar replied, his concern for her bringing out his fighting spirit.

"And will you take care of his father, too?"

If that's what you ask of me, then yes, I'll take care of his father, too."

"If so," Martha responded with a heartbreaking sigh, "I'll consent to your marriage."

"But…" Molnar was confused, "that's not what I asked for."

"But it's the least I can do for you right now, Paul. You're a good man. You deserve to enjoy the wonder of having children. And I can't promise you anything. Certainly not that."

"Martha!"

"Paul, soon I'll be leaving for Budapest. I don't know what will happen to us there, and so I want you to stay here, create a life for yourself, but, more importantly, don't allow our trading company to collapse. My parents are too unhealthy to move away. My sisters won't leave either. Please,

I'm asking you to take care of them, give them money or anything else they may need. I'll talk to my parents, I'll let them know that if the situation gets worse they should give you their collection of paintings to sell off, one at a time, in order to save any of them. Don't hesitate. I'll correspond with you by letter. If there is any problem, you can always consult with me."

"Martha," Paul held her hands tightly, his eyes reflecting deep fear, "do you believe it'll come to that?"

"It's not the time for beliefs, my dear," Martha's eyes filled with tears. For the first time in those dismal years, she was allowing fear to seep into her consciousness. "Things have already happened and will continue to happen, whether we believe in them or not. The reality of our times is impatient, it won't wait for our imagination to catch up with it."

"If so, how can you put such a heavy responsibility on me? Me, the small, dull accountant from a remote town? I'm sure you'll find someone stronger than me in Budapest to help you."

"Paul, you're not at all a small man. You'll grow and develop precisely to bear the responsibility I've placed on your shoulders, perhaps even more." As she said that, she leaned over and kissed him on the lips, "Our love will give you the strength."

***

A few weeks later, Yoshka and Martha packed their belongings and headed for Budapest. The passengers on the train witnessed an intriguing situation: A beautiful and noble woman was sitting and looking out of the window, her expression tragic and reflective, while the man and boy who accompanied her, also fine-looking people, were playing around and cheering like a couple of carefree children.

Peter did all he could to make his mother laugh, but she appeared even more distant. On normal days he would have been worried about her, but that day was very different. The fact that they were moving to Budapest, the big city, had aroused his sense of adventure, which he must have inherited from his father. He was already picturing himself organizing the other boys on their new street to play all kinds of different and strange games, which he'd learned from the many books he'd read recently. It never occurred to him that he may not become the head of the group. Peter had been a leader from the day he could stand up for himself. Even the older boys would do as he said. Not because he was domineering, which he wasn't, but because of his charismatic and easygoing nature, his love of people, and his developed sense of justice that formed a kind of aura around him.

After arriving in Budapest, they first lived with Mark and Gizi, whose home was large enough to accommodate three more families. Mark was doing well at the sausage stand he ran in the central train station. Thanks to the fact that one of his most enthusiastic customers was a high ranking official in Admiral Horthy's government, he was allowed to keep his stand and to even employ his brother.

Yoshka soon proved to be a valuable employee. His blue eyes and amusing ways attracted plenty of women who would get off the train to discover, much to their surprise, how much they loved sausages. Gizi used to joke sometimes that the women of Budapest and the surrounding area gained an average of twelve pounds in weight between 1942 and 1944.

Although Peter did not become the leader of the Andrassy Avenue children, he didn't mind. In any case, he found his cousin Marika more interesting. She had read even more books than he had, although most of them were romances for women. That's when Peter finally understood what his parents were talking about that eventful night.

Martha also found her place in Budapest, at least at first. As a sworn consumer of culture, she thoroughly enjoyed living in the big city. She visited museums and theaters, and her new experiences filled her with excitement and joy. Nothing bad could happen in such a cultural country, she told herself whenever she was overwhelmed with worry. Her relationship with Yoshka was also improving. She began feeling pleasantly warm again whenever their eyes met across the dinner table. Her fury at him was slowly subsiding, and she was even beginning to believe he'd been right to urge her to move to Budapest. As time passed, she began reading the letters she received regularly from Paul Molnar with just a cursory glance, checking to see that he'd transferred her family's earnings from the trading company to her parents. She would send him short letters in reply and almost completely ignore the passionate love poems he added to his letters. Only occasionally would she comment jokingly that he was showing a surprising degree of lyricism for a bookkeeper. She also promised to collect all his poems and keep them, and perhaps publish them when the time was right.

***

One day, in 1944, Martha was passing Peter's room on her way to her own, when suddenly her ears pricked up and she stopped. A smile crossed her lips. She thought she could hear Peter and his cousin Marika reading a dialogue from *Romeo and Juliet, and she was filled with pride in her son, who preferred the classics to getting up to no good on the street.*

She was about to move away, when she heard Marika command, "Now you have to kiss me, silly."

"It doesn't say that in the play," she heard Peter's reply.

"What kind of Romeo are you?" Marika grumbled, "If you really love your Juliet, you have to kiss her. You don't have to follow the play so strictly."

Martha could feel the rage rippling through her veins. She debated whether to barge in and put an end to the whole thing or talk first to Gizi, the mother of that seductive Jezebel. But the sudden silence coming from behind the door and the gasps that broke it made her lose her composure. She burst into the room and roared angrily, "What is this? You are cousins, you know!"

The two recoiled in panic, and Marika answered without thinking twice, "Romeo and Juliet were also cousins!"

"No, they weren't," Martha seethed. "You really should learn the play better before you rehearse it with others."

"Mami, I'm sorry," Peter moved over to her. "It's my fault. I asked Marika to act out *Romeo and Juliet*. He looked so embarrassed and humiliated that Martha's anger dissipated in an instant.

"There, there, I shouldn't have burst in on you like that," she mumbled, subdued, "after all, you're both big now. But perhaps you could find less-romantic plays to perform?"

"All right," Peter answered softly and glanced at his cousin. From the brazen look she gave in return, Martha could see that she had plenty to worry about, even more than she had imagined.

She ran off to find Gizi and told her how distressed she was, only to discover, much to her surprise, that it did not bother her sister-in-law in the least.

"I know that they're very close, Marika told me so a long time ago."

"How close? Close in that way?"

"Yes, why are you surprised? Peter is a charming, handsome, smart, and sensitive boy, and if you tried, you could find a few good qualities in my daughter too."

"Gizi, it's not funny. They're too young and they're cousins, it could even be dangerous if it goes too far."

"What harm is there in it, Martha?" Gizi burst into sardonic laughter, "They're only children playing games. I wish that going too far was the worst thing that could happen to us,"

***

As it turned out, Gizi was right, but she still couldn't persuade Martha of that. Before Martha could find a way to keep Peter away from Marika, fate intervened. In October of 1944, Ferenc Szálasi, the leader of the notorious Arrow Cross Party, came to power, and his first decree was to transfer all the Jewish men over the age of fourteen to Hungarian army labor camps. Although this kept Peter away from Marika, it didn't make Martha any happier. She was so worried about him that she almost had a nervous breakdown. The idea that his future was to be entrusted to those green-shirted Arrow Cross thugs, who guarded and commanded the camp, threatened to drive her crazy.

In despair, she wrote an anxious letter to Paul Molnar, begging him to volunteer to the Arrow Cross. Even though her request was unreasonable and extreme and required Molnar to abandon his family, uproot himself, and give up his salary, he didn't argue, he only asked who would run the business in his absence. Martha answered him firmly that there were more important things to deal with. She even ordered him to sell all the fabric they still had in stock and to use the money to bribe some Red Cross senior punk to make him an officer.

As always, Molnar did as she asked and had himself stationed him in Budapest at the transit camp where the Jewish men were being held.

Molnar may not have been a particularly strong man, but his mind was sharp. Immediately after being stationed at the camp, he was appointed an adjutancy officer, and his job was to allocate the work to the forced Jewish laborers. He immediately sent Peter and Yoshka to the kitchen, assuming they could both cook because he knew that Martha had never been able to make a dish more complicated than noodles with cheese.

***

On her part, Martha didn't rest for a moment. She heard rumors that underground members of the Zionist Relief and Rescue Committee were handing out fake documents and rushed there to buy documents making her and Marika Christian. Gizi didn't need such documents as she had never bothered to convert.

Martha, so proud of her black hair, dyed it blonde. She told any of the neighbors who asked why that she was beginning to turn gray. Every day, she would appear at the gates of the camp where Yoshka, Peter, and Mark were being held and bring them food that Gizi prepared. Molnar claimed that her visits were putting everyone in danger, and, in any case, Yoshka and Peter weren't exactly starving, since they supervised the food supply for the entire camp. Still, he organized a pass to the ghetto for her, and Martha went every day to see for herself that they were alive and well.

One day, it paid off. She was walking through the Jewish ghetto on her way to the camp, when she saw a long line of people being led down the street. A man was calling out names, all Jewish. She walked toward them, her heart sinking. By that time, she was well aware of where those Jews were being taken and the intense pain that she felt forced her to look and see if she could save anyone. Suddenly, she noticed Yutzi's son Tibby in the crowd. Martha stepped back and hid in the shadows of a building. Her back was covered in cold sweat, and a voice inside was telling her that she had to move if she didn't want to put her husband and son at risk. In any case, there wasn't much she could do for her nephew. But another voice that came straight from her heart cried out that she wouldn't be able to live with herself if she didn't try to save the boy.

Her heart pounding, Martha walked up to one of the Arrow Cross soldiers. She showed him her fake ID, which said that she had a fifteen-year-old son, and, pointing to Tibby, said, "There's been a mistake. That's my son. Please release him!"

The soldier looked at her suspiciously, and then at Tibby, looking for similarity between them. The crowd was becoming difficult and a nervous officer yelled to him over the megaphone to leave her alone.

"He's my son, and I'm taking him," Martha insisted and walked quickly toward Tibby, who looked confused, as if in his own world. "If you have a problem with that, call Paul Molnar, a senior officer at the camp, and he'll speak to you in a language you can understand."

The soldier turned his back on her and walked away. Martha held her breath in anticipation, waiting to see if an officer would now come to see what she was up to, but nothing happened. The soldiers continued to sort the despondent people into groups. Martha grabbed Tibby's arm and pulled him along, rushing away from the ghetto.

That day, she did not visit Yoshka and Peter. She arrived with Tibby at the house on Andrassy Avenue, and her heart broke when she heard the boy's story.

***

"You have to go to Baja today!" was the first thing she said to Molnar the next day when she saw him at the camp entrance.

"Why?" he asked. There was a rebellious spark in his eyes, and she nervously asked herself how much longer he would act on her behalf.

"Paul, my darling," she softened her tone and lowered her voice, noticing that his eyes were puffy and red. "I received terrible news yesterday. We have no time to waste. Your thug friends murdered my sisters and their husbands."

Molnar felt his heart sink. He wanted to hold her tight and squeeze all the pain from her heart. But circumstances didn't allow it, so he bit his lips and answered bitterly, "My friends? You asked me to join them!"

"Paul, don't get angry with me when I'm upset. I've lost half my family, and I can't even grieve properly. I need your help! My parents have managed to stay alive, even though they're ill, and I'm asking you, please, go to Baja and help them. Ask your wife to move into my parent's house with your children, hide my parents in the basement, and provide for their needs. I also want her to take care of the house, especially the art collection. We'll be needing it soon."

He thought quickly, trying to work things out in his mind, but without much success. The reality of living in the camp in Budapest wasn't an easy one, but it least it wasn't covered in blood. He'd heard rumors that the Germans were planning to speed up the transport of Jews to the death camps in Poland, but he didn't believe them. His dreamy, thoughtful temperament didn't match the spirit of the times. He'd always preferred to see things in a positive light and not to stare into the dark shadows around him. Meanwhile, life in the camp was relatively calm. Some of the officers and guards would even play cards in the evening with the Jewish laborers. Yoshka, who was one of the best players, would often keep them amused with his jokes. If you didn't look too closely, you could imagine a completely different reality. And Molnar tried as hard as he could to do so.

"I'll go, Martha, don't worry," he finally answered, taking her hands in his. His heart went out to her. There was so much pain in her eyes, he was afraid her heart would break.

"I'll be fine, just take care of yourself," she answered, standing tall. Usually, at this time of day, Peter and Yoshka would pass by on their way to their hut. She didn't want them to see that she'd been crying all night. She knew that they would soon need all the mental strength they could muster.

***

The time Paul Molnar spent in Baja was one of the most difficult periods of his life. Without wanting to, he found himself investigating the chain of events that had led to the execution of thousands of Jews. It wasn't the horror stories he heard that caused him to shudder but the tone of voice in which they were told. The townsfolk who had joined the Arrow Cross—his old neighbors and friends whom he used to play friendly games of cards with—talked about the events as if they were also just a game. He felt sick to the stomach, a feeling that remained constant throughout that year, as if he were pregnant with a monstrous and distorted creature just waiting to erupt from him.

Worst of all was the horror he felt when he walked into Martha's parents' home. They were so shocked and desperate, they didn't even protest when he told them to move to the basement, nor when he explained that, from then on, they were not to be seen by anyone other than his family. Martha's father, whom Molnar remembered as an impressive, elegant man, was a pale shadow of himself and her mother looked even worse. Molnar felt that were it not for Martha's adamant insistence, he would have turned around and run away. He kept his promise, though, and stayed there that terrible night, explaining to his terrified wife what to do. Together, they looked through Mr. Goldberger's magnificent painting collection and he took half for himself. "Only if you're facing a disaster," he instructed his wife, "bribe anyone you need to. Under no circumstances waste this ammunition in a moment of hysteria." He left her copies of documents proving that he was a senior Arrow Cross officer, just in case she needed to use them.

Then he took the most expensive-looking paintings, kissed his baffled children ,and left the house. He couldn't bring himself to sleep there, especially with Martha's parents sleeping in the basement.

***

The next day, Molnar waited for Martha at the camp, but she was late. He was crushed with worry. He knew that if something happened to her, he'd lose any will to live.

Hours passed before he saw her moving slowly toward the camp gate. His heart skipped a beat. When she reached him, he ignored his urge to sweep her up in his arms. The guards at the gate could have reached the wrong conclusion and tried their luck with her when he wasn't in the vicinity.

Martha held a limp hand out to him. "You did it," she whispered to him, her voice trembling with tension.

"Yes," he squeezed her hand in encouragement, strangely drawing strength from how limp it felt, "I did as you asked. Your parents are in a safe place, and I also brought a few paintings with me."

Martha's eyes lit up with hope. "Wonderful," she said, and that single word was worth more to him than anything he could imagine.

"I've just come from Raoul Wallenberg's place," she said, and when she saw the confusion in his eyes, she immediately explained that he was a Swedish diplomat who was taking abandoned homes in Budapest, those of evicted people, and turning them into neutral territory under the Swedish government's rule. "I left my nephew Tibby there, and I want to move Peter there too."

"But Martha…" he tried to explain that it was impossible.

"No buts," she snapped, her eyes turning to steel, "he'll be much safer there."

"Yes, perhaps, but how will we get him out of here? It'll put us all in danger."

"Let it, I'm willing to take the risk for my son."

"What do you want me to do?" he asked in despair. The thought that Martha may have lost her mind after the terrible tragedy in her family made him feel weak.

"Sell one of the paintings. You can give the money to the camp commander. Tomorrow, at dawn, I want to take Peter away from here."

"But Martha, he's safe, I'm looking after him. Why waste precious ammunition now? Besides, it will draw a lot of attention to us that…"

"Paul," the desperation in her voice froze his blood, "I have to get him out of here, even if it's the last thing I do in this life."

As usual, Molnar did as Martha instructed, and Peter moved to Raoul Wallenberg's shelter. A month later, when transports began leaving the camp for Auschwitz on a daily basis, it became clear to them both that Martha had been right.

Frantic, Molnar began to sell the paintings. He knew that the price of leaving Yoshka and Mark in the camp could change in an instant, in the bloody market that was being run there.

He had to pay the camp commander and his deputies every day to keep Yoshka and Mark safe.

Martha, on the other hand, no longer visited as often. Sometimes the ghetto would be closed without prior notice, when the lines for the death trains filled the streets. Molnar knew that she was trying to raise more money to help him protect Yoshka and Mark, but he felt weak when she wasn't there. He was losing strength, and not being able to share his fears with anyone didn't help. At night, while playing cards with Yoshka and his friends, he sometimes felt the urge to bash the awful truth into the man and wipe the smug smile from his face. It never occurred to him that Yoshka's smile had nothing to do with optimism. Yoshka was well aware of what was going on around him. He also understood what the reduced quantities of food he was required to cook every day meant. The only thing he didn't realize was the reason he had not yet been led out of the camp himself. He knew nothing of the paintings or bribes that Molnar was using to keep him alive. He naively believed that the camp officers were in dire need of his cooking skills, which in truth, no one else in the camp could compete with.

Molnar grew more and more desperate as he ran out of paintings. Knowing that his wife had not yet sold any, he was planning to visit Baja again, but he was afraid that if he left the camp for even a day, Yoshka may not be there when he returned.

Martha told him she would go instead, but he was concerned she wouldn't be able to return. Baja was chaotic, people were being shot in the streets and their bodies tossed in the Danube. Even worse, Martha was too well known there, so her fake documents would be of no use. Even the young people remembered the beautiful Jewish woman who used to walk like a princess through the streets, her posture perfect.

Gizi also thought that Martha was being reckless, when she got up one night and informed her that she was going to Baja.

"Think rationally for a moment," Gizi tried to stop her as she watched her put on a white lace blouse and a gray skirt that covered her ankles. "If anything happens to you who will take care of Peter, Tibby, Marika, and Yoshka? They're all in much greater danger if you're not here."

"Nonsense," Martha shook her blonde hair, which she had had enough of. "The children are safe now and Yoshka…" Her eyes filled with tears. "If I don't hurry, he and your Mark will be sent off to the death camps."

At that, Gizi's hands started to tremble and she dropped the cup of tea she was holding. It shattered as it hit the floor. They had both heard about what went on in those camps, but they'd never put it into words. It was as if just talking about it made the horrific facts more real.

She sank into a chair, bent over, and as she was picking up the pieces of the shattered cup, they heard someone banging at the door. Martha shuddered for a moment but immediately regained her composure, took measured steps to the door, and opened it.

"Who's there?" she asked, opening the door just a crack, but it was dark and she couldn't see who it was.

"Angelika," she heard the answer whispered in a strange and foreign accent.

Martha was stunned for a moment but immediately snapped out of it, thinking that it was about time she changed the way she responded to unexpected events, since nothing could be worse than what may eventually happen.

"Just a moment," she whispered and opened the door. She tried to fight the fear, which was slowing her down as it spread to her limbs. She stared aghast at the sight of the slim, fragile woman wearing a dark robe, it's hood pulled over her head. Her face was so pale that it glowed under the shadow of the hood. She looked like a ghost from the Dracula books she used to read in secret as a child.

"*Ishtenem*," she gasped and stepped back, bumping into Gizi who had emerged from the kitchen.

Angelika blurted out a few, quick sentences in broken German and Hungarian, took the hood off her head, and they stared horrified at the beautiful nun's face, whose head was covered in a white wimple.

"Come in," Martha said, recovering first, and she took the girl's black robe. She was no longer afraid of her, only extremely curious.

Clutching a huge satchel, Angelika came inside. Gizi quickly closed the door behind her. Mumbling incoherently in a variety of languages, Angelika opened her satchel and pulled out a large bundle of papers. Martha and Gizi didn't know what to make of her, and they couldn't understand a word she said. Uneasy, they didn't say anything as they watched what she was doing.

"Here," she finally said, and waved an object in the air. Martha and Gizi held their breath. It was a beautiful oil painting of the nun standing in a bear's booth.

"Imre painted this!" Martha finally said and pointed excitedly at the scrawled signature in the corner. "This must be his most spectacular painting yet, I'm convinced."

"Ahh!" Angelika responded enthusiastically, "Imre, Imre," and she babbled on in her strange language.

"Maybe it's Latin," Gizi tried to guess.

"Do you speak Latin?" this led Martha to ask in the perfect Latin she'd learned at the gymnasium.

"Yes," Angelika nodded happily, and immediately explained that yes, it was Imre's painting, but Shandor had told her to send it to them.

"Shandor?" Martha wondered, "Doesn't he live in America?

"Yes," Angelika confirmed, "but before he left, he made us swear to do all we could to help you, the Schwartz family."

"How nice of him" Martha grunted. "He runs away to save himself and asks you to put yourselves in danger to help us. What a truly admirable show of responsibility!"

"No, it wasn't like that!" the fire in Angelika's eyes sparked, making Martha flinch away in fear. She made a note to herself to remember what a spirited temperament the radiant nun had. "Shandor didn't want to go at all! He insisted on coming here himself, on sneaking across the German lines to help you. I convinced him to abandon his insane plan. I knew that he was desperate, and I feared for his life. I believed he may risk himself since he had already lost his will to live."

"Lost his will to live?" Martha mumbled. Angelika's explanation didn't fit what she knew about Shandor's life in Paris. "Shandor said that he was having a wonderful time in Paris, with Imre and the woman they both… loved?"

She immediately stopped talking and looked closely at Angelika's face. A crazy thought popped into her mind that this nun was that very woman.

Angelika nodded as if reading her thoughts. "Yes," she said, her voice catching at the unspoken question, "I am that woman."

"But, how? You are a nun!" Gizi exclaimed, confounded. Martha was too embarrassed and confused to speak. Yoshka's stories of his life with his brother in Paris sounded intriguing and exotic. How could she have known the woman they loved was a nun?

"We were lovers in spirit alone," Angelika explained as Martha's stunned eyes shifted from her beautiful face to the picture with the bear. Then she understood why she believed it to be the most wonderful painting Imre had ever painted: It conveyed precisely the feeling of desperate love that would never be realized.

CHAPTER 12

As the German army closed in on Paris, Shandor grew more distressed. After the passionate night he'd spent with Angelika, he moved in with Hugo Scott, who wouldn't stop imploring him to come with him to America for a while. Shandor, however, who was well aware of his friend's debatable courage, knew that Scott had no intention of returning to Europe. He knew that his compulsion to leave Paris was because he was afraid that the Germans would invade the city.

Scott didn't try to hide his plans when Shandor confronted him openly, and he thought that his friend was behaving foolishly by not trying to save himself by fleeing. "In America, you'll be able to take better care of your family in Hungary," he tried a different method of reasoning.

"But what about my family here?" Shandor thought. His hope of ever getting his family out of Hungary had long since died.

"What do you mean by family?" Scott asked, "Imre or Angelika too?"

"Imre won't leave without Angelika," Shandor explained, not wanting to elaborate too much regarding his own relationship with the nun.

"If so, you'll just have to get Angelika to leave," Scott said firmly. "I can try to organize papers for them both."

Shandor began trying to persuade Angelika to emigrate to America, if only until the war was over—a mission he considered crucial to his life.

He knew that Imre spent his afternoons with a few of his artist friends in a café in the Tuileries Garden, so he chose that time to visit her at his old home.

Angelika looked surprised to find him at the door. "Shandor, what are you doing here?!" she asked.

"We ran out of wine at Hugo's," he attempted to joke, trying to ease the loaded situation. "I thought maybe you'd have a glass to quench my thirst."

"Shandor, seriously! We agreed we'd never meet on our own."

As a matter of fact, they hadn't agreed on anything, other than his excuse for leaving home. They both explained to Imre, separately of course, that Shandor had fallen in love with one of Hugo Scott's woman friends, and that's why he was moving in with him. Imre didn't even raise an eyebrow. Deep inside, he'd always believed and even hoped that something like that would happen one day.

"Angelika, believe me, if I didn't have a critical reason for being here, I wouldn't have come, certainly not alone."

"Well, then," she said, avoiding his eyes, finding the intense love and affection in them hard to bear.

"The Germans are closing in on Paris, Angelika—"

"I thought you came to tell me something I don't already know," she sighed.

"—and Hugo is urging me to leave with him for America."

"Have you come to say goodbye?" she whispered, glancing up at him, her eyes suddenly filled with tears.

"No, how can you think that?" he quickly grabbed her hands, 'I'm not budging without the two of you!"

"Shandor," her hands were shaking and she pulled them away, "I am asking—no, I am begging you—please, leave Europe!"

"I'll go only on the condition that you both come with me! Hugo promised to arrange visas for you for America. You'll be able to stay there."

"It's impossible!" Angelika shook her head, "I couldn't possibly run away!"

"What?!"

'I want to stay and fight the Germans!"

"Have you lost your mind? Those criminals have a big, strong army. The battle for Spain was child's play compared to what is going to happen here, and soon!"

"Yes, Shandor, they have a big, powerful army. And that's why there won't be a war here, but a brutal and terrible occupation instead. Such situations force the civilian population to rise up in the end. And how can I stand by and not do the very least I'm capable of?"

"You're right," Shandor bowed his head with a sigh. "You mustn't run away, you have to fight, to rise up. If so, I'll stay too and contribute my part to the struggle."

"Shandor, no! I don't want you to stay!" she shouted straight from her gut. Looking at his confused expression, she added softly, "Someone has to tell the world what's happening here, someone has to win over the American public opinion so they will fight against the Nazis."

"Hugo can do that on his own, he's better at that than I am."

"Shandor, I'm begging you to go and to take Imre with you."

"He won't go without you."

"Then please, go on your own," she begged, bursting into tears again. Shandor watched as they rolled down her cheeks, and he couldn't help but be struck by her extraordinary beauty, despite her tears, or perhaps because of them.

"I don't understand you," he muttered in confusion. "You insist on staying and fighting and describe fleeing as cowardice, but you want me to be the coward and run away from the struggle."

"What don't you understand?!" she cried out, "If anything happens to you, I…I'll simply want to die!"

"But that's precisely how I feel about you," he said softly, moving closer to her.

"No, Shandor, nothing bad will happen to me. God is watching over me," she pulled away and pointed up. "But if you stay, I can't guarantee that…"

"That what? That he'll continue to watch over you? What are you afraid of, Angelika? That if I stay in Paris, you won't be able to resist the temptation, and we'll make love again, and you'll feel the wrath of God?" The thought of that was a joke to Shandor, but, to his astonishment, he noticed her nodding, her eyes wide.

"I'm astounded! I can't believe that you're capable of believing in that—"

"In that what? That nonsense?" She tried to smile, "Shandor, my love, that nonsense protects us all. Believing that something is going to happen is what brings it upon us, don't you see? You never planned on staying here and fighting, and you aren't even sure that you'll be able to survive if you do. I cannot drag you into a dangerous mission that you never even considered being a part of. I can trust only myself and my faith to strengthen me and protect me from all evil."

"I don't understand what you're saying," Shandor replied despondently, "but I'm also incapable of refusing you."

"Good," Angelika smiled through the tears, "I'm glad you can't."

"But, my love, you have to promise to do something for me in return."

"I'll take very good care of Imre, I promise!"

"No, I know that you'll do that even if I don't ask you to, but…I want to ask you to do something that involves…risk."

"Darling," Angelika burst into sardonic laughter, "I'm planning to risk myself for people I don't even know, so doing so for you will bring me nothing but joy."

"Well," Shandor hesitated, "I'm not talking about the present but about the future. I have no idea what is going to happen, but I know that things will not improve any time soon. On the contrary, and I'm concerned, very concerned…for my family in Hungary."

"For Peter and his parents?" Angelika encouraged him to continue. She knew from his stories that he deeply loved that boy, a youth by now, and was very attached to him.

"Yes, mainly for them, but for others, too. And as far as I know, their situation at the moment is better than ours will be within a few days…but things are likely to change, and I believe they will need help. I don't know what kind, and I don't want to make you promise anything with far-reaching consequences. But since you'll probably be joining the underground, when it gets here, and since the underground movements across Europe are…they're connected to each other…"

"Shandor," Angelika was running out of patience, "please make your point, are you asking me to help Peter and the family with anything they may need?"

"Yes, but—"

"No buts. Your request is sacred to me, I'll fulfill it with love."

***

A week later, Shandor and Hugo Scott left Paris. The Nazis invaded the city a few days after that. Imre surprised Angelika, who thought that he was out of touch with reality, and found a refuge for them in Menton, a picturesque and popular resort town on the border of France and Italy. One of his painter friends invited their entire group of artists to stay at his family home until the situation improved.

Since she wanted to stay in Paris, at first Angelika tried to talk him into leaving without her, but Imre wouldn't hear of it. "If you stay, I stay," he said stubbornly, refusing to listen to her arguments.

Angelika found herself in a huge old house with a spectacular view of the beach and snowy mountains instead of in the dark basements of the Paris underground. At first, she felt terrible about it, but she slowly began to roam around the town getting to know its residents, only to find out that there, too, secret organizations had sprouted in anticipation of what was to come, and they were preparing a network that would rise up against the Nazis.

***

By the time all of France had been occupied, Angelika's band had formed close ties with the Italian freedom fighters who had rebelled against Il Duce, as well as with a small, bold Yugoslavian group who were risking their lives in order to hurt the Nazis throughout central Europe. When Angelika heard about a young Hungarian nicknamed the Suicide Attacker because of his eager willingness to embark on the most dangerous of missions, she asked to meet him in person.

At first, Shani was baffled and shy, but when he found out that Angelika was Imre's close friend, his reluctance gave way to enthusiasm. He painfully told her about the hardships his family in Hungary were forced to bear and how his sisters had been murdered by the Arrow Cross, noting that he'd strangled a few with his own bare hands in revenge. He added that he had nonetheless not found peace and that he agonized constantly over not being there when the heinous murder took place and for doing nothing to prevent it.

Concerned, Angelika mistakenly thought that Martha had also been murdered, because Shani didn't mention their names, but when she asked what became of Peter, Shani paused, his face blank. "Peter survived, as far as I know," he finally growled. "My older sister Martha took care of herself and her own little family, just not her sisters."

"And that makes you angry?" Angelika was surprised, struggling to hide her relief. She didn't want to anger him any further, "Why aren't you glad that at least she's alive?"

"What is there to understand?" Shani snapped "She's having an affair with one of the murderers, an Arrow Cross man, enjoying the good life and protecting only her son and her husband, yes…and our parents, in the end she did remember to take care of them, but in my opinion, she was too late."

"Shani, listen to me. These are not ordinary times, no one can do any more than they're doing! Shandor left for America, and I'm not at all angry at him. Imre, your friend, is sitting here in the next village, enjoying himself painting. Why are you not furious with him?"

"It's not the same," Shani growled, "Imre's paintings provide us with enough money to buy ammunition to fight the Germans, and Shandor, well…I don't know enough about the way things developed to express an opinion…what I do know for certain is that Shandor wouldn't have left Hungary were it not for Martha's dear husband Yoshka getting into trouble, with his own stupid and adventurous love affair!"

At that point, Angelika realized that there was no point in arguing with Shani. His anger at his sister and her husband stemmed from deeper and more complicated issues than she could comprehend. She took comfort in learning that Martha had found a way to protect Peter and his father, and she made Shani swear to tell her immediately about any changes in their situation. Not without grumbling, Shani promised to do so, and she believed him.

Indeed, a year later, Angelika received news that Martha was in desperate need of money, having sold all the paintings in her possession, and she had no funds left to pay for Yoshka's life.

She was at a loss, for she realized that as the end of the war approached, Martha would need more and more money. She thought of sending her a few paintings but sending them across enemy lines all the way to Hungary would not only make her mission more difficult but also more dangerous. She went to Shani and begged him to organize a band of men for her, so that they could each carry just one or two paintings, but he refused, saying that his partisans had more pressing matters to deal with, angry at her for wanting to sacrifice so many of Imre's paintings for anything other than to purchase weapons to fight the Germans with.

Angelika decided to do it on her own. She took the painting of the nun and the bear, which she'd already been offered thousands of francs for, and set off on the dangerous journey to Budapest. It hurt her to part with the painting, the first of sentimental value to her and the only memento she had of her dear friend Adrianus. The thought of the painting being sold to some Nazi pig was intolerable to her, but she eventually convinced herself that God would take care of the painting and it would eventually find its way to people who could appreciate it.

***

Martha and Gizi, stunned and silent, listened as Angelika finished her story, stopping now and then so that Martha could translate for Gizi. Martha's eyes filled with tears when she realized what a sacrifice Angelika was about to make for her. She tried to decide if it would be right to accept the painting and give it to Molnar. Knowing that Shani was angry at her for staying alive only made her more hesitant.

"I really should go to Baja," she said at last, after giving it some thought. "There are more paintings at my parents' house. Although they aren't as valuable as this one, I believe they would fetch enough to keep Yoshka alive for a few more months, and that's all the time he needs. The Allies are on their way."

"Martha, you should be ashamed of yourself!" Gizi scolded her.

"Angelika has risked her life to make it here to give you the painting. Is this how you repay her? By endangering your own life?"

"But you heard how precious that painting is it her," Martha mumbled anxiously.

They were speaking in Hungarian so that Angelika wouldn't understand their conversation, but she surprised them and added in Latin, "I want you to take this painting." Then, placing her hand tenderly on Martha's arm, she elaborated, "I made a vow to Shandor to help you in every way possible. Our longing for the dead cannot come before our commitment to the living."

Surprised, Martha took some time to respond. The tears welling in her eyes grew bigger. Then she looked at Angelika's wise eyes and nodded. "Thank you," she said softly, "I'll do as you say, but I want you to know I will always be indebted to you for the huge sacrifice you're making for us."

The next day, Martha wrapped the painting in paper and left for the camp to give it to Paul Molnar. He took the painting from her trembling hands and promised to sell it for as much as he could get and to use the money only to buy Yoshka Schwartz's life.

A few days later, the three women received the upsetting news that Yoshka had been sent on the train to Mauthausen.

**

I looked at Gizi's face. She looked sad. I could feel her grief permeating my skin.

"That's it, that's all I know," Gizi sighed and paged through the bundle of papers she'd taken out of the parcel. "These are the letters Molnar wrote to Martha at the time, and even later. Unfortunately, I can't find any explanation for what happened, my child, just one letter from two decades ago, saying that that painting and others from Mr. Goldberger's collection are waiting for Martha at her family home, which naturally Molnar would be happy to return to Martha as well. He also wrote that he never stopped loving her and asked her to forgive him for the mistake he made."

"I…understand," I muttered in bitter disappointment, not really understand anything. "So what can we do, since Grandma Martha passed away long ago?"

"I think that…you should go to Baja yourself," Gizi said thoughtfully. "Old Molnar also passed away years ago, but he must have left a will regarding the property."

"Could you come with me, perhaps?" I asked.

"I can't, my child. I would happily join you on this trip, but I'm too old. And I still have to work for a living," she continued and pulled me back to the small kitchen. "The pension laws in Hungary are not developed enough for an old woman such as myself to live nicely without extra income, so I bake cakes for the small café downstairs." She opened the oven door and proudly showed me five homemade roulades. "You see, my oven's not big enough to bake more than five at a time, so I'm tied to the house, and it's hard for me to leave."

Her tone was so joyful that I found it hard to feel sorry for the little woman, who must have been close on a hundred.

"Come," she said as she packed up the roulades, "let's go to the café. At least have a decent breakfast before you head for Baja."

∗∗∗

It wasn't until I was sitting on the train, in an old but comfortable and empty carriage that I again began to puzzle over the strange mystery, which had seemingly never been solved. Why didn't Paul Molnar sell the painting intended to save my grandfather?

Gizi and I had discussed that question over breakfast: She thought that Molnar had only just begun to understand that the war was almost over. He was probably afraid that the Allies would put him on trial and wanted to make sure he had enough money to bribe the prosecutors or hire a decent lawyer.

"Whatever the reason," Gizi concluded our talk, "you'll have to ask Molnar's grandson Otto. I hear that he's the only one still living in the Goldberger house. You must make it clear that he has to return your property to you. Demand it."

"I'm not very good at that," I muttered nervously, scanning my memory for all the times I'd ever had to be demanding, but I'd never been any good at it. My mother excelled at it, and maybe that's what made me so lame.

"Think of your sister and the money you need to save her eyes," Gizi said firmly. "That'll give you the strength, just as the necessity to save Peter and his parents gave Angelika the courage and fortitude to travel that bumpy road and risk her life just to deliver the painting to Martha."

"And what happened after that?" I asked, trying to postpone the exercise in courage that Gizi had recommended, "What happened to all of you after the Russians liberated Hungary?"

"That's a very long and winding tale," Gizi smiled, her eyes misting over. "If we begin, I'm afraid you won't be in such a hurry to get to Baja, and I think that accomplishing the mission you came here to do is more pressing. In any case, we need to stop somewhere before you get on the train. I promise, when you return, I'll tell you everything, if you're still interested in listening, that is."

CHAPTER 13

The train station in Baja was small and old, and the splendor that characterized its counterpart in Budapest was entirely lacking. A few people were standing on the platforms waiting for passengers from the big city. Hesitantly, I approached an elegantly dressed young woman who looked as if she may speak a little English. I asked her how to get to my grandfather's home. Luckily, she spoke excellent English and gave me good directions. I had to take a tram and get off three stops later. There, on a small street, surrounded by a big and well-kept garden with the Danube as a backdrop, loomed a huge, picturesque stone house.

I walked slowly along the path to the entrance, my heart pounding so hard, I feared it could be heard all the way to Israel, but there was no indication from inside that anyone had heard me. I stood at the door, which bore no identifying sign, and I tried to guess what Molnar's grandson would do when he realized why I was there. He would probably throw me out, elegantly at best. And what would I do then? I took a few deep breaths and tried to bring my heart rate down to normal.

Think about Noiki, I instructed myself, as Gizi had suggested. *Think only of her and of the fact that you have to find the money to save her!*

I raised my hand to the door and knocked loudly three times. A man's voice called out from inside, "Who's there?" and before I could decide what to say, the door opened wide and a blond man with broad shoulders was standing there, staring curiously at me.

"What—" he began to ask, when suddenly his curiosity was replaced by excited astonishment. "Martha?! You're Martha Goldberger?!" he continued, his voice sounding choked.

"What?!" I started laughing, the crazy situation giving me the strength that Gizi had told me about, "How can I be Martha?! I'm Darya Schwartz, her granddaughter. Martha passed away a long time ago."

I spoke in English. I could never have explained everything so quickly and efficiently in Hungarian. Remarkably, his English was perfect, which is impossible to say of his math, if he thought I was Martha.

"Come in, come in," he said.

"You must be Otto Molnar," I continued as I marched into the spacious entrance hall. Two seconds later, I froze when I saw two big oil paintings on the main wall of the huge room hanging above the unlit fireplace. The first was the painting of Angelika and the bear. My grandmother stared at me from the second, and my resemblance to her was amazing.

Now I understood why Gizi had insisted on dragging me to her hairdresser before I left for the train station. "You look very much like Martha when she was your age," she told me, even though I'd never been able to see it in the old photos. "It's just your hairstyle isn't classic like hers was."

"A haircut doesn't change a person's appearance that much," I argued back, mainly because I didn't want to give up my wild hair, which, in my opinion, depicted everything I liked about myself.

Gizi reminded me again that I was in the middle of an important task and that it wasn't the time to be concerned with my self-image. "The more you look like Martha," she said, "the easier it'll be for young Molnar to recognize you and believe that it's you. I think it'll make it less difficult to achieve your aim."

Gizi had been right, of course. Otto Molnar, who looked a little older than me but was much better looking and impressive than I'd expected, reacted with an obvious lack of confidence when I unexpectedly burst into his home.

Instead of putting me in my place and asking me why I was standing there and behaving as if I owned the place, he stood there staring at me, moved and amazed, glancing now and then at the painting of my grandmother.

"I asked you if you're Otto Molnar," I repeated demandingly, his helplessness giving me incredible confidence.

"Yes, I am," he answered submissively, focusing his blue eyes on me.

"Good," I said, "I'm Darya Schwartz, and I'm here to talk to you about a very important matter."

"I assume you're here to take what belongs to you," he replied, "this house and those paintings on the wall are yours."

"What?" I was stunned. "Aren't you going to bargain with me? Ask me for proof?"

"No," he sank onto the sofa next to the fireplace, "you're the only proof I need."

***

Strangely, my hostility dissipated as soon as I realized that Molnar was serious. He looked at me again, shook his head, stood up, and said that he would get the documents to sign the house over to me, but I quickly stopped him.

"Hold on, wait a minute," I said, anxious suddenly that it was a trap. "Firstly, I don't read Hungarian, so, we'll have to have them translated before I think of signing. Secondly, could I please have something to drink?"

"My apologies," he smiled for the first time since I'd arrived. Unfortunately, this made him even more dazzling. "I'll get you something to drink right away," he said and walked toward what I guessed was the kitchen. "Coffee or tea? Or perhaps a cold drink?"

"Coffee would be awesome," I replied, following him with my eyes, "and something cold, too, and…could you make me a sandwich or something? I'm starving!"

"With pleasure, I'll make you anything you want," I heard his warm voice coming from the kitchen. This only made me more apprehensive: Everything was going too smoothly, and, as the daughter of a woman with a tendency to expect the worst, I couldn't stop feeling that it would end badly. I tried to shake off my nervousness by looking around the room and trying to appraise the beautiful house. Nothing helped.

First of all, I should call home, I thought frantically, *I'll tell Dad, Mom,* and Vered the whole strange story, and maybe they'll tell me exactly what to do to avoid falling into traps.

"May I call Israel from here?" I asked Otto when he returned carrying a tray full of food.

"Of course," he responded, pointing at an old telephone by the sofa, "tell me the number and I'll talk to the switchboard."

A few minutes later, I was talking to Vered. She sounded awful.

"Darya, where are you?!" she demanded, "You have no idea what's going on—"

"Wait a minute, Vered, let me talk, I have wonderful news!" I interrupted her, "I'm in Baja, at the house that belonged to Grandma and—"

"Darya, listen to me!" I suddenly noticed that she sounded breathless as if she was crying, "I don't have time for your nonsense! Noa's condition has deteriorated. She was having terrible headaches all night, so we dashed her off to the hospital. The doctors said that they have no choice but to perform surgery immediately! Are you listening?"

"Yes," my heart sank quickly, and my hands started to tremble. Molnar noticed and took the coffee mug from my hand, "So…when are they… operating?" I stuttered.

"They don't know yet, they're terribly confused. From what they saw on the previous MRI, it doesn't appear to be a malignant tumor, but now they don't understand why it's growing so rapidly. Anyway, the head of the department still thinks that Professor Salzman has to perform the surgery, and his deputy claims there's no time to wait for him to arrive—"

"Vered," I tried to get a word in, "what does that mean, there's no time? How much time do we have, exactly?"

"Tell me, do you really think this is the time for games?"

"No, listen to me, I can probably get the money right away. I'm with Molnar's grandson, and he's prepared to transfer the house and some paintings that are worth a fortune to me. I'm convinced it'll cover the cost of surgery. If you say it's urgent, I won't wait until the documents are translated, and I'll go to the bank tomorrow to transfer the house and mortgage it. Tell the doctors to speak to Professor Salzman and to fly him out immediately, okay?"

Stunned silence. That's all I heard on the line, and then she spoke, her voice steadier and more optimistic. "I didn't understand a word, Darya, but are you serious about the money?"

"Totally," I said, looking at Otto Molnar, who was still looking at me with concern.

"Fine," she gasped, "I'll go to the hospital right now, but how can I get hold of you? On your mobile?"

"No, I forgot my charger at home," I replied, "call me here, at Molnar's house. Hold on, I'll ask him for the number."

Otto jotted down the number for me on a slip of paper, and I read it out to Vered.

"Okay, got it," she said at last. "Stay by the phone, I'll get back to you as soon as I can."

"What's wrong?" Otto asked after I put down the receiver. "You look extremely upset."

"Yes," I nodded, still trying to decide whether to tell him the story immediately or wait until Vered called back. I didn't want to give him any excuse to take advantage of our predicament and try to get rid of us with peanuts. Then again, I trusted his sincere willingness to give me the house and paintings right away before hearing what I had to say, just as I trusted the tender, thoughtful expression he was looking at me with when he pointed at the sandwich and coffee. "You should have something to eat and drink, it'll help you calm down."

"I can't eat a thing," I said, taking a quick sip of coffee.

"I thought you said you were hungry."

"I was, but..." I hesitated again, then finally decided to tell him what had happened. Talking about it may help me feel a little better. Otto listened intently, and, as the story unfolded, he took my hand in his and squeezed it encouragingly. When I was done, he opened his mouth to speak, but then the phone rang.

Otto quickly picked up the phone, and after a few brief words, he handed it to me and said, "It's for you, from Israel."

My hand trembled as I took the handset from him. The other was still in his.

"Darya," Vered said, in a voice that didn't sound optimistic, "listen, we spoke to the doctors, and they spoke to Professor Salzman. He says that he can't possibly get here in time and that if Noa's condition is so bad, she should be flown to him in the States."

"But the doctors said it could be dangerous for her to fly," I could barely mumble the words.

"Well that's the thing—now they're saying that with it spreading so rapidly, it's becoming much more dangerous."

"God!" I couldn't breathe for the tears. "So why did they wait until now? What kind of doctors are they, Vered? Don't you dare let them touch Noa."

"We may not have a choice, Darya," Vered was also finding it hard to talk. "They want to do a few more tests and then call a meeting with all the department's doctors and with Professor Salzman on the phone before making a final decision on how to proceed. Meanwhile, you should get here with the money."

Cold fear was making me mute. Tears were pouring down my face and wetting my clothes, and I couldn't bring myself to speak. Vered noticed and added, "I'm sorry, but I have to get going, Mom and Dad need me with them. See you soon," before she hung up.

"Bad news?" Molnar asked.

"No worse than before," I sniffed. "My sister needs surgery as soon as possible, and there's a professor in the States who wants her to come there, which means it's urgent we transfer this house to me so I can sell it."

"No problem," he replied and handed me the plate with the sandwich, "eat and I'll fetch the papers."

I didn't think I'd be able to eat, with the huge lump of fear and pain sitting right where my stomach was. But after a few minutes of thinking how by starving here I would add to my family's problems, I took a few hesitant bites.

"Drink your coffee too," he encouraged me when he returned holding the papers, looking at me with compassion and empathy. "It'll give you a boost."

I gave him a piercing look, finding him hard to understand. A strange Israeli girl walks into his house one evening with no warning. At first, she behaves condescendingly, as if she thinks she deserves everything she wants, and suddenly, following a phone call, she tells him a heartbreaking story and starts crying as if her world has collapsed. Someone less sensitive and considerate would have referred me to a psychiatric institution. Could that be what he was planning?

***

Otto put on his glasses, adding intelligence to his good looks, and his eyes scanned the papers. "Actually, they've already been signed by my grandfather," he explained as he read. "It's a kind of will stating his wishes to transfer the house and paintings to Martha Schwartz's legal heirs. I hope it's enough for you to take to your bank in Israel so you can mortgage the house. Hold on, I should check that with my attorney."

He picked up the phone and dialed. A moment later he was chatting away in Hungarian. I couldn't understand a word.

I watched his expression as he spoke, debating again whether I could trust him. His face conveyed innocence and sincere honesty, but maybe my brain was picking up that message only because he was so attractive. For some reason, we tend to trust beautiful people more, as if we assume that God had good reason to create them with such perfect physiology.

"Okay," he said after putting down the phone, "my attorney says that your father has to go to an attorney in Israel to sign a notarized document confirming that he's Martha Schwartz's only legal heir. Then he'll have to send the documents here and give you power of attorney authorizing you to take care of matters on his behalf. And then, after we have the property and paintings appraised, you can go to the bank and get a loan."

"But that'll take too long," I said desperately, "and I want to go straight to Israel with the money for the surgery."

"Then you'll have to trust me," he replied, looking pensive. "I'll try to arrange everything quickly so that I can take out a mortgage on the house and transfer the funds to you within a few days."

"Otto, are you really willing…to do all that for me? For us?" I stared at him, and when he nodded confidently, I went on, "You don't realize how this is going to save us, you have no idea…but really…please, try to get it done as quickly as possible, all right?"

"You have my word," he said, smiling reassuringly this time, which miraculously managed to erase any remaining suspicion I had of him. "Now go to sleep, you have to get up very early tomorrow."

"Yes, I actually should be going," I said and looked at the clock on the wall. It was almost ten o'clock and I had to get to the airport at least three hours before the flight. "Can you find out when the next train to Budapest leaves?"

"You aren't catching the train. I'll take you to Budapest," he said adamantly, "I'll just have some coffee and we'll leave."

"Are you insane? Do you have nothing better to do than drive to Budapest? You probably have to work tomorrow!"

"I've already asked to be replaced," he replied briefly. "Would you like another drink?"

I agreed to more coffee, and Otto suggested I have a good, strong cognac as well. The cognac did a good job of opening me up and loosening my tongue, and I found myself telling him about my quest and about Shandor Bachi and Gizi's stories. Then we left in his old, green Skoda. I looked at his beautiful face as he concentrated on the road, and, much to my annoyance, I again found myself thinking that this man was too perfect to be true.

"Otto," I heard the cognac speaking from my throat, as if I had no control over the words, "why did you wait until I came to you? Why didn't you try to find us?"

To my relief, he didn't look angry at all when he replied, "Because my grandfather thought it was the only way—to wait until someone showed up. At the time, he tried to contact Martha and return everything, but… she refused to even see him. She was furious."

"And rightfully so, from her point of view," I mumbled.

"True," he agreed, his face clouding over.

"I'd like you to tell me…" I took his free hand, the one that wasn't on the steering wheel, and squeezed it tight, trying to show that I hadn't inherited my grandmother's anger, certainly not toward him, "why did your grandfather not save mine? Why didn't he sell the painting, since that's what he'd been given it for?"

Otto hesitated but he didn't pull his hand away, "Are you sure you want to hear about it now?" he asked, "It's not an easy story."

I focused my eyes on his somber face and nodded quietly. Otto leaned back in the driver's seat, and still driving, began to talk. By the time he was done, the light of dawn had broken, as if wishing to reveal all the dark secrets of our families.

CHAPTER 14

Paul Molnar did not reveal to Martha that an order to send Yoshka to Auschwitz had already been given and that he'd used his own money to delay the terrible decree. The day she came to him with the painting, he chose to comment only on how stunning it was, agreeing with her that it was the most beautiful Imre had ever painted. *His unrealized love has certainly permeated the painting, that's why it's so remarkable*, he thought to himself, comparing it to his own, unrealized love for Martha. She looked more beautiful than ever, even though she had wasted away and her cheeks were pale. He still hoped that after the war, when sanity returned to the minds of any survivors, Martha would realize that he, not Yoshka, was the right man for her, precisely because of how true his love for her was. He believed that Yoshka cared mainly about himself, but not for a moment did he wish her husband dead. He was a decent man at heart and all he wanted was a fair chance.

When he returned to his room, he placed the painting opposite his bed and then sat there for an hour, looking at it. He thought about their lives, going back to the brave friendship he and Martha had shared when they were children. He searched his mind for the precise moment when things went wrong. His heart ached when he remembered the evening he was walking with Martha through the woods on the banks of the Danube and that group of ruffians dressed in dark masks appeared out of nowhere. He ended up behaving like a coward, even though he could be forgiven for that, because he was basically still a child, and he ran away from the fight. Yoshka saved her from them and rightfully won her heart.

As the day wore on, however, Molnar felt the resentment building up in him. Can a person's entire future be determined by a single event, he asked himself, did he not prove his courage every day after that, every hour? After all, he risked himself and joined that vile criminal organization called the Arrow Cross, only because Martha asked him to. He could meet his death at any moment if anyone found out that he wasn't a true believer in their ways and that his only reason for joining the party was to watch out for the Jews.

That evening, while playing poker as usual, he looked into Yoshka's blue eyes and felt his anger grow even stronger. His opponent looked smug, maybe because Molnar was always losing to him.

It was already late at night, and Molnar was over the moon, with four queens in his hand. He was finally going to win, which would relieve a little of the discomfort in his chest. All the other players had folded. It was just him and Yoshka left. With a very uncharacteristic and triumphant cry, he spread his cards on the table and looked up to meet Yoshka's eyes. He wanted, just once, to see what they looked like when defeated.

But Yoshka didn't even blink as he spread his own cards on the table, and Molnar immediately understood why: He had a royal flush. Again, he had been defeated by his opponent. His mouth tasted sour.

Then Yoshka surprised him by laughing so hard that his body shook, "How easy it is to fool you!" he said, his tone mocking, and pulled another deck of cards out from under the table. "You're so gullible, Molnar. You always were, and you always will be. If you'd bothered to count the cards, you would have seen it for yourself!"

At that, all the others laughed too, and only Molnar was shocked and left speechless with rage. "Why did you tell me?" he eventually mumbled, his throat dry.

"Because it's so easy to deceive you, it's not as enjoyable anymore," Yoshka retorted mockingly. "You've always been gullible, even when we were children, otherwise—"

"Otherwise what?" Molnar demanded to know, when Yoshka suddenly stopped speaking, looking like he'd said more than he wished to.

"Nothing, not a thing…" Yoshka insisted. "Here's your money, keep it, for God's sake!"

"Gentlemen, leave the room," Molnar commanded the others, and they did, but with blatant reluctance. Yoshka remained seated, with the same, smug and condescending expression on his face.

"If you're such a hero," Molnar addressed Yoshka, "tell me what you wanted to say before?"

"Let it go, Molnar, you may have another heart attack if I do," was his answer.

"Stop your bombastic performance this minute!" Molnar shouted furiously, banging the table. "Your arrogant smile would have been erased long ago if you knew you were still here only thanks to your wife!"

"My wife? What do you mean?!" Yoshka yelled back, his face now showing no trace of a smile.

"Your wife…you're still alive only because of her, thanks to our affair… hers and mine…"

His eyes blazing, Yoshka took his time responding. But then he smiled again, mockingly, and asked, "An affair, you say? Do you mean the crumbs she threw you just to upset me? She loves me, and she always will, Molnar, it's time you understood that. Perhaps none of this would have happened if you weren't so gullible. Do you still want to know what I was going to say before? Well, here's the story. Do you remember that night by the Danube, when you were attacked by those masked boys? Then listen well! Those were my boys, from my gang! They were following my orders! I told them to stage an attack on you, because I knew you'd scurry away like a little mouse, I knew you'd be a coward! For quite some time, I was afraid you'd realize what had happened. But you were a fool even then, Molnar! A gullible fool!"

Molnar felt like he was about to suffocate, like his heart had stopped beating. The room was spinning, and Yoshka's words seemed to be surrounding him: Coward! Coward! You fool, you gullible fool! As pale as the wall, he leaned on it while Yoshka poured a glass of water over him, trying to help him recover. The room began to look normal again, but the humiliation, pain, and shock that Molnar was gripped by only grew stronger. "Get out of here!" he ordered Yoshka quietly. "Get out of here before I kill you with my bare hands!"

Yoshka smiled again and left the room. Molnar dropped to the floor and stayed there all night. The next day, when he finally managed to drag himself to his office, he found a list on his desk for the next transport to Mauthausen. Yoshka Schwartz's name was in the fourth column from the right. His hands trembling, Molnar picked up his pen and signed it. Then he returned to his room and drank himself into a stupor, all the while staring at the painting of the nun and the bear.

***

"What happened that night," Otto summed up the unfortunate story, "was that two men whose feelings had been hurt were stupid enough to lock horns, their love for the same woman driving them crazy. My grandfather regretted it the following day, after he sobered up, but it was too late. Your grandfather was already in Mauthausen and your grandmother refused to ever see him again."

"I can understand her," I said softly.

"Yes, so can I," Molnar agreed, "and my grandfather did too. That's why he didn't try more than a couple of times to see her. All he wanted was to tell her he'd like to return all of her family's property to her, but even that she didn't want to hear."

"Maybe she thought that if she accepted it, your grandfather would feel that she'd forgiven him."

"Maybe," he said, deep in thought. We could see the airport in the distance. Otto parked the car in the adjacent parking lot and insisted on escorting me to the check-in counters. "Just to check that you don't take a flight to Australia by mistake," he explained with a smile. "You look like you're in a daze."

"That's because of your cognac," I yawned, letting him throw my bag on his back. A sense of relative calm washed over me as I walked beside him. Somehow, I'd managed to convince myself that he was completely trustworthy.

In the passenger hall, before boarding, I was overcome with a new, dizzying feeling of excitement, when he leaned down and gave me a kiss that seemed to last forever, as he held me close to his warm chest.

"Otto, I have to tell you something…" I said after I managed to catch my breath.

"You'll be late for your flight," he smiled, as if he knew exactly what I wanted to say.

"No, it's important. I…want you to know that I have…a boyfriend. In Israel," I stammered, blushing.

"A boyfriend?" he rolled the word in his mouth as if it had a strange and exotic flavor.

"Yes, a boyfriend, a partner, you know," I thought he hadn't understood what I meant.

"I understand, Daryakum, it's all right, I didn't think otherwise," he grinned cheerfully, his smile lighting up the passenger hall. "Clearly a girl as lovely as you can't walk around alone for long."

"Well, I just wanted you to know that…" I said, no less embarrassed.

"Have a good trip and take care of yourself," he said and squeezed my shoulder, "and most importantly, I hope that your sister gets better!"

"True," I agreed, having trouble moving my feet, as if they were stuck to the stone floor tiles.

"Go on, you'll be late for your flight," he hugged me again, this time kissing my forehead.

"*Szervusz*," I said goodbye and turned to go. I could feel his blue eyes watching me, burning my back.

I boarded the plane and sank into a chair, looking forward to a good, deep sleep to take me under its wings. But for some reason, I had trouble falling asleep. Of all the important things in the world, I couldn't get that kiss and the brief talk that followed out of my mind. What did it mean to him, I wondered. Why did the boyfriend I mentioned make no impression on him? In fact, after the intense and emotional night we'd spent together, I felt that the kiss was definitely in place, but the shiver of excitement that it came with was an overreaction on my part. *Maybe I shouldn't have told him about Oren*, I thought, embarrassed in retrospect. *He must have thought I was acting like a baby, making a big deal out of a kiss.* But I was convinced he was also moved when our lips touched and…*Cool it*, I reprimanded myself, *you really are behaving like a baby. All in all, it was just a kiss from an incredibly good looking and attractive guy, but why are you getting so carried away with enthusiasm and doubt? A minute after he gets back into his funny car, he'll forget that kiss, so just hope that he'll still feel something for you when he gets back to Baja and that he'll keep his promise to transfer the money.*

Still, despite the tongue-lashing I gave myself, I found it difficult to relax. I couldn't stop thinking about Noa, although my thoughts were constantly interrupted by Otto Molnar, that charming, strange Hungarian who I didn't even know existed until yesterday.

CHAPTER 15

Vered picked me up from the airport, which was really nice of her, since I was on the verge of collapsing, both physically and mentally.

"I love your new hairstyle," she ruffled my hair.

"Yes," I replied, surprised that I'd forgotten about it, after being so vehemently opposed to it. "How's Noiki?"

"Not good, she's on pain medication and asleep most of the time."

"And what about the doctors' meeting? When is it?"

"This afternoon, when it's morning in the States. What's new? Do you have the money?"

"I brought a kind of will, old Molnar's, it says that all the property that belonged to Grandma Martha is to be transferred to us," I answered almost mechanically. When I noticed that she was staring at me in the mirror, I continued and told her the whole story, the beginning of which I had heard from Gizi and the end from Otto Molnar.

By the time I was done, we'd arrived at the hospital. Vered parked the car and looked at me excitedly.

"So basically, you're telling me that you met the grandson of Grandma Martha's lover?! That's incredible!"

"That's not like you, Vered," I snapped, "getting excited over a shady love story, instead of the fact that we'll soon have enough to pay for Noa's surgery, maybe even more."

"Don't expect too much," she responded dismissively, "go figure how much the house is worth now, probably less than a shack in Petah Tikva, being so close to Tel Aviv. I only hope we'll have enough to pay for Noa's surgery."

"What, are you kidding?!" I attacked her with unexpected fervor. "You should have seen the house! It's stunning! And Otto took care of it all on his own!"

"You seem very impressed with the grandson," she said, her eyes narrowing. "What's he like? Is he hot?"

"What does that have to do with anything?!" I became even more annoyed.

"What do I know? Since when are you so materialistic, getting excited over houses? That's my job in the family, if I'm not mistaken."

"Another thing you inherited from Mom," I bit back.

"Yeah, yeah, only you're like Dad in this family," she grimaced at me, and immediately voiced my deepest fears, "but let's just hope that you're not as gullible and that this Otto person will really send you the money and not disappear with it to some exotic island."

"Vered, you have no idea what you're talking about!" I shouted. "Why would he do such a thing, now of all times? After he told me the whole story and gave me the papers?"

"Maybe he wants Dad to sign them and give you power of attorney authorizing you to take care of the inheritance, and then he'll be so charming that you'll agree to not take anything from him? Have you thought of that, for instance?"

"Stop it, he's not like that, really," I muttered despondently, but my misgivings were rearing their heads again. It looked like I'd be stuck with them until I saw a big fat sum in my bank account with my own two eyes.

***

Dad was pacing up and down the hospital corridor when we got there. He was pale and looked tense. "Dad," I rushed over and hugged him. He stared at me as if he were having trouble recognizing me.

"Daryakum," he said wearily, at last. His face was bristly and his eyes red, "how are you?"

"I'm fine, Dad, what's with Noiki?"

"She's sleeping, Mom's with her. I'm waiting for the doctors to arrive."

"Do you have a phone charger?" I asked.

"What?" Dad stared at me, his eyes confused. I realized that he wouldn't be much help, so I went into Noa's room. She looked like an angel, sleeping there. A very pale angel. Her light hair was fanned out around her face and Mom was sitting by her side, holding her hand.

"Mom," I whispered and kissed her cheek.

"Darya," she stood up and hugged me, "how are you doing? Did you get a haircut?"

"Yes," I answered quickly, "and it seems like I've also secured the money for Noa's surgery. It should go into my bank account soon, and I need a phone charger to check. Is Dad's here?"

"Yes, sure," she went to the corner and took out a charger from the blue travel bag, "but how…"

"I'll tell you everything in a few minutes," I said as I grabbed the charger from her. I rushed out to the balcony, where there was no danger of bumping into any of the hospital staff. I didn't want to make anyone angry at me for talking on my phone in the hospital.

Within no time, I found a wall socket, and within three minutes, I was hearing Otto's warm voice again.

"It's good you called," he said, breathlessly, "I just got out of the bank and I was meaning to call you. You see, the appraiser has estimated the value of the house to be two hundred thousand dollars, but the bank is only prepared to loan me a hundred and fifty, because they don't believe I'll find a buyer who'll pay the full valuation price. What do you want me to do?"

"Take it," I replied, "we'll decide what to do after the surgery."

***

"Everything will be fine," I informed Mom, Dad, and Vered, who were huddled in the corridor outside Noa's room, "Otto is taking out a loan at the bank and he'll transfer the money to my account within a few days."

"What?" Dad said, surprised, and Mom, her eyes suspicious, followed suit and said, "Who is this Otto?"

"What? Didn't you tell them?" I said to Vered, annoyed.

"I wanted to wait and make sure that we really have something to tell them," she glared at me. Even though her answer reminded me that I, myself, had decided to wait to tell our parents the story until I saw the money in the bank, I immediately started to tell them everything. By the time I was done, they were both looking stunned and excited.

"You don't say!" Naturally, Mom was the first to recover. "This young man, the grandson of a Nazi, is prepared to give you the house and all the property that they stole from Grandma Martha?"

"First of all, he wasn't really a Nazi," I jumped to Molnar's defense, may he rest in peace, "he only joined the Arrow Cross because Grandma asked him to keep an eye on her family."

"That's true," Dad said, his eyes scanning the will, which he was now holding, "it turns out he was a decent man. As someone who knew my father's annoying behavior very well, he probably managed to drive him insane at that card game, which probably made him momentarily forget his commitment to Grandma."

"Is that all you have to say?" Mom raised her voice, "You're defending the goy who had an affair with your mother and almost broke up your family?!"

"He was no more guilty than my father. She initiated the affair with him because of Yoshka's affairs."

Mom looked shocked but she didn't respond, probably because she'd heard too many references to affairs in the family. It wasn't that she didn't already know about some of them, but she always preferred to suppress the details, since they didn't match her moral perspective.

"I still don't understand why you're acting like a UN inspector," she continued, "your father could have died in that camp!"

"He could have, but he didn't, he lived for way longer than Molnar, and today, looking back, I think that we can forgive him, especially in light of his grandson's generous behavior," Dad retorted, waving Molnar's will.

"Too true!" Mom immediately forgot her moral dispute with Dad, "At least we can pay for Noiki's surgery now. When will those doctors get here!"

My phone rang on the balcony, making me jump. I hoped it was Otto letting me know that he'd transferred the money, but it turned out to be Oren.

"Hi," he didn't try to hide how happy he was to hear my voice, "where are you? I've left you like a thousand messages!"

"I'm at the hospital," I replied, "and where are you?"

"I'm in Paris. How was Hungary? I haven't been able to get hold of you for two days."

"I forgot my charger at home," I said, a slight tone of apology in my voice, and immediately went on to tell him what had happened.

Oren sounded both worried and enthusiastic. "Then, you have the money for the op?!"

"Yes," I answered wearily, "now we're waiting for the doctors to decide if Noa goes to the States or if Professor Salzman comes here."

"And when will they decide?"

"Soon," I said, feeling the tension seeping through my limbs. Only now that all my rushing about was over, did I feel the full force of it.

"I'm so sorry I can't be with you all now," he sounded discouraged. "I wish I'd known how bad the situation is, I would have got someone else to take the flight."

"You couldn't have known; we didn't know either."

"Yes, but…all this stress…it would be much easier for me to bear if I were there with you."

"True, but that's just the way it is. Anyway, I'll keep you updated."

"Okay, I'll be back tomorrow morning, so you can call any time. And Darya, do me a favor, don't go anywhere without a charger."

"Okay, Oren, bye, kisses," I said quickly, when I heard the many voices coming from Noa's room. I assumed the doctors had finished their consultation.

I went back to the room. They were all standing around Noa's bed, talking between them. Mom and Dad were standing to the side and whispering with Vered.

"Noa," I went and stood by Dad's side. He seemed torn between hope and despair.

"She'll probably fly to the States tonight," he said softly. "They're concerned that the tumor is spreading so fast…it's growing from one test to the next. Professor Salzman is prepared to operate on her as soon as we arrive, but he can't come here on such short notice, so it seems we have no choice."

"Cheer up," I said, putting my arm around his slumped shoulders, "it'll be fine. You and Mom should go with her."

"Yes," he nodded, "you can come too, and Vered, if money's no longer an issue."

"Yes," I said, hoping with all my heart that the money would be deposited in my account soon, "I'll go home now and book your flights, and then I'll pack a few things for you to take with you, okay?"

"Sure," Dad looked like his spirit had just returned from a trip to another world, "go, and call us later."

Mom had a lot more to say before she let me go. "Pack only warm clothes for me and my green nightgown, the one that looks like an evening dress," she instructed, as if dictating a list to me. "I'll probably sleep at the hospital, so I should at least look decent. And pack all of Noa's stuffed animals and all that, you know what a baby she can be."

"Hold on, what about Mickey?" I asked. The dog couldn't stay behind on his own.

"I'll talk to Gilad, I'll tell him to pick him up tonight," Vered said. Gilad was a lecturer at the Technion in Haifa, so he couldn't be with us at the hospital in Petah Tikva.

"All right, then," I said and turned to leave as Mom called after me, "And try to get a good discount on the tickets, after all, why else did we send you to be a flight attendant?"

"Yes, Mom," I answered impatiently. All I wanted was to check with the bank to see if anything had been deposited.

***

At eight that the evening, I went back to the hospital with three carry-alls and a suitcase. I was very pleased with myself, and with Otto, who'd faxed me copies of the mortgage applications he'd submitted and a copy of the transfer to my account in Israel. All the tension that had been building up in me over the last few days evaporated in an instant. And after I managed to book Noa a first-class ticket at a huge discount that the CEO himself gave me after he was brought into the picture, I felt that I deserved a medal.

"Can we get going already?" I asked, gasping for breath when I saw my parents and Vered standing outside Noa's room. The door to the room was closed.

"Not yet," Mom replied gloomily, "they're treating her now, trying to prepare her for the trip. She woke up and started screaming in pain, I really don't…"

Suddenly, Mom burst into tears, making it startlingly clear to me that the situation was far from good. Dad quickly put his arms around her, and they stood there, as still as a tragic statue.

"They're not sure she'll be able to fly in her condition," Vered said softly when she saw the panic in my eyes, "things are bad."

"So why didn't you let me know!? I've moved heaven and earth to get you on a flight tonight!" I complained, my heart pounding in my ears.

"Is that what concerns you?" Vered barked as she glanced at Dad, who looked as if his world had fallen apart, then she lowered her voice and whispered, "Sorry, Darya, we're all just so confused."

"I'm going in," I said and moved toward the closed door. I couldn't stand the situation for one more second. I couldn't bear the fact that a bunch of disinterested doctors who were just as confused as us were about to determine my sister's fate, and we, her immediate family, had no say at all.

"Darya! Are you crazy?" Vered grabbed the back of my shirt and tried to stop me, when the door opened and two doctors, one young, one old, came out, their expressions undecipherable.

"What's going on?" Mom and Dad quickly let go of each other and rushed over to them.

"We're sorry," the younger doctor said, his expression softening when he saw my mother's tearstained face, "it appears she won't be able to manage the flight in her condition. The surgery will have to be done here."

"And Professor Salzman? Will he come here?" Mom was sobbing now.

"I'm sorry, Mrs. Schwartz," the older doctor responded, "the professor won't be able to make it, and we have to operate on Noa tonight. We'll do our best!"

The corridor spun around me for a moment, and I thought I was going to pass out. But a moment later, the black dots that were racing before my eyes disappeared, when I remembered that I shouldn't be adding more problems for the medical team and my family to deal with. I had to be a rock for the family to lean on.

***

An hour later, the four of us gathered by the operating room, afraid and bewildered. Gilad walked in with four cups of steaming coffee and gave them to us without a word. Mom took a sip, as if trying to draw courage from it.

"We can't carry on this way," she said, "we have to send positive energy to Noiki."

"Mom, really!" I protested and took a sip of coffee myself. It tasted like coffee from a machine, which it was.

"No, I'm serious!" she declared, "I heard about this method, of sending positive energy through thought, and it helps to strengthen the person having surgery. We must relax and concentrate on positive thoughts. Picture Noa regaining her health and her sight."

"I'll picture it outside," I announced. The situation was unbearable, even without that mystical nonsense. Although I was tired, I felt I had to do something, such as measure the diameter of the hospital's lawn and breathe fresh air.

"You can do it outside too," Mom's voice had become worryingly calm, but she caught my eye and added, "Go out, Daryale, if that's what you feel you need to do, but keep those positive thoughts coming."

"Okay, Mom," I answered and dashed outside to breathe. I walked around the lawn a few times and then tried to concentrate on positive thoughts, but it didn't really work for me. All I could think about was what the doctor had meant when he said that they'd do their best. Was he implying that they'd do their best to help her regain her vision? Or, heaven forbid, to save her from death?

***

The terrifying thought made my legs tremble, so I sat down on a bench and tried to think about other things. Positive things, as Mom had instructed me. I stared at the restaurant at the gas station near the hospital entrance, and I tried to imagine all of us, the whole happy and healthy Schwartz family, including Noa, walking in to eat dinner. But instead, I found myself wondering how other people, who I couldn't see clearly, were walking into that very restaurant to have dinner now as if nothing was wrong, while my sister hung between life and death on the operating table just a few feet away.

Who's the idiot who opened a restaurant right in front of the hospital? I wondered, when suddenly I saw Dad walking toward me.

"Any news?" I almost pounced on him.

"No," he dropped down next to me, his face gray, "I just…also needed some fresh air."

"There's plenty here to go around," I said, trying to sound cheery.

"I don't understand," he mumbled and buried his face in his hands, "how does a girl who's never done anyone any harm, suddenly become so ill?"

"She'll be fine, Dad," I put my arm around him. His shoulders were shaking from trying not to cry. We were interrupted by my phone ringing, and I grabbed it out of my purse, thinking maybe it was Vered, and that she had news for us. I wasn't expecting to hear Oren's voice, sounding like it was from another galaxy.

"Darya, how are things?"

"Not wonderful," I answered, glancing at Dad, who had sat up and was now leaning against the bench, his eyes dry and questioning.

"What do you mean? Are you going or not?"

"No, Noa's condition is a little…worse. The doctors decided to operate immediately, she's in the operating room right now."

"You're kidding! Why didn't you let me know?!"

"What do you think, that's the first thing that entered my mind? As soon as they told us?!" I attacked him with a fury that surprised even me. "I've been under so much pressure, spending all day booking flights and packing…"

"All right, all right, I'm sorry," Oren said, minus the accusing tone he'd used before but sounding despondent and sad, "so what happens now?"

"Nothing. We wait."

"Okay, let me know as soon as she's out of surgery, will you?"

Fine," I assured him and quickly hung up. Dad was staring at me, his eyes wide.

"It was Oren," I explained. "He's in Paris, and he's too stressed out to sleep, so he's taking it out on me."

"It seemed to me that you were the one taking things out on him. What's going on between you, Darya? You don't seem to be doing very well."

"Dad, do you really have nothing better to worry about?" I said, "Does it matter what's happening between me and Oren?"

"I'd rather discuss matters I can help with, rather than think about… other things," he answered gloomily. Then my phone, which I was still holding, rang again.

This time I noticed a row of zeros on the screen, indicating that the call was from abroad. I guessed it was Oren again, and I tried to sound patient so that Dad could relax and give up his plan to talk about it.

"Hello, Darya," I heard Otto's singsong Hungarian accent, "how are you, my dear?"

"Otto!" I was suddenly filled with joy, even though I'd almost forgotten his existence.

"Yes, Daryakum, how are you? Did you receive the fax I sent?"

"Yes, but…in the end my sister couldn't fly. Her condition deteriorated and they decided to operate on her right away."

"I'm sorry," his voice sounded grim and empathetic. "When will they start?"

"They've already begun, now we're waiting."

"I see," he replied, then after a long pause, continued, "so I won't bother you now with mundane issues."

No, no, it's no bother," I clarified, desperate to hear his voice for a little longer. "I'd actually rather be talking about anything other than the op."

Dad gaped at me, his eyes wide with astonishment, but he kept quiet. I really wanted to walk away and find a quiet place to talk to Otto, without Dad listening in, but I couldn't leave him there alone, with his face so sad.

"It's nothing serious," I heard Otto on the other end, "I just wanted to tell you that I've put the house up for sale, and I spoke to the curator from the Budapest Museum of Fine Arts. I arranged to bring her the paintings tomorrow for her to evaluate."

"Otto, you're an angel," I sighed, "thank you!"

"Well, Daryakum, I'm glad I could help in some way, even though I understand from what you're saying that money is no longer the problem. I hope that your sister's surgery is successful and that she makes a full recovery."

"Me too, and you should really cancel your mortgage application. When I come, after all this is over, we'll take care of everything together."

"Fine, I guess that for now you'll be busy with more important things," he continued softly, "but if it's not too difficult, try to send me a message sometime and let me know how your sister is, and how you are. Because I, how should I put it, I'm a little worried about you all, and—"

"Sure, I'll let you know," I promised excitedly, "as soon as we know what's going on, okay?"

"Okay, then, Darya, thanks."

"No, I should be thanking you," I argued with him, trying to draw out the conversation. But when I looked at Dad's face, which had become somewhat derisive, I decided to end it, and in any case, Otto hadn't said another word. "All right, then, bye," I said.

"Bye," he responded, "and I hope to hear from you soon."

I hung up, trying to hide my excitement, but as usual, Dad's piercing eyes were reading me like an open book.

"Was that Molnar's grandson?" he asked, as if he didn't know.

"Yes," I nodded, "he's put the house up for sale, and tomorrow he'll take the paintings of Grandma and of the nun with the bear to an art museum in Budapest to have them evaluated."

"That's very nice of him," Dad said, adding, "Did you notice the difference in your tone when you spoke to him, compared to how you spoke to Oren?"

"Ugh, Dad, really!" I snapped. "Is this really the right time? With Noa lying on the operating table?"

"You're right," he sighed heavily, the pain flooding his eyes. He was suffering so deeply that his shoulders seemed to be weighed down. I couldn't bear it, so eventually I said, "No, you're right, I'm sorry. We can talk about anything you want, as long as the damn time passes, somehow."

"What do you want to talk about?" he asked, an innocent expression on his face, a heartwarming and naughty glint in his eye. Despite the difficult situation, I saw his expression as a sign that he'd be all right.

"About the odds of finding life on Mars," I said sardonically. "Stop playing games, Dad, you wanted to talk about me and Oren, so go on, talk."

"I thought perhaps you would talk about it."

"There's not much to say, Dad," I sighed. "We're in the same place as we've always been: We love each other, we fight, drive each other up the wall, and in the end, we kiss and make up. Just like any other couple that's been living together for twelve years."

"And Molnar's grandson? What's he like? Tell me a little about him."

I took my time responding. Dad's reason for asking was clear, and the way he cut straight to the chase got my back up. Still, I felt an almost uncontrollable need to tell him all about Otto Molnar. I wanted to see it in his eyes, the positive opinion I was sure he'd arrive at, regarding the wonderful and sensitive man I met in Baja. Dad didn't say a word, he just listened intently to every detail of my story. The only thing I left out, for obvious reasons, was the kiss that Otto gave me at the airport, the memory of which was washing softly over me.

"And what would have happened if you'd met him under different circumstances, say if you weren't in a twelve-year relationship with Oren? Could you see yourself falling in love with him?" he asked when I was done.

At a loss, I looked at him, surprised only that he'd expressed thoughts that I hadn't even dared to have.

"Dad," I sighed eventually, "what kind of question is that? That's really unfair."

"In my opinion, it's a good one, and fair. You should always ask yourself tough questions, otherwise you'll find yourself in a situation you've given no thought to and find yourself in trouble."

"What kind of trouble? Do you think I'd have an affair with Otto behind Oren's back?" I said, annoyed again.

"I didn't say that, but—"

"Then I'll have you know, I told him I have a boyfriend," I stated triumphantly, "and he said he didn't think otherwise, because I'm so lovely…" I stopped suddenly, feeling that I'd gone too far. The question of why I even had to tell Otto that I had a boyfriend hung in the chilly, night air. I felt my cheeks go warm, a telling sign that I was blushing, and I avoided Dad's cynical gaze.

"I see," I heard him say, "he's behaving just as I thought he would, like any other European Don Juan."

"He's not a Don Juan, and he's certainly not like anyone else," I jumped to Otto's defense. "He's a wonderful, generous man and I couldn't have dreamed of anyone behaving better, considering the way we met."

"He behaved like that because he's an old-fashioned romantic. His grandfather told him a sob story and asked him to fulfill his will. And that's what he's doing. It's certainly very nice of him, I'm not saying it's not, but that's not a reason to fall in love with him and to forget who you are."

"I haven't fallen in love with him, Dad, not at all! It's just…he seems interesting, that's all."

"Interesting—and attractive?"

"Yes," I admitted, "but that's not to say that I'm going to have an affair with him, and I certainly wouldn't leave Oren for him."

"So why do you think you're being so impatient with Oren? I've never seen you like this before, only now, since you got back from Budapest."

"That's not true, Dad," I sighed, "things between us have been off for a long time, and…maybe I really have been a little more confused lately about what I feel for him, but that's not because of Otto. It's…maybe it's all the romantic stories I've heard recently, about Grandma and Grandpa, Grandma and Molnar, Shandor and Angelika. All these stories about love that is larger than life have made me think that my feelings for Oren are so…shallow. They don't feel as intense in comparison, and it's frustrating."

"Oh, Daryakum, my child," Dad sighed, "Shandor Bachi and Paul Molnar were romantics that grew up in a different culture, a culture you can't understand. A culture that developed as a result of Goethe and Schiller's works, of young Voltaire's suffering, and the more I think about it, it was a culture that sanctified death, not life. My father's another story, he certainly had an appetite for life, but he was also a product of a culture that you can't understand, not now, or ever."

"But I want to understand that culture. I feel that if I can't, I'll never be able to understand myself either."

"You're wrong, Darya, you grew up in another, simpler and perhaps healthier culture, because it takes into account the unfortunate fact that we're mortal; that the time we're given here is very short, and if we don't make the best of it, we'll miss the opportunity for more meaningful experiences. I'm not belittling the good old European culture, you know how much I appreciate its classical music, literature, theater, but…somehow… when it comes to real life, there's something morbid about it. In my opinion, it wasn't by chance that the drive for destruction consumed people, in of all places, the center of Europe's cultural life, and was expressed as Nazism and fascism. I don't think it was because of the economic crisis. It was the result of bad education and the sanctification of the darkest urges of the human psyche, and it didn't start in the '30s, my child, it had much deeper roots in our overly romantic culture."

"Really?" I asked curiously. Suddenly, I was finding the theoretical side of what Dad was saying more interesting than my own emotional affairs.

"Really and truly," he nodded, "and I think that you're making a mistake, although a common one, by allowing yourself to fall in love with this man, who with all his kindness and generosity, belongs to a completely different world, one that you have no ability to understand."

"I haven't fallen for him, Dad," I objected immediately. "I barely know him, and I have no idea what's going to happen between us. Maybe I'll get back to Baja and find out that he has a girlfriend or something…"

"Well, that's precisely the problem. Even if he has a girlfriend, I don't think it'll bother him to have a fling with you."

I wanted to respond right away, to tell him that if that was the case, under no circumstances would I agree to it, and nothing would happen between us. But then I remembered Otto's lighthearted reaction when he heard I had a boyfriend, and I kept my mouth shut.

"Dad, let's go inside and see if there's any news," I said nervously, when I looked at my watch and saw that it was close to midnight. Dad's face grew somber and he stood up. We entered the corridor and walked toward the operating rooms. Mom, Vered, and Gilad were sitting in a triangle opposite the glass doors, each of them seemingly deep in thought—positive thought, naturally.

"What's happening?" I whispered to Vered, who glanced at me.

"I have no idea," she whispered back. I watched as Dad went up to Mom and stroked her head. "A doctor comes out every now and then, goes off somewhere and then comes back, but no one's told us anything. To be honest, it doesn't look great, I would prefer you to take Dad away again…"

"But I want to be here, see which doctor is brave enough to tell me what's happening!" I said angrily, but Vered quickly silenced me.

"Drop it, Darya, your crap really won't help matters now. It's best if you're outside with Dad, see how he is…and try to find ways to distract him."

I looked at Dad sitting silently next to Mom and hugging her, tears streaming down his face.

"Come on, Dad, let's go back into the fresh air, we have a few more things to discuss," I went over and took his arm. Puzzled, Dad looked at me and then at Mom, who nodded, "Yes, Peter, go outside, the air will do you good. We'll call you as soon as we hear anything."

Dad got up and dragged himself toward the exit, "Would you like us to get you anything to eat or drink?" he stopped and asked.

"No, thanks, who could eat at a time like this?" Mom said, and we went outside again.

"It's brain surgery," I said to him, making a considerable effort to calm us both, "it takes a lot of time and patience. But it'll be all right, I have a feeling."

"Yes…" Dad looked like he was about to burst into tears again. I gripped his arm and pulled him toward the bench we were sitting on before.

"Come, let's sit down and continue our discussion. It was just getting interesting. What did you want to warn me about before?"

"What?" he looked like he had no idea what I meant.

"Come on, Dad, we were discussing Otto, Molnar's grandson. You said that I don't understand the cultural codes that he grew up with, and you tried to explain to me why I shouldn't fall in love with him," I said, careful not to mention Oren.

"Cultural codes?" Dad repeated, as if not understanding.

"Yes," I replied, "the romantic European cultural codes, the…Dad, you know what? Gizi told me all about your family's story, until the end of the war. Could you tell me what happened afterward, about how Grandpa got back from Mauthausen? Why did you stay in Hungary after the war? How did you manage under the communist regime? And why did you immigrate to Israel only in 1949, and miss all the action, the Palmach and all that if, in any case, you didn't like the European culture?"

"Do you think I have the energy to go into all those stories now?" Dad sighed, but after I nodded vigorously and squeezed his hand in encouragement, his eyes suddenly brightened, he sat up and began to speak. Slowly at first, but as the minutes passed, his voice grew stronger, steadier, and more focused.

CHAPTER 16

Budapest was liberated by the Red Army one freezing day in January. No one even considered dancing on the streets, where the snow was painted red. The injured and dead were lying on every corner, the conquerors beside the defeated, the oppressors with the oppressed. Russian tank and gun shells didn't distinguish between their blood.

Martha, Gizi, and Angelika huddled by the radio, listening to the constant announcements concerning the curfew imposed by the Russians and to the repeated warnings to locals not to violate it. As usual, Martha was impatient. She longed to hold Peter in her arms, make sure he was safe and sound, and discuss with him how to find his father. They hadn't received any sign of life from Yoshka since that damned day he was sent to Mauthausen.

Angelika and Gizi almost had to use force to stop her. Gizi told her that nothing good would come from being killed on the street, and Angelika reminded her that Gizi herself was in the same situation, as Marika was also at the Wallenberg shelter like Peter and Tibby and her husband Mark had been sent to Auschwitz only days before Yoshka was sent to Mauthausen.

Martha said she preferred to die quickly, rather than to go slowly out of her mind, but the two women remained skeptical and the argument grew more passionate. There was no telling what would have happened if someone hadn't come knocking at the door late one night. They opened it to find Peter standing there on his own, breathless and gasping. He, too, like his mother, could no longer stand being away from his family just when the bells of freedom had begun to chime.

"What were you thinking! You could have been killed!" Martha fell into his arms, hugging him so tightly she almost choked him.

"And where are Marika and Tibby?" Gizi asked him anxiously, after Peter managed to break free of Martha's arms.

"They stayed there," the boy explained. He was very thin, but his face was surprisingly flushed. "I persuaded them that we shouldn't all run the risk."

"Peter, meet Angelika," his mother said, taking him by the hand, and then suddenly a scream escaped her. "What's wrong with you? You're burning up with fever!"

Peter shivered and dropped to the sofa. Angelika went over and felt his forehead while Martha, terrified, ran to get a damp cloth.

"He has a very high fever," the nun agreed, looking at Gizi, who was watching nervously as Martha pressed the damp cloth to Peter's forehead.

"What are we going to do?" she muttered repeatedly. "How will we get a doctor to come here, with the curfew?"

"Let me examine him," Angelika suggested. She'd taken care of ill people before. She sat down next to Peter, whose teeth were chattering uncontrollably, and opened the collar of his shirt. In the dim light of the lantern, she noticed a red, slightly bumpy rash on his chest and nodded to herself in recognition. "He has scarlet fever," she said, watching the boy tremoring. "We should get him into bed and find a doctor. It's urgent."

The three women supported Peter on both sides and from behind. They led him to the bedroom and helped him climb into bed. Martha was as pale as he was red. She wiped his feverish forehead with the cloth as tears rolled down her cheeks. "Rest now, Peter, just rest, you'll recover and be all right, don't worry," she murmured, her voice cracking. "Mami's here, relax, I'll take care of you and of everything...."

"Has Marika also come down with the fever?" Gizi asked aloud. Peter stared at them both and tried to lift his head to speak, but his voice died and his head dropped.

Angelika pulled Martha and Gizi out. "Do you really think it'll help him if you behave in this way?" she reprimanded them, keeping her voice down, "From the looks on your faces, he could conclude that he's dying, the poor boy. It's better you think about where to find a doctor."

"We don't stand a chance," Martha said, "even if we find someone, how will we persuade him to come out with the curfew and all?"

"All right, stay here," Angelika said and rushed to the kitchen. Martha returned to Peter's room, and Gizi followed Angelika.

"Look for old, leftover bread," Angelika instructed her as she rummaged through the kitchen.

"Why?" Gizi asked.

"Here, I found some!" Angelika announced triumphantly, taking a loaf of bread wrapped in paper out of a cabinet. Gizi had been meaning to throw it out, after finding green mold on it.

"The mold will cure him," Angelika explained to Gizi, who was watching her in horror. "Mold has curative properties. We'll dissolve it in a drink and feed it to the boy with a spoon."

At the same time, Angelika brewed tea on the stove, to which she added the last two spoons of sugar left in the almost-bare pantry. She waited for the tea to cool down and carefully crumbled the moldy bread crust into it.

"Here!" she said encouragingly and ran to Peter's bedroom.

Throughout that night, Angelika and Martha did all they could to get Peter to drink the murky tea. As Angelika had expected, the poor boy couldn't drink much, because his throat was infected, but he obediently licked the liquid from the spoon they held up to his mouth, and, by the time dawn broke, his fever had started to drop and he fell into a deep sleep.

**

For days, Martha didn't move from Peter's side waiting for him to get better, even though Angelika kept warning her that she may contract the disease herself.

"I don't care," Martha replied, "If I do, I'll also drink your wonder drug. After all, we have enough mold here for an army."

"But Martha, this is a childhood disease, and if an older person becomes infected, it's twice as dangerous. The bacteria could even damage your heart."

"My heart is already immune to damage," Martha replied firmly, refusing to move from her son's bed. She didn't reveal to Angelika that when Peter was awake he must have been terribly confused, because he told her in detail about a three-way romance between himself, Marika, and Tibby, which had carried on while they were at the shelter. Martha was beside herself with anger when she understood what had happened. Peter had tried to avoid having an intimate relationship with his disgruntled cousin, especially after Martha had made her opinion perfectly clear, but then, just to make him angry, Marika threw herself into Tibby's arms and that was something Peter couldn't ignore. "She's beautiful and delightful," he explained to his mother, when he noticed her lips stiffen. "None of the other girls were as captivating!"

"Peter, please, calm down," Martha stroked his hair, still sodden, "you need to build up your strength and recover, and I'm not angry with you, only with Marika. When she returns, we'll be leaving this house."

Peter didn't argue because Martha told him they'd be returning to Baja, although she had no idea how she would get the house back without talking to Molnar. But before she had the chance to catch Gizi on her own to tell her how angry she was with her daughter and inform her of her plans, she came down with scarlet fever and was incapacitated herself.

Meanwhile, the curfew was lifted and Gizi called Doctor Tadeusz, who lived down the road. The doctor looked troubled when he informed them that Martha would need several doses of penicillin, which was difficult to obtain even on the black market, but Angelika prepared another batch of mold, which worked more slowly this time, and Martha hovered between life and death for a week. She then needed another two weeks to recover, during which tempers kept flying in the house at 35 Andrassy Avenue.

One day, Tibby and Marika showed up at the house. They were holding hands. Gizi was happy to see them, and so was Peter, but he was secretly worried. He hoped that Martha wouldn't be able to hear them from her room, which would only annoy her and making her fever rise. Angelika wanted to return to France, where Imre was waiting for her, and Peter feared that with her gone, there'd be no one there to stabilize Martha again if her condition deteriorated. He decided to talk to Angelika and explain, somewhat awkwardly, how complex a situation they were in.

Angelika thought that Peter should meet with Paul Molnar and try to reclaim the Goldberger family home. That way, he and Martha would be able to move as soon as she regained her strength. Peter went to the camp where he was previously imprisoned but was told that Molnar had been taken with the other surviving Arrow Cross members to a Russian detention camp. On his way home, exhausted and tense, he noticed a silhouette in the distance, a shadow of a man who looked like his father.

"Papa!" Peter exclaimed and ran toward the hunched figure, who was showing no sign of hearing him. "Papa! Papa!" he continued to shout, his chest bursting with hope and happiness.

The figure stopped. Peter was panting by the time he reached him, and he couldn't believe that the hunched and emaciated skeleton was really his father—not until he looked into the blue eyes that glinted back at him, not dulled by all he'd been through, and the shadow whispered his name, "Peter? My son, Peter?" Then his father fell into his arms, sobbing with joy before losing consciousness.

***

Although Yoshka made it to Budapest, one could say he was there in spirit only. His body was barely skin and bone, and that, too, was ridden with typhoid. No one understood how he'd made the long trip from Mauthausen to Budapest on his own, in his condition. He also didn't provide reasonable answers, and when asked to elaborate, he replied, "I just… walked…through the snow…"

Angelika decided to stay in Budapest, until Yoshka and Martha had regained their strength. After Doctor Tadeusz made another house call and examined Yoshka, he said there wasn't much he could do, but Angelika decided to fight for his life, no matter what.

"Apples!" she said to Gizi, Peter, Marika, and Tibby, who were sitting around her looking desperate. "Apples can save Yoshka's life. Go out and look for apples!"

"Where?" Gizi asked, her voice desperate. "It's still the middle of winter…"

"There must be apples in the nearby villages!" Angelika stated firmly, and Peter jumped up and shouted, "That's right! There were always apples at the Swedish shelter, I'll go there and ask the cook where he found them!"

"I'm coming with you!" Marika quickly announced, "I have a good relationship with the cooks."

"Tibby, you stay here," Gizi ordered the boy, when she saw the intention in his eyes to join his cousins. "We have two patients to take care of, and we'll need your help."

Tibby, whose mischievous and wild nature had completely changed since losing his parents, nodded obediently and remained seated.

Marika and Peter left the house and headed for the shelter. It was evening by the time they got there. Much to their dismay, they discovered that the shelter had been turned into a Russian military camp. Peter was desperate, finding it hard to believe that the soldiers would agree to give them apples for free.

"Who said anything about getting anything for free?" Marika asked, a cheeky glint in her eye, "You may have nothing much to offer, but I certainly have."

"Marika, I'm not going to let you put yourself in that kind of danger!" he shouted. "This is not a game, those are Russian soldiers! They don't understand Hungarian and certainly not our way of thinking. They may try to rape you and then brutally kill you, or think that you're a whore and exile you to Siberia. I've heard countless stories about them!"

"They may not speak Hungarian, but I speak a little Russian," Marika reminded him of the close friendship she'd had with the Russian refugee boys at the shelter. "We have to try, Peter, otherwise your father will die!"

"Then I'm coming with you," Peter insisted, thinking it was unfair to let her take the risk all on her own.

"No, it's not a good idea," Marika argued. "If you really want to help, then I should enter the kitchen from the back, and while I'm talking to the cooks and distracting them—I may even be able to get them out of the kitchen for a few minutes—you can climb in through the window and steal a sack of apples."

"Excellent idea!" Peter said enthusiastically. He knew the kitchen well and knew the perfect spot to sneak in through without being seen. Luckily, since the kitchen was on the edge of the camp, they wouldn't have to cross it to get there.

Peter stayed by the window while Marika headed toward the back door, pinching her cheeks on the way to add a crimson tinge. Then she let her hair down, trying to look as attractive and beguiling as possible. Peter, who was watching her through the kitchen window, thought to himself that she'd never looked so beautiful. Her green cat eyes stood out against her loose black hair and pink-stained cheeks.

The cook, a tall Slavic-looking Russian stared at her in surprise as she walked over to him with a smile. Peter held his breath and tried to pray, but, not knowing how, he just stared at them. Marika stood close to the cook, took his hand, and spoke to him in flowing Russian. The cook listened to her, nodding occasionally, then held out his free hand and pointed to the door. Marika turned around and walked toward it with the cook behind her. Despite his concern for her, Peter wasted no time and immediately climbed through the half-open window. He took a quick deep breath, then looked around for the sacks of apples where they used to be kept. It took him seconds to realize that the kitchen had been reorganized and that they were now using huge sacks to store the produce. He rummaged through several before he found one full of green apples. He heaved it onto his back, which almost collapsed under the weight and, gasping for breath, dragged himself to the window as fast as he could. There, he took the sack off his back and started to tie it closed, so that the precious fruit wouldn't fall out when he tossed it out. But then he heard steps approaching and he threw the sack out with what remained of his strength before climbing out the window. Then he bent over and collected the apples that had rolled away on the ground and put them back into the sack.

When he stood up again, he peeked through the window and saw Marika giving the cook a goodbye kiss on the cheek. She was holding two bags of apples, and her eyes smiled at him from behind the cook's back.

"You see, that wasn't difficult," she told him when they met at the fence, outside the camp. "The cook, Ivan, was very nice and generous after I told him that I needed the apples to cure my father of typhus. He took me to the pantry and told me to take as many bags as I could carry."

And what did you give him in return? he wanted to ask, but overcame the malicious impulse. Marika had acted heroically, and he had no reason to accuse her of anything. Besides, what could the two of them have done during the ten minutes they spent outside the kitchen? "But why did you want me to steal a sack," he asked, finding it hard to conceal his unwarranted anger, "if you knew that you would get what you wanted from him in return for a smile?"

"First of all, I wasn't at all sure," she kissed him on the cheek, "and besides, I wanted you to feel like you were contributing something to saving your father."

***

Yoshka and Martha recuperated within a few weeks. Their recovery filled everyone with joy and optimism, and Angelika decided to return to France as soon as she could, because she'd heard that the Russians were beginning to give the clergy and laity a hard time. Peter and Marika, who had become closer than ever since the night they went out for apples, decided to hide it from Martha, at least until they knew if the scarlet fever had done any damage to her heart.

Tibby felt that Peter and Marika were paying no attention to him, and, for the first time in months, he realized that he was alone in the world. He spent days brooding over it, and when Angelika started packing for her trip, he came to her and asked boldly, "Will you allow me to come with you?"

"What?" Angelika said, taken aback, as were they all. Martha told him he was all she had left of her family and that she had no intention of letting him leave her.

Baffled, Tibby said, "But you have Peter," as if his thoughts were clear to everyone but her, "whereas Angelika and Imre have no one. I wanted to ask them to adopt me."

"I'd be delighted to adopt you, Tibby," Angelika went over to him and hugged him. Highly sensitive, she could sense how lonely and vulnerable he was, despite being surrounded by relatives who didn't want him to leave.

"But, Tibby, what will we do without you?" Marika and Peter asked in unison. Martha raised an eyebrow at Marika's flirtatious tone, which reminded her how dangerous it was for Peter to stay there much longer.

"You'll be fine, you have each other," Tibby mumbled embarrassedly. He hadn't expected such intense resistance to his innocent proposal, which had come from the bottom of his heart.

"What do you mean?" Martha barked, glancing demandingly at Peter.

"Martha, what does it matter now?" Yoshka intervened, unaware of all the finer details. "The boy has made a request, and we have to give it serious consideration. After all, it is his future in the balance."

"I'm sorry," Martha said and gave Angelika an apologetic yet determined look, "Angelika you know that I'll always be grateful for all you've done for us. I will never be able to repay you. But I cannot give Tibby up. My sisters and brother-in-law were murdered, I'm estranged from my younger brother Shani, and my elderly parents will also never forgive me if I allow the boy to go with you, it could take a serious toll on their lives."

No one spoke. None of them could bear to tell Martha that while she was lying on her deathbed they had received news from Baja that both her parents had died just days after the liberation. Angelika looked sternly at Tibby, warning him not to tell Martha the awful news. Then she spoke, her tone measured, "You're right, Martha, Tibby should stay with you. It would be better for him to grow up with his immediate family. And there is no need to feel indebted to me, my dear," she continued, her eyes bright, "and certainly not to feel that you must repay me. I did what I had to, what any person of God would do."

After she finished, she hugged each of them warmly, threw her bundle over her shoulder, and left for the train station.

"What a wonderful woman!" Yoshka said after Angelika left the house. "Shandor is a fool! How could he let such a woman go?"

"You're the fool," Martha snapped, even though on second thought, she realized how inappropriate it was to talk like that in front of the children. "Don't you realize that Shandor never did give her up?"

"No," Yoshka shrugged and went to the kitchen to make himself breakfast. Since his recovery, he was constantly hungry. Martha looked at him and sighed. She knew that he would never understand what she was trying to explain. He couldn't see things abstractly. Still, she had never loved him more.

***

A few days after Angelika left, Shani showed up. He asked to speak to Yoshka in private, but he treated Martha like she was invisible. When the two of them were alone, he told Yoshka that his parents had passed away and that his only brothers to survive were Imre and Shandor. Yoshka felt a sharp stab of pain, but Shani gave him no time to mourn. He went on to say that, in his opinion, all the survivors of the distinguished Schwartz family should leave Hungary and immigrate to Palestine, that godforsaken country full of camels that Yoshka had refused to immigrate to before the war. Yoshka was furious at Shani's insensitivity and impudence. "Who are you to dictate to us?!" he raised his voice.

"I'm not," Shani changed his tone, realizing that he'd gone too far, "I just think that it's best for all of us to leave this terrible place, which has always been anti-Semitic. Our families were murdered here, some not even by the Nazis, but by the Hungarians—our own people—who have always hated us. All they needed was the opportunity to act on it."

"Shani, you're as reckless as ever," Yoshka replied gravely. He was still finding it hard to digest that of the enormous Schwartz family, only Shandor, Imre, and the six of them in Budapest had survived. "I want to stay here, at least until I'm convinced that what you're telling me is true, and that no one else from our families has made it through…"

"It's true, believe me!" Shani gripped his hand tightly, "Do you believe I'm capable of saying such horrible things without first verifying them? For weeks, I wandered through all the liberated territories, I risked running into Nazis and collaborators looking for easy prey, but I did all I could to find your brothers. I spoke to survivors, I went to registration offices, I looked through thousands of names of survivors. Believe me,

Yoshka, I wouldn't have come here if I wasn't convinced of the magnitude of the disaster. I'm sorry that I have to be the bearer of such bad news, but I think we have to be brave and cope with these things, not run away from them and hide."

"Cope?" Yoshka repeated. "Is this your way of coping? You just suggested I run away with the family!"

Shani, feeling awkward, avoided Yoshka's eyes. He was better with actions than words, especially when faced with Yoshka's convoluted and sophisticated use of language.

"Well, then, what do you suggest?" he asked at last.

"Hold on, Shani: Firstly, there could always be a mistake in the records and in the survivors' stories. I believe that some people who were at Mauthausen would be willing to swear that I also died there. Sooner or later, a Schwartz will appear out of nowhere and there'll be no one to tell him where to find us. Besides, who knows what tomorrow will bring in Hungary, even regarding the way the Jews are treated. Word on the street is that we'll be compensated for our property and money, and we'll certainly be treated well after the horrific hardships we experienced. I suggest we wait and consider your suggestion at a later time. It wouldn't do any harm to your immigration plans if we had a little more money, right?"

"Possibly," Shani admitted reluctantly, "but some things are more important than money, such as the children, Peter, Marika, and Tibby. They're still young, and moving to a foreign land will certainly feel like an exciting adventure. Not only that—the odds of them becoming well integrated into a new land are higher while they're still young and strong and have the will and curiosity to learn new customs. The longer they stay here, the harder it'll be."

"Leave the children out of it for now!" Yoshka slammed his fist on the table, "And don't dream of trying to tempt them away behind my back! Do you hear me? Be very careful! Otherwise you'll lose us as your family too."

Shani, who hadn't considered this possibility before, decided at that moment to change his approach. Instead of answering Yoshka aggressively and boldly, he softened his tone and assured him that he wouldn't do anything behind his back. Then he proceeded with the same sanctimonious tone and asked Yoshka to apologize to Martha for him for ignoring her and explain that he only did so because of the shock and pain he felt when he heard about the deaths in their family. Yoshka agreed and did all he could to appease Martha and to reconcile her with her brother, believing that Shani really did regret his wayward intentions.

***

A month later, when he was wandering around the Budapest provisional administration office for the department in charge of locating concentration camp survivors, Yoshka bumped into Paul Molnar. He saw him immediately as he looked through the door, sitting like a lord in his spacious office, behind a heavy mahogany executive's desk. Yoshka was taken aback. He'd never imagined that running into his arch enemy could ever be helpful. He turned around to leave, but Molnar called his name, and when he didn't answer, he ran after him.

"I'm so glad to see you survived that hellhole," he gasped when he reached him.

"How nice of you!" Yoshka responded with anger designed to hide his fear.

"I mean it sincerely, Yoshka. What do you think about putting our resentment behind us and turning over a new page? After all, this is a new age, one of forgiveness and absolution."

"What do you want, Molnar?!" Yoshka snarled, even though he guessed that Molnar had a senior position in the interim administration.

"I'd like to help you, Yoshka, you and Martha. I tried to get a message to her saying that she could have her family's home in Baja back, and the paintings, but she didn't answer me."

"Nor will she, Molnar, she doesn't want anything to do with you, ever!"

Molnar's face twitched in pain for a moment before turning deadpan again, "If so," he said, "I would like to compensate you for the property. In my capacity as the manager of the department that compensates people for property stolen from them during the war, I can arrange a house and employment for you."

"If so, I want a hardware store again," Yoshka quickly clarified.

"A store?" Molnar responded hesitantly and looked left and right, checking that no one was eavesdropping on their conversation, "That will be a little difficult…Yoshka, the new administration believes more in manual labor and less in…trade."

"I'll be doing manual labor in the store," Yoshka looked at him uncomprehendingly, but after a few seconds, he realized what Molnar was trying not to say. "Listen, Molnar, let's be practical. Budapest needs builders, renovators…I've been walking around the streets for months wondering who's going to fix all the damage from the war. People are living in the ruins. Doesn't your administration think that someone should fix it?"

"The administration believes that everything will come in its time," Molnar replied, but with a flash of comprehension in his eyes.

"Look, we don't need a house, we have a place to live. If you find me a place to open a store and give me a permit to sell building and renovation products it'll compensate us for all our property in Baja. Think about it, Molnar—it'll cost your administration almost nothing, and your conscience will also be clean."

"I'll think about it," Molnar promised and reached out his hand to shake. Yoshka hesitated, then shook it.

A week later, an official letter was delivered to the occupants of the house on Andrassy Avenue, stating that the temporary administration of Budapest was hereby granting administrative permission to live in the house. Three lines had been handwritten on the printed letter stating that Yoshka Schwartz was hereby authorized to run a construction materials trading house in Horthy Square and that he was permitted to employ any of his relatives to work for him.

All the household members were delighted by the temporary administration's generosity, all except for Shani and Martha.

Shani was concerned that establishing themselves in Budapest would sabotage his plans to take them with him to Palestine, while Martha was troubled that Peter and Marika's relationship would grow too strong, especially with them living in the same house.

***

They all began working at Yoshka's store, except for Gizi, who was in mourning and pining for Mark. For months after Yoshka confirmed that his brother had perished in Auschwitz, she stayed sitting by the window overlooking the street, waiting for him to return.

Marika, on the other hand, processed the bad news of her father's death much faster, and the only thing she didn't do was continue her studies at the gymnasium. She found the store much more interesting, and she found it comforting. She explained to her mother that being engrossed in her work distracted her from thinking too much and becoming overwrought. School, on the other hand, was so boring that she was afraid she would drown in sorrow.

Gizi didn't argue with her. Her grief was so intense, Marika wasn't sure she'd even heard her excuses.

Peter and Tibby returned to school, the former with enthusiasm, the latter under duress. Neither of them dared to oppose Martha's insistent drive to see them complete their high school education.

***

Yoshka called the new company "Schwartz Ignetz & Sons" to forever commemorate his late father and murdered brothers' name. Yoshka, Shani, and Marika worked mornings, while Martha, Tibby, and Peter took care of the afternoons, but Marika's eagerness to stay until evening caused issues. Martha didn't like how overly diligent she was, suspecting that it was because she wanted to spend time with Peter. The fact that the two of them would occasionally disappear without explanation made her blood boil. One evening, after everyone had gone home, Martha took Marika aside and told her in no uncertain terms that her presence at the store in the evenings wasn't wanted. Marika grimaced, stamped her feet, and even asked Yoshka and Shani to explain to Martha that she contributed to the sales. But in no way did Yoshka want to upset his wife who, ever since she'd been ill, felt pain in her heart when she was angry.

Shani viewed this controversy as an opportunity to carry out his plans. He had a furtive conversation with Marika after her confrontation with Martha and managed to calm her down by telling her his plans to emigrate to Palestine. When he left, he explained to the miserable girl that Martha would have to take over for him during the day, which was busier than the evening. Then the evenings would be left entirely to the three youngsters, Peter, Tibby, and herself. Marika stared at him with her bright green eyes and asked curiously why he was planning on going away. Shani described how amazingly joyful the new land of countless possibilities was, especially for adventurous young people like her.

"Groups of Jewish youth who survived the camps are streaming in every day," he explained when he noticed her enthusiasm growing. "Wonderful, talented, and beautiful young people just like you, and since they leave their families behind, the new group becomes their family."

"And what will they do there, in that distant land?" Marika asked inquisitively.

"Live and work," Shani explained. "There are groups of young socialists who have established colonies where everyone lives, works, eats, and sleeps together, and at night they dance and sing."

"Dance and sing?!" Marika's wild imagination was sparked, and already, she, too, was dying to leave for that special place. Then Shani explained to her that Yoshka and Martha were vehemently opposed to going and warned her not to say a word to anyone, lest they rush off and upset Gizi, who was already falling apart and would forbid Marika to go.

On the other hand, Shani did permit Marika to tell Peter and Tibby about the wonderful new land, but only if she insisted that they keep it secret.

Shani shrewdly thought that Marika would be able to persuade Peter and Tibby to leave with him for Palestine, and then Yoshka and Martha would have no choice but to follow since they wouldn't be able to bear being separated from their son.

He didn't, however, take one thing into account, which was that Peter was a very devoted son. Although he was very enthused by the stories, when he realized that his parents were against it, he refused to leave them on their own.

Marika found him difficult to understand, and she even became angry at him. As a result, they slowly started to drift apart, much to Martha's delight, even though she had no idea why.

Meanwhile, the temporary administration of Hungary was dissolved and elections were held. At first, Shani was glad that the new government had to include the communist party in its coalition, even though it had received only seventeen percent of the votes. His joy didn't last long, however, when he realized that communism also had its more unpleasant sides. One was the establishment of the secret police force, and the second, which stemmed from that, was the fear that Hungary's borders would soon be closed to anyone wishing to leave.

At the time, Yoshka's business was flourishing, thanks to the extensive relationships he'd forged with the new government's officials, who helped him to obtain plenty of restoration projects in Budapest, and even beyond.

Shani became gravely concerned, especially after discovering that Yoshka had repeatedly rejected his brother Shandor's offers to join him in the States. Yoshka said straight out to anyone willing to listen that he had no intention of ever leaving Hungary. He thought that their situation was excellent and would only get better. He would also add that they were morally obliged to their dead relatives to stay in the land of the people who had wanted to expel them and to thrive and prosper as well as they could, proving that no one could annihilate the Schwartz family.

When Shani began to feel the hourglass running out, he decided to take Peter, Tibby, and Marika aside for a talk, so he could make his urgent intentions clear. He knew that he'd be old and gray by the time he reached the borders of Hungary if he waited until Marika convinced Peter to leave.

One evening, when Martha was feeling ill and decided to stay home, Shani said that he'd take over for her at work and supervise the youngsters. To his surprise, he found only Tibby behind the counter. Marika and Peter were in the storeroom having a lovers' tiff. Marika was in tears, claiming that Peter had been ignoring her and had even started taking evening walks with girls from the gymnasium. Peter, in his defense, argued that Marika was the one causing them to drift apart, by trying to persuade him to leave for Palestine.

"If you want to live in Palestine, then there's no point in our relationship," he added, just as Shani walked into the storeroom, determined to put an end to the silly squabble.

"Children, why are you arguing?" Shani demanded. "Peter, if you come with us, you and Marika will be able to stay together. And it's clear to us all that it's what you want. You do love her, am I right?"

"Yes," Peter mumbled, embarrassed and feeling cornered. He'd actually been feeling less attracted to his beautiful cousin for a while, but he didn't dare tell her. He even dreaded admitting it to himself. He liked the girls he'd met recently at the gymnasium much more because they loved classical music, literature, and the theatre, none of which interested Marika, who was adventurous and jittery and had difficulty sitting in one spot for more than five minutes.

"Then come with us! That'll solve the problem," Shani gave him a winning smile. "I know that your parents are against it, but I believe that when they understand that your mind is made up, they'll give you their consent and even come with."

"It won't be that simple," Peter said gravely, "Mami may give in and agree to go, but Papa will never agree to it. And I can't do anything that would harm my family on my conscience."

"Peter, you're a young man! Your whole future is ahead of you!" Marika cried passionately. "How can you give up all your plans because of your father's stubbornness? It's just so selfish of him not to understand that Budapest is too small and stifling for us."

"I don't feel that way, Marika," Peter confessed, "although the stories about Palestine do spark my more adventurous side, I don't find Budapest stifling at all. On the contrary, lately I've been feeling that I should complete my schooling before making any plans for my future, such as emigrating from here."

"Oh, you and your studies! What nonsense!" Marika grumbled. "That's just your sneaky way to meet new girls and neglect me!"

"That's not true, Marika, I really do think I should complete my studies before I leave. With all due respect to the new wind fanning that fireplace, what will you do there? Where will you work? You'll have to work for a living wherever you are, you know."

"She can work in the fields, or the kitchen, or the children's nursery," Shani interjected. "Those are jobs that don't require academic training, and they're in demand in the socialist societies of Palestine. That's the greatness of the place—everyone is immediately put to work as soon as they arrive, no one remains unemployed."

Marika glanced at Peter's face, eager to find a hint that he was wavering. In fact, she had no desire whatsoever to work at any of the jobs that Shani had mentioned. What she really wanted was to get to Palestine and find a man who would fall in love with her and support her financially if Peter wouldn't. Otherwise, what was she taking such good care of her sensual appearance for?

"I'm sorry, Shani," Peter shrugged adamantly, "although it all sounds very alluring and exciting, I can't do it to my parents. I love them too much."

"I don't believe you'll have many opportunities to change your decision," Shani replied. "Hungary's gates may close soon, and you and your parents, whom you're so concerned about, will have to bear the consequences. No one can assure you that things here will remain as they are. There are changes happening every other day here, and who guarantees that a communist government won't come into power soon and confiscate all private property?"

"I don't believe it'll come to that, Peter responded thoughtfully, "the Hungarians are a determined people. If they don't feel that they're being allowed to manage their affairs for themselves, they will rise up and revolt, even for appearance's sake."

Shani felt for the boy. He was precisely the kind of person they needed in the new state that he believed would eventually arise in Palestine. He tried again to convince him and repeated his thoughts aloud, but Peter stood his ground. Although he agreed with his uncle that he and other young people like him would have a new and promising start in that distant land with the exotic name, he couldn't bear the pain his mother would feel if he forced her to choose between him and his father. Despite his astute and sharp mind, he had no idea how much pain he would cause his mother, precisely because he chose to stay in Budapest.

CHAPTER 17

For a few days, Marika thought about leaving for Palestine with Shani. Then something surprising happened that made her decide: Her half-sister Sophie, who had been taken from Gizi by her father when she left Poland with Mark during the Great War, suddenly appeared on their doorstep. Although she didn't know her mother, Sophie seemed to have inherited her strong sense of justice and courage. When the Nazis invaded Poland, she ran away from home and joined the resistance. She told the family how she was caught helping Jews in Warsaw and sent to Auschwitz when the war was almost over, where she met a number of Jewish women from Budapest, one of whom was Gizi's neighbor. The woman told Sophie that her mother hadn't been harmed by the Nazis, so she decided to go to Hungary to look for her after she was released. Sophie was already thirty-two, but she looked much younger. She was thin and pale, her cheekbones and round blue eyes prominent in her small, gaunt face, and her clothes were too big and hung off her.

Seeing Sophie again brought Gizi's zest for life back. She abandoned her permanent spot by the window facing the street and put all her energy into caring for the daughter she had lost. She'd abandoned all hope of ever seeing her again, and, now, she seemed godsent. All the letters she'd mailed to her over the years explaining how her cruel father had kept them apart had been returned unopened.

With Sophie back, Marika felt completely abandoned, since even her mother now showed no interest in her, not to mention Peter, who was having long conversations into the night with their new guest. Sophie had attended the music academy in Warsaw before the war and even showed him—only him—the songs she'd written.

One morning, the family woke up to find a letter telling them that Shani and Marika had left for Palestine. Only Tibby and Gizi cried, although Gizi's tears dried up a few minutes later when Sophie came over and hugged her. Nobody thought about Tibby until Peter noticed how upset he was and whispered to Martha to console him. Martha did as he asked, but it was too late. Tibby felt abandoned, and a week later, he, too, disappeared. Martha, who couldn't stop blaming herself for losing him too, fell ill. She recovered and regained her strength only after she received a letter from Shani, telling her that Tibby had arrived at their transit camp in Italy and had boarded the ship to Palestine along with them.

***

Some of Shani's fears were realized when Hungary's gates were shut and no one could leave. These developments didn't bother the Schwartz family. In any case, they weren't planning on going elsewhere at the time because, although governments were rising and falling, none of them had dared to nationalize private property. On the contrary, most of them encouraged small businesses as well as agricultural reform. Yoshka Schwartz's small business was doing extremely well in that friendly climate. The only problem was with his permit to employ only family members, and, with three gone, he didn't have enough workers. Gizi together with Sophie, who had been formally recognized as family, filled Shani and Marika's places, but since there was no one to replace Tibby, they still needed one more. Yoshka thought up a creative solution for this: He asked Peter, who was still spending much of his time with his friends from the gymnasium, to declare his engagement to whichever female friend he was closest to at the time and to offer her a job at the store. Most of the girls needed an income and were also very fond of Peter, so his plan usually worked well, except once or twice, when the girls started arguing over their turn at the title.

No one suspected the secret behind Peter's wanton behavior was that he had fallen deeply in love with Sophie, his step-cousin, who was more than double his age. Knowing that his mother would make twice the fuss she'd made over Marika if she found out, he decided to keep it to himself. Even Sophie remained unaware until they decided to buy a piano so that she could play for the family. She was an excellent pianist and made the evenings at home much more enjoyable.

Peter had always wanted to learn the piano, and he asked her to teach him. Sophie was happy to, and the two of them began spending every night together, sitting side by side by the piano. After the lessons, they would have long, deep conversations.

One night, after Peter successfully played a complicated piece from Tchaikovsky's Swan Lake, Sophie, feeling triumphant, hugged him and kissed him on the lips. Peter felt a wave of heat wash over him, and without thinking, he put his arms around her and returned her friendly kiss with a passionate and exciting one. Shocked and flustered, Sophie could barely breathe. She hadn't expected the seventeen-year-old youth to behave like an experienced lover. When he loosened his confident grip on her for a moment, she tore herself away and fled outside. Peter ran after her, afraid that he'd hurt her feelings. He found her sitting on the steps, clutching her face in her hands and crying.

"Sophie, I'm sorry," he stroked her arm, "I just couldn't control my feelings any longer. I love you."

Sophie responded with stifled wails, and he felt his heart break. "Forgive me, Sophie, please, I'm sorry, I didn't mean to hurt you. I promise I'll never come near you again, just forgive me for going too far, please."

Sophie only started to cry harder, and then she jumped up and ran toward the Danube. Terrified, Peter ran after her.

***

Peter caught up with her in the woods by the Danube, and afraid that she may throw herself into the dark water of the river, he grabbed her arm. To his surprise, she stopped crying and murmured a few broken sentences in Polish, and all he could understand was the name Vladek.

"Sophie, Sophie, I'm sorry, I'm truly sorry," he whispered in her ear, mustering the willpower not to embrace her again.

"You have nothing to be sorry about," she finally responded in the broken Hungarian she had learned so quickly, "nothing at all, Peter. It's not your fault. I'm not crying because of you, but for my poor Vladek."

"Vladek?" Peter asked, "Who is he? And why are you crying over him?"

"Vladek was a man I loved in Warsaw," Sophie explained as she sat down on the wet grass. Peter quickly sat down beside her. "We were going to get married, and then the war broke out," her eyes filled with tears again and her voice choked with emotion, but she continued. "He was the love of my life. I never loved anyone but him. When the Nazis took over Warsaw, I persuaded him to join me in helping the Jews from the resistance movement. And he…was shot…I thought I'd never recover from his death, that I would never fall in love with another man, even if I survived that horrific period. I loved him with all my heart, Peter, but earlier, when you kissed me—suddenly, for a long moment, I forgot about him. I forgot about Vladek! May God forgive me." She stopped talking and buried her head in her hands again as she burst into tears.

Although relieved, Peter felt uncomfortable. He had never believed in God, especially the kind who gets angry at people for choosing to go on with their lives after their loved ones die, and he felt unable to comfort her.

"Sophie, God has nothing to do with it, it's between you and Vladek," he said eventually, after thinking a little. "If you could ask him what he thought, he would probably tell you that he wants you to go on living after he died. After all, staying away from men and never falling in love again will not bring him back to life."

"I know," she mumbled, trying to steady her breath. She looked up at him, her huge eyes shining in the dark, "I know that nothing will bring my Vladek back to life, and I didn't decide to abstain from men because of him, I was simply surprised by your kiss. It made me feel like I used to, young, vibrant, and passionate, as if nothing bad could ever happen to me again, to me, to us…as if we were two young people in love in an optimistic, good, and wonderful world. And that scared me, Peter, because it's nothing but an illusion."

"It's not an illusion," Peter answered fiercely as he took her damp hands in his, "the world is being re-created now, it's going back to the starting point, and it can't be worse than it has been already!"

"You're so young, Peter," Sophie stroked his head, and he felt his blood boiling in protest, "I don't want to dampen your optimism because, in this day and age, it's a valuable and important asset. But I'm afraid, my dear—I'm afraid to fall in love again, I'm afraid that I'll bring disaster upon the head of any new man I love."

"Nonsense," Peter exclaimed just as he recalled his mother's weak heart and the possibility of it growing even weaker if his love for Sophie was discovered. He hoped his mother would be able to accept it. She was a sensible woman and, although she'd need time to get used to the idea, in the end she'd understand that nothing should stand in his path to happiness. Sophie was not a blood relative like Marika, she was merely a few years older than him. His mother may find it difficult to accept, but she would, eventually. No one can see Sophie in a negative light. She seemed like an angel, to all of them. Peter, as usual, remained optimistic.

He had no way of foreseeing the disaster that was coming, one much worse than his mother's potential anger at his relationship with Sophie.

***

Sophie and Peter decided to hide their relationship from everyone until Peter completed his education. Then, they assumed, no one would have any excuse to stop them from expressing their love for each other openly. Peter expected Sophie to tell him to continue seeing his old female friends so that they wouldn't raise suspicion, and she did. She didn't think she would feel hurt when he flirted with girls half her age since it was a different girl each week. Peter thought the same, knowing that he'd never felt so strongly and deeply for any girl or woman before her. Much to his surprise, he discovered that emotions can arise in a number of ways, and sometimes he found himself intensely attracted to one of his young friends. There was no denying it. To his relief, his attraction to them would dissipate as quickly as it appeared, and his enormous love for Sophie would take hold of his heart again. Having to hide their love and to meet secretly on the banks of the Danube only fanned the flames even more.

As a result of the fleeting flings he was having, Peter's confidence and strength began to grow, and he started feeling like the more mature of the two.

Time passed, and Sophie also started feeling her confidence growing. For the first time in her life, she was experiencing how it felt to be surrounded by a family that loved her and wanted the best for her, and this added color to her cheeks and made her stand taller. At a certain point, she even adopted the lighthearted way in which the Schwartzs would joke and flirt with the customers at work. Everyone loved the change in Sophie, even Peter, who believed that in time it would help his mother understand what he loved about her. He was planning to share his secret with one and all after he completed his studies at the gymnasium, because he believed he would seem more mature to them then. He had no idea that the change in Sophie may eventually become an obstacle.

Sophie's new attitude attracted suitors, but they were too young and far between to compete with Peter for her affections. Most of the men her age had died in the war or had been captured, and those who returned from the camps in Russia were scarred and unattractive.

One day, a handsome man in his thirties entered the store and introduced himself as Alexander Molovsky, a high-ranking officer of Ukrainian origin who was serving in the Russian army and had been stationed in Budapest. His headquarters, he told them, needed extensive renovations, and he was in charge of having them done. He spoke Polish, which helped his friendship with Sophie develop quickly, and he continued to visit her at the store after the renovation work was completed. Sophie only realized what a mistake she'd made in being friendly to him when he started to openly court her. Alexander, who knew nothing of her relationship with Peter, became an ardent and insistent admirer.

He would show up at the store in the evenings with flowers, chocolate, and a variety of other small gifts aimed at melting Sophie's heart. She would accept his gifts with a smile of gratitude, but she repeatedly refused his invitations to see him after her shift. She didn't want to hurt him, and so, one evening, she told him about Vladek and how her heart had died along with him, which was why she could never fall in love with any man ever again. Alexander, or Alex as he had asked everyone to call him, was very touched by her story, but not enough for him to give up. He still thought that he could heal Sophie's heart and make her fall in love with him, if only he were given the opportunity.

He believed in taking women by surprise, like on the battlefield, a belief he based on his vast experience in both fields. He started devising a way to surprise Sophie by using a less conventional method of courting. For this, he needed information on what she got up to after work, so he began following her in the evenings. What a huge shock it was to find out one night that her heart was not only not frozen, as she'd told him, but that it had belonged to young Peter Schwartz for quite some time.

Alex was stunned and hurt, but not for long. He hoped that his love for Sophie would die a quick death. Unfortunately, that's not what happened. Instead, his desire to hold her in his arms and see her look at him the way she looked at Peter only grew stronger. He was angry with her, yes, but at the same time, he longed to embrace her, to crush her to his chest as he squeezed lustful moans out of her—for him, Alexander Molovsky, the distinguished Russian army officer, not for that light-haired boy who he felt nothing but disdain for.

However, as the days passed, and especially the nights, and he watched the lovers from a safe distance, he became overwhelmed by frustration and anger, especially after failing to find a way to sabotage their relationship. Then one day, his headquarters received an order to recruit young Hungarians of eighteen years or older for a military unit that would guard the borders. Lieutenant-Colonel Alex Molovsky felt his blood rushing through his veins as he looked at the document. Peter Schwartz appeared to be just the right age to recruit, and he was in excellent health and great physical condition. He would have Peter recruited as soon as he graduated from the gymnasium and stationed as far away as possible. That would clear the way for him.

***

Peter, who had no idea what was going on in Molovsky's mind, would be graduating soon from the gymnasium, and because he wanted to excel in all his subjects and to do excellently on his exams, he was spending night and day studying and memorizing the material.

He rarely saw Sophie on his own, but, precisely because of that, their few rendezvous were even more exciting and loving. On those few evenings, as he held her in his arms and kissed her face, he imagined them becoming more intimate in a room of their own.

At the graduation ceremony, he looked at Sophie sitting with his parents and Aunt Gizi. She looked stunning and was obviously thrilled for him. He was over the moon, and he couldn't help but think that no one in the hall was more fortunate than he. He'd received excellent scores in all subjects and he wanted to show them to his parents after they went home, before he told them about his relationship with Sophie.

He went straight home with his family, happily foregoing the graduation party with his classmates. Along the way, his parents debated his future. His mother thought he should continue his studies and attend university, whereas his father thought he should start working full-time in the family business, both at the store and doing renovations with him. Peter didn't interfere in the argument. He knew full well what his plans for the future were: to be and live with Sophie, the woman he loved, no matter what.

When they got home, his parents walked in first, followed by Gizi. He and Sophie took a moment outside. He gave her a hug and whispered in her ear, "In a few minutes, my love, we'll be together forever."

Sophie kissed him quickly, her cheeks flushed, and then they heard his mother's heartbroken cry. At first, they thought she was screaming because she'd spotted them through the window and caught them. They jumped apart and Peter rushed into the house, his heart racing. If his mother reacted that way just at the sight of them hugging, how would she respond when she found out that they'd long past that stage. He tried to think of a way to placate her, but then he noticed that she was sitting on the sofa, holding a piece of paper and trembling all over. His father was sitting beside her, his arm around her shoulder, trying to calm her. "It's not the end of the world, Martha, it's not the end of the world," he muttered.

"Yes, it is!" she exclaimed and burst into tears as soon as she saw Peter, who naturally, appeared anxious. "It's an induction order," she wailed, "for you, Peter, may God help us, after the atrocities we went through, they want to take my boy away…and kill him!"

"Calm down, Martha," Yoshka said firmly. "No one is going to kill Peter, these are days of peace and there is no war in sight—"

"Peace?" she interrupted him, "You call this peace? There are soldiers on every corner, there's so much tension in the air I can't breathe, and I'm not prepared to let my son fight against the enemies of the party!"

"Shh, Martha, you mustn't talk like that…" Yoshka lowered his voice, his eyes widening with fear. Peter cringed in the armchair facing his parents. Out of the corner of his eye, he could see Sophie leaning on the lintel, her face an abysmal well of anguish. He had mixed feelings. He didn't share his mother's concern for his safety, and he wasn't afraid. What he didn't like was the idea of serving in the Hungarian army, which in actual fact, was the Russian army's willing slave. Peter didn't have much interest in politics. His love for Sophie made him almost impermeable to the stench coming from Mother Russia's kitchen. But now, when he was called to serve the army and to enforce its coercive policies, he was forced to face a reality that he found not at all pleasant. For a long while he had felt, as all Hungarian citizens did, that the control over their homeland, which not that long ago had been lost to the Germans, was now slipping into the hands of the Russians. The last elections had been a resounding farce. That was obvious from the low-spirited whispers echoing through the streets. Although his father insisted on ignoring politics and concentrating on their own personal situation, which was improving, his developed sense of justice prevented him from doing so completely. Sometimes he felt bitter, especially when everyone around him continued to behave as if everything was perfectly fine. But being so absorbed in his studies and in his love for Sophie, his feelings of frustration would subside and become just a minor resentment. Now Peter had to decide which side he was on, and for the first time in his life, he felt that his place was not there. He'd received a few letters from Shani, Marika, and Tibby since they'd left Budapest for the tiny land in the Middle East. He found one from Tibby particularly perturbing. Tibby wrote that he'd been drafted into the Israeli army and had fought in the brave country's War of Independence against seven of its neighbors, ensuring that Jewish lives would no longer be forsaken. Tibby wrote that when he went into battle, armed with a rifle and wearing a uniform, he couldn't help but think about the boy he used to be, and how he'd watched his parents being murdered before his very eyes, unable to save them. He wrote how horrific it had felt to stand in the line for Auschwitz until Martha came along and saved him. "At the time, I didn't know that life could be different," he wrote to Peter, "and even though I was a hooligan and I'd been in dozens of street fights, I was paralyzed when faced with an organized group of gun-toting murderers. Today I know that I'll never again allow myself to feel so helpless. Being a soldier in the Israeli army is the permanent answer to all those criminals who murdered my family and tried to murder me too."

Reading Tibby's letter, Peter had felt a twinge of envy, but he immediately repeated to himself that, unlike his cousin, he had been saved from a similar fate, thanks to his mother's courage and resourcefulness, and as such, he could not hurt her by leaving for Israel.

Now, however, as he watched his mother sobbing, he thought that if in any case he was being forced to join the army and fight, it should rather be there, in the only place in the world where Jews had fought for their lives and won.

***

They walked silently through the dark forest that marked the border between Hungary and Austria. There were eleven young men and two women. They'd been told to keep quiet, and in any case, they preferred to keep their thoughts and feelings to themselves. They were to follow the guide across the border, and they were hoping not to be discovered and captured by the soldiers guarding that border.

Peter knew that if he hadn't done something drastic, he would have been stationed right there, on the Hungarian border; that he would have had to obey orders and shoot dead anyone on their way to freedom. For the first time, he knew he had chosen the right path. He couldn't imagine anything worse. *People should be free to choose where they want to live*, he thought, *and no one should stand in their way*.

His thoughts wandered to his father, who was furious when he heard he was planning to leave Hungary. "Under no circumstances, do you hear me?!" he raised his voice before immediately lowering it as he remembered the informers who were infesting every corner. "You will put us all in danger because of your foolhardy nature!"

"Then come with me," Peter retorted. He had had the same argument earlier with Sophie, and it had taken the wind out of his sails. All he felt was sadness, which he was trying to shake off. "Uncle Shani left me details of his contacts. He said that they were willing to help anyone who wanted to escape, including children and the elderly."

"We're not old," Yoshka said furiously, "and the journey there doesn't scare me. What worries me is what we'll do when we get there, to that country, with its stories that you're so excited by."

"We'll work, like everyone else. It's a new country and they're still founding it. You would certainly have plenty to do."

"But how would I work without knowing the language?" his father growled. "And why would I give up all my wealth to replace it with an unknown future in an unknown country?"

"Papa, I've made up my mind—I'm going and that's that!" Peter declared wearily. The argument he'd had with Sophie had exhausted him.

Although she hadn't asked him irritating questions like his father and wasn't at all troubled by her own future, she was concerned about Gizi. "If Mami agrees to come along, I'll go willingly with you," she said with tears in her eyes, "but if she refuses, I can't leave her here. I'm the only family she has left."

"And what about me, Sophie? What about our plans to build a life together?"

"It seems that your new plan has taken its place," she answered, lowering her somber eyes. "You're so eager to go to the land of the Jews, you've forgotten that I'm not even Jewish. Have you stopped to ask yourself if they'll agree to take me in?"

"Nonsense," he answered dismissively, "why wouldn't they? Come with me, I'd like to see anyone dare to turn you away!"

"Is that the way you want to begin your life in a new country?" she scoffed. "With fights between Jews?"

"Sophie," he held her to him, "you know how much I love you, more than anyone in the world, but even if I stay here, I'll be far away serving in the army. Who knows where I'll be posted."

"Your father said that he knows people who can arrange for you to be stationed in Budapest."

"Sophie, don't you see what's happening around you? The situation is terribly unstable, and the officials and managers are being replaced on almost a daily basis. We never know what's around the corner. My father's contacts could be nothing but yesterday's news, or even not even that."

"So maybe I could try…I could talk to Alex for you…" Sophie thought aloud, "the lieutenant-colonel. We're friends, he's been trying to win my heart with flowers and gifts, and he's a good man. I'm sure he'd help you if I ask him to."

"Don't you dare!" He felt his blood boiling, but he couldn't understand quite why he was so angry. Maybe because Sophie had a serious suitor and she hadn't even bothered to tell him. "I don't want you drawing his attention to me now—they may suspect that I'm planning to run away."

"Are you determined to leave, then?" Sophie said, tears welling in her eyes, "To give up our love and your entire future for some nationalistic ideal?"

Lost in thought, Peter just hugged her without saying a word. He felt his heart racing. He knew that she was right. If he fled from Hungary, he would have to give up not only the woman he loved and his family but also his culture and beliefs. What did he know about Israel, apart from the fact that Jews could hold their heads up high there? Religious and national affairs had never been that important to him. He had been raised as an atheist of Austro-Hungarian culture and had been utterly shocked when his religion had been held against him. After the war ended, he persuaded himself that it had been an anomaly in history, that it could never happen again. That is until he was faced with that damn induction order, which brought other feelings to the surface. He longed to belong to a place that people could call their homeland, even though they hadn't been born there; to belong to a society that had risen from the ashes and rubble and built itself up.

***

Yoshka was furious and called him an incorrigible romantic. Peter was fine with being called that and responded by saying that he could only blame himself, as he was the one who'd raised him. He reminded him how he and Martha would always marvel when he chose to play Nemecsek, the blond boy who sacrificed his life for the group in The Paul Street Boys story.

Martha cried quietly and took no part in their arguments, but one day, she woke up and stated that she'd rather Peter emigrate to Israel. She'd had a dream, she explained, in which she'd seen Peter driving a tank through the streets of Budapest when, suddenly, a Molotov cocktail was thrown at him, and it exploded loudly and killed him. Yoshka scoffed and told her she was becoming neurotic, that it was far more likely that Peter would find himself driving a tank in Israel rather than through the streets of Budapest. Martha stood her ground and even tried to convince Yoshka to go with Peter to Israel.

When Peter saw how his greatest fear was becoming a reality, and his parents were fighting because of him, he decided to leave as soon as he could, without saying goodbye.

And so, five days after receiving the recruitment order, he left the house under cover of darkness, never to return. His parents and Gizi were at friends playing cards. Only Sophie was at home. He went into her room, looked at her sleeping there like an angel, and kissed her forehead. Without waking up, Sophie fumbled for his hand and pulled him to her.

He felt his heart leap. A small voice in the back of his mind whispered to him to stay, even for one night, to sleep in her arms just once. But Peter immediately chose to silence that voice. He'd made his decision, and he couldn't back down now. He felt himself choking as he pulled his hand carefully out of Sophie's. She sighed and turned over. He stood for a moment looking at her, then tiptoed out of her room.

He left the house and went to meet up with the group. In a few days, they would be crossing the border into Austria. Along the way to the meeting point, feeling deep grief and regret for not saying a proper goodbye to his family, especially to his dear mother, he encountered a dark figure emerging from the alley.

"Ishtenem!" he let out a strangled scream, fearing that the army had heard about his plan and had sent soldiers after him.

But then he heard Martha whisper, "Peter, it's me, Mami." She was smiling tenderly, "I was afraid you'd do this, run off without saying goodbye," she said without a trace of reproach in her voice. "I would have done the same if I were you."

"Mami," he hugged her warmly and felt the tears welling in his eyes, "I'm sorry—"

"No, no, there's nothing to be sorry about. If you'd waited even a few days longer, the Hungarian army would have taken you away by force. Gizi told me this evening that Sophie was planning to talk to Alexander Molovsky about your case. Silly fool. In fact, I rushed home to warn you, but when I saw that you weren't there, I realized that you'd left."

"Mami," he held her to his chest, "you're so clever and brave. Won't you come with me to Israel? They need women like you there."

"And what will your father do without me? He'd go out of his mind and act stupidly. We have tough days ahead of us here, Peterkum, and his charm and connections won't always be able to help him. In fact, I'm afraid his ties with the current officials are too strong, and as a result, he'll have problems with those who follow, but he doesn't understand that, and he's as sure of himself as ever."

"Then why haven't you talked him into leaving?"

"Because he's so pigheaded, Peter, pigheaded and arrogant. Still, he's your father and I love him. I won't leave him to his fate and leave, I can't do that. He needs me here, and I'll stay by his side through thick and thin. But you need to leave with a light heart. So long as I'm by your father's side, nothing bad will happen to either of us. And I'll do all I can to convince him we should join you as soon as possible."

"Szervusz, Mami," Peter could barely tear himself away from her.

"Wait, son, do you have any money?"

"I have precisely enough for the trip."

"I wanted to take the money your father hid in the store for a raining day, but it would have delayed me and I was afraid I wouldn't reach you in time," she said regretfully and started rummaging through her purse.

"It's all right, Mami, I'll be fine. I'm young and healthy, and I'll find work when I get there."

"Still, it worries me," she replied and took out a brown pouch of jewelry from her purse. She handed him a gold necklace with a Star of David pendant on it. "I sold all my jewelry during the war," she apologized. "This is the only necklace I kept, a memento from my grandparents, who were practicing Jews. I want you to wear it, Peter, as an amulet, but don't hesitate to sell if you're in urgent need of cash."

"Fine, Mami," his tears welled up again, but he tried to smile as he put the necklace on. Martha answered with a smile, but her eyes, too, were damp.

"Go in peace, Son, and may God be with you." She hugged him again, then turned around and walked away. Peter stood there and watched her go. She feared for him so much, he thought, that she'd decided to entrust him to God, whose services she had never before used. Only a few minutes later, he realized that he may miss the train the group was planning to catch, and he started walking quickly to the meeting place.

***

Only when they arrived at the transit camp in Vienna, did the young group of immigrants shed their shells and make friends. Peter, who was still deeply saddened by leaving his beloved Sophie and his family, had caught the attention of Aniko and Eva. The two girls noticed how sad he was and tried to make friends with him and cheer him up. Jano, also with the group, was a big muscular brute with the face of a child, and he had tried everything possible to get closer to Eva. When he realized that befriending Peter would achieve his goal, he, too, started to prance around him day and night.

Peter now had three close friends, even though for the first time in his life he wanted to be alone just to think. Saying that, they were entertaining and generous company, and he quickly forgot that he preferred his own company.

Aniko and Eva told him that they wanted to join a kibbutz, and they even knew its name "Givatuz," they called it, stressing the last syllable until the Jewish Agency guide explained that the name was "Givat Oz," and that the kibbutz was near Megiddo, which used to be a biblical city. All that was left of Megiddo was ruins.

Peter wondered out loud how they'd fit in on the kibbutz, that had actually been a city back in biblical times, and received a roar of laughter from the group. That's when he started to feel better and more optimistic. He slowly regained his confidence in his ability to fit in wherever he chose to live.

Vienna disappointed him, which also helped to raise his expectations of Israel. He had heard so much about the Austro-Hungarian capital in his childhood. His parents spoke of it admiringly, almost in holy reverence, whereas he discovered a city like all other cities, certainly no more beautiful than Budapest. Many of its magnificent buildings were still in ruins, and scaffolding had become their main feature. Peter felt despondent whenever he thought about how his parents longed to see it. The whole time he was there, he couldn't help but think that the old world's era of glory had passed.

His new friends didn't leave him much time for thoughtful introspection. They surrounded him with the joy of youth, and soon Peter became Aniko's boyfriend—at least that's what Jano decided, since he wanted Eva for himself.

Peter had no objection to that. Although he was secretly attracted to Eva, who was the prettier of the two, he wasn't that intent on having to fight with Jano. In fact, he was only looking for female affection and attention so that he could forget Sophie, who would appear in his mind mostly at night when he was alone. Aniko served this purpose perfectly, as she was amusing, sweet, and bouncy, so much so that he forgot that she was too short and thin for his taste.

Then one day, a week before they were scheduled to fly to Israel, Jano and Eva asked them if they would like to switch couples. Peter was a little shocked but realized that Jano was quite enthused by the idea, and he gave in to Eva's sensual and bold charisma. Aniko also seemed enthusiastic, as she almost disappeared in Jano's tanned and muscular arms.

By the time they boarded the boat to Israel, the four were already a close and happy clique, and after a couple of days at sea, they decided to settle in the kibbutz with the exotic name Givat Oz and to live a romantic life in what was kind of a commune. They never imagined that people in the exciting new land would turn out to be much more conservative and old-fashioned in their outlook than anyone back home.

CHAPTER 18

Peter took a deep breath. They had arrived. To his surprise, the new air didn't make him feel any fresher. It was too humid, and there was a hint of sourness hanging in the air, which made Peter wheeze. He was a little discouraged, but it was nothing compared to the bitter disappointment he felt when faced with the Jewish Agency official, who was registering all the new immigrants and handing out temporary IDs.

"What's your name?" the official asked in English, without even raising his head to look at him.

"Schwartz Peter," he answered in the Hungarian fashion, giving his surname before his first name.

"Peter? Peter? We have no such name here," the man said firmly. "What does it translate to in Hebrew?"

"It doesn't have a Hebrew translation," Aniko, whose English was better, came to his aid, "but in Hungary, it's considered a nice name."

"This is not Hungary!" the official declared as he wiped the sweat from his forehead, "How about Pinchas?"

"Pin-ghas," Peter awkwardly tried it out, having trouble deciding how he felt about the name, which had a throaty sound to it he found foreign and unusual, "I...I don't...know..."

"Fine, then what's your father's name?" the official continued impatiently.

"Schwartz Yoshka."

"Yoshka is Joseph in Hebrew," Aniko quickly explained to the official, who finally raised his head and stared at her.

"I know that," he snapped impatiently, "so your name in Israel will also be Joseph."

Peter didn't understand why he had to give up his first name, which had been part of his identity for twenty years.

"We don't have all day," the official urged him, "Is it Pinchas or Joseph? Decide quickly!"

"Joseph, make it Joseph," Peter muttered despondently.

"It's not bad," Aniko consoled him in Hungarian, "it's only for registration purposes, you can still ask people to call you Peter."

"What about Schwartz?" the clerk demanded to know, "It's Shchori in Hebrew."

"That, I'm not prepared to do. Not under any circumstances!" Peter told Aniko in no uncertain terms. "I fled Hungary to live in a free country, so why on earth do they want to change my surname?!"

"Leave it as Schwartz," Aniko told the official, "it's all he has left of his family. Almost all of them perished in the war."

"All right, Schwartz, if you want," the official said, a trace of hostility in his voice, "even when we want to help you, it's not good enough. All I wanted was to help you feel more comfortable, with a sabra name, that's all!"

Peter had no idea what a sabra was, but he could see that the official was angry, so he chose not to argue when he saw him write the name Joseph Schwartz.

On the same occasion, Aniko and Eva became Hanna and Chava, but all it did was amuse them. They stood and watched when Jano bent down to look into the eyes of the official and growled, "You will not change my name, is that clear?!"

The official looked up in surprise, and when he noticed the gigantic proportions of the man standing over him, he decided to back down. After Jano was registered as Jano Kolodny, the four of them went to the truck that had been sent to take them to Givat Oz.

Peter's mood began to improve on the way to the kibbutz, as he looked out through the edges of the tarpaulin covering the truck and saw that he was not in an arid desert as he'd expected. Green fields stretched away from the road, dotted occasionally with sandy, yellow patches, which only made them more interesting.

A young man and a middle-aged woman were waiting for them at the kibbutz secretary's office. Perhaps Givat Oz had been built on the ruins of a biblical city, but it looked and smelled like the country. The man and woman were nice and smiled a lot more than the sweaty official at the airport, and they immediately agreed to Peter, Eva, and Aniko's request to be called by their original names, rather than by those on their papers. However, their request to live together, all four of them in one room, was met with astonishment.

"Mixed living quarters are not acceptable here," the woman said, "and besides, we don't have a free room right now. Girls, you will join Rina and Bella, two nice girls from Tel Aviv—"

"Who were in the Palmach and so they haven't had time to get married yet," the man added jokingly, much to Aniko's astonishment, who could understand his English but didn't get the joke.

"And you," the woman said to Peter and Jano, "will live with Yoji and Shmulik, immigrants from Poland who were also partisans in Yugoslavia and who speak a little Hungarian. They will help you to fit in quickly."

Jano wondered why the four people who Saraleh the kibbutz member had mentioned couldn't live together, and then there would be a free room for them. But Aniko didn't even bother to translate his suggestion into English. The embarrassed and skeptical look they received when they asked to share a room was enough for her to realize that such an arrangement wouldn't be readily accepted.

Later that evening, when Peter and Jano met Yoji and Shmulik and told them what happened at the office, the two of them burst out laughing.

"You thought that you could live together, in a romantic commune, here on the kibbutz?" Yoji rolled around laughing on the bed.

"You're lucky they didn't send you to a re-education camp!" Shmulik added.

"Do they have such camps here?!" Jano was shocked. Back in Hungary, he'd heard of the notorious camps they had in Russia.

"No, but what were you thinking? And to make such a suggestion to

Saraleh, my God!" Yoji started laughing again, imagining the face of the esteemed head of the social committee when she heard their request.

"Kibbutz society is the most puritanical one could imagine," Shmulik finally explained, when he realized that their own reactions were even more embarrassing for the newcomers. "Here, only men and women who are married can live together, and sometimes they have to share their room with another person, when there aren't enough to go around."

"But," Peter insisted, confused by the flood of new information, "they said that there are communal showers for men and women, so how does—"

"There are communal showers, yes, but we shower separately," Yoji explained. "The women shower between six and seven-thirty, and the men from seven-thirty until nine. The afternoons are also divided: women between two and three, and men between three and four. And anyone caught peeping when the women are showering is thrown off the kibbutz."

"Peeping?" Peter repeated in surprise, "Why would anyone want to do that?"

"Are you being serious?" Shmulik looked at Yoji with a glint in his eye.

"You'd be surprised, but there have been quite a few incidents," Yoji added sardonically. Peter realized that he should keep his naïve questions to a minimum, if he didn't want to become a source of ridicule and mockery in this strange place. He could see that the cultural gaps were much wider than he'd foreseen. He would have to undergo a fundamental change in perception, and he was not so sure he was either capable of it or willing to.

***

A month after Peter arrived in Israel, he felt confident enough to start looking for his relatives. He already knew enough Hebrew to understand the meaning of the word sabra, which was slang for Israeli-born but actually meant prickly pear, because Israelis were considered prickly on the outside but sweet on the inside. To his delight, he now almost looked like one too. A month of working in the fields without a wide-brimmed hat had turned his skin color a burning red, but eventually, his pigment succumbed to his stubbornness and changed slightly. One evening, when he was shaving in front of the mirror in the communal shower, he was pleased to discover that his face had turned a reddish-brown and that his straight, pale hair had a few even paler stripes. His muscles, too, had changed and had grown bigger from doing hard physical labor.

One day, as he was passing by the secretariat's shack, two strangers approached him, and without hesitating, spoke to him in Hebrew, as if taking him for a born and bred sabra. He could taste the victory in his mouth. At least externally, he was fitting in well in his new country.

Yet he still found the cultural aspect bewildering. Although he'd discovered an old record player and classical records in the clubhouse, and he could listen to music in the evenings after work, if he'd chosen to do that every evening as he longed to, he would have had no young friends, because they preferred folk dancing in the dining room to the sound of Motke the kibbutz member's accordion.

Peter also wanted to join in, but he didn't think he could learn the dances, as the steps seemed incredibly complicated and confusing, even to watch. Jano, Aniko, and Eva, who had no desire to be part of that circle, tried to persuade him to give up and explore the forests around the kibbutz with them. Occasionally he would, but as time went by, he lost his enthusiasm for their games, and he found himself sitting on his own in the dining room in the evenings, hoping for a little attention from the sabras, especially the women. The only way to fit in well in Israel, he thought to himself, is to make friends with its sons and daughters.

One day, he was given a window of opportunity, when he was sent to work in the grove picking oranges. Noga, one of the kibbutz girls, was working nearby. She wasn't particularly pretty, but she had long, tanned legs and a thick, black braid, and he remembered seeing her before, wearing an army uniform.

In the afternoon, after he'd watched her all day, she waited for him under a tree, holding a juicy orange. "Would you like a segment?" she asked with a smile, revealing sparkling white teeth. Peter eagerly said yes, and they sat side by side next to a crate and talked. By the time the head of the grove came and urged them back to work, Peter had already asked Noga to meet him in the clubhouse that evening. She looked hesitant, but he quickly reassured her, "I'll be there, I haven't listened to the music I love for a long time. I'd love you to join me."

***

By about ten o'clock, he'd finished listening to all the new Beethoven and Brahms records, which a Polish immigrant by the name of Schimek had brought with him from Poland. Noga was nowhere to be seen, and he guessed that she'd probably chosen dancing to the accordion over joining him. Earlier, he'd turned down Eva, Jano, and Aniko's suggestion to go to a café in Afula. Now he felt lonely and slightly despondent, realizing that making friends with the kibbutzniks was going to be very tough, perhaps even impossible. Noga herself didn't particularly excite him, but he saw her as a way to achieve his plans. It was also the first time he'd ever had to make any effort with a girl, and his failed efforts made the task even more challenging.

In the end, he decided to go to the dining room to see if she was there, and on the way, he ran into her by the playground. Noga looked like she'd been dancing for hours. Her long, unkempt hair hung loose on her shoulders, which gave her an excited look. Her cheeks were red and hot, and her eyes were dancing contentedly. Happily, she was alone.

"I was beginning to think that you wouldn't come," he pretended that they'd met in the clubhouse.

"I wanted to get here earlier," she sounded apologetic, "but the gang caught me on the way and made me go dancing with them. So anyway, why don't you ever come to the dining room?"

"I've been a few times, but I gave up. I don't know those dances."

"They're easy, I can teach you," she offered and sat down on the bench, still trying to catch her breath, "but not now, I'm exhausted."

"When then?" he felt both eager and inept.

"Next Saturday, when I come home from the army." She answered, then added, "Do you want to go for a walk?"

"I'd love to!" he felt his face get hot and was worried that he'd blushed.

Noga looked cheekily at him and then blurted out, "I heard that you have a girlfriend, one of the Hungarians that you came here with."

"Aniko?" Again, he prayed his cheeks wouldn't give his away by turning red, "She's…not really my girlfriend."

"I heard that, too. They say that the other girl, the dark-haired one, is also your girlfriend."

This time he knew he was blushing.

"Is there a rumor mill here?" he protested.

"Yes," she giggled, "it's one of our most successful industries. Unfortunately, it doesn't generate any profit."

"Maybe it does," he retorted, "you seem very pleased with this titbit of information."

"Look," she said, seriously, "I usually hate gossip, but I like you, and I want you to know that you don't stand a chance with me if you continue that…friendship…with the two Hungarian girls."

"Why?" he felt slightly irritated. Noga barely knew him and she was already dictating conditions to him.

"Because it's unacceptable here to behave that way," she explained simply, "no self-respecting sabra girl from the kibbutz would go near a…Don Juan."

"Really? I thought I noticed your men, the sabra men, I mean, changing girls every dance, like that Tarzan, the tall one with the mustache whose pockets poke out of his trousers."

"You mean Arik?" Noga waved her hand dismissively, "he just likes showing off. When his girlfriend Shula is in the vicinity, he becomes that small, and anyway, everyone knows they'll be getting married soon."

"Oh, so that's the way things are here. First you decide to get married and then you become a couple?"

"Don't exaggerate!" she laughed again, and then leaned toward him and gave him a long kiss on the lips. Then she pulled away and added, "You see? We're not that conservative."

Peter watched her as she walked away, still giggling. He was spinning inside. Noga was so good at flirting, that for a moment he had found her irresistible.

"Why are you still stuck to the bench?" she taunted him when she turned around. "Have I managed to confuse you?"

"A little," he admitted and awkwardly walked toward her. "So what happens now? Do we have to get married?"

"No, but that's all you'll get from me if you prefer to continue your romantic relationship with your two Hungarians."

"They're not mine," he protested, "but I don't understand why I should have to give up my…friendship with them. Although we didn't know each other back in Hungary, we were smuggled over the border together, and we've been very close ever since."

"Then stay with them and be done with it!" her eyes sparked. "I'm not going to make a fool of myself!"

"But, Noga, I don't want you to make a fool of yourself, I just don't understand why—"

"And nor will you!" she snapped angrily and ran off. Peter stood there, bewildered. He really didn't understand how things worked in that strange place. Why couldn't he kiss a girl without promising to marry her, or at least to be exclusive? Yoji and Shmulik had mentioned how straight-laced the kibbutz society was, and he had internalized that knowledge as best as he could, so he hadn't expected Noga to act as freely as Aniko and Eva. But he also didn't think that anyone should consider marriage before tasting the lips and body of their loved one. What if they didn't like each other, what then? Lost in thought, he walked slowly back to his room. It made no sense at all to him—deciding to create a new society in Israel with laws as conservative and puritanical as the laws of the Orthodox Jews in Hungary.

***

Peter only became more confused when they were sitting in the dining room, and he told Jano about his walk with Noga. Jano laughed dismissively and told him that he'd had a similar experience with a kibbutz girl by the name of Rotem. She didn't even kiss him during their silly talk, but that didn't stop her from explaining that the kibbutz viewed their relationship as serious.

"I felt like a high school student being reprimanded by a middle-aged teacher," he added with a smile, "and that's when I realized I was wasting my time with those odd girls. I didn't want to go anywhere near her again, even though I thought she was very attractive until then. Forget them, Peter, you'll never understand the girls here, and we have no reason to try. Our girls are no-less beautiful, and I find them so much more attractive and beguiling, with their vivacious wit and lust for life. Why do we need complications with girls who may look young, but who sound like old nags from an isolated village in the south of Hungary?"

"But Jano, why did we come to this country if we're only going to create our own little European enclave here?"

"We came here to live as Jews, in the only place where Jews can walk with their heads held high, but that doesn't go to say that we have to behave like the Orthodox."

Jano finished his speech and his black coffee and went off to find his co-workers. Perplexed, Peter was left sitting in the dining room. He looked around, feeling like there was an invisible yet impermeable wall of gloom dividing him and his immigrant friends from the kibbutz members, even though his friends also looked like they'd been born there. They dressed like sabras, their skin was brown from the sun, and they were tall. He felt so despondent, that he began to miss home, Budapest, Sophie and his parents, even Gizi, who had approved of his romance with Marika, he remembered well. In Hungary, everyone loved him. Even the girls from the gymnasium, the girlfriends he would replace every week, never grew angry or resentful. And now he had to cope with disapproving looks and whispers behind his back, only because he had two close female friends, girls he considered his true friends. It was nobody's business what they did in the woods at night.

That day, while working in the field, he decided it was time to look for Shani, Marika, and Tibby. He hoped that they would make him feel better. Then, he thought, he would leave the kibbutz. After all, there were cities in Israel too, and he hoped that they were less restrained, more liberal, like European cities. Basically, the kibbutz was a society of hard-working farmers—no wonder the laws they'd chosen to live by were so harsh.

***

A week later, he contacted Shani, who had written to tell him that he was living in Jerusalem. Marika had long been married and lived next door to him, and Tibby was still serving in the army. He was stationed at a camp not far from the kibbutz, and he would be able to visit him.

Peter smiled to himself when he read that Marika was married. He figured that she'd had no difficulty in overcoming her disappointment when he chose Budapest over emigrating with her to Israel, but even he couldn't have predicted quite how easily. And then, when he read where Tibby was, he remembered that he also wanted to serve in the Israeli army. The next day, he reported to the secretariat and asked to enlist.

The kibbutz secretary, the young man who'd welcomed them with a smile the day they arrived, was delighted to hear his decision. He gave him a letter and a few pennies for the bus, then explained that he should go to Sarafand, a base in the center of Israel.

Peter packed a small suitcase, said goodbye to his friends, and set off. The secretary had promised to keep his place in his room, but Peter didn't know if he'd be back. He felt like he was embarking on a new journey.

It was almost dusk when he arrived at Sarafand, after having to change buses twice. The guard at the gate said that he was too late and that all the recruitment offices were closed. Peter was tired, hungry, and thirsty, and asked if he could eat and sleep at the camp, but the guard allowed him only a drink of water from the nearby faucet. Since Peter wasn't a soldier, he didn't have the authority to let him into the camp, he explained to him, then suggested he go back to where he came from and return early the following morning. Peter was overcome with despair. He had used all the money the secretary had given him, and the aroma coming from the falafel stand across the road was making him drool. He sat down at the bus stop and tried to decide what to do next. The option of sleeping on the bench until morning didn't seem so bad to him. When he traveled from Hungary to Austria, he'd had to sleep in much worse conditions. But he was being driven insane with hunger, and it wasn't passing. Eventually, he walked over to the falafel seller and asked him if he'd buy the gold necklace that his mother had given him. The surprise on the seller's unshaven face was blatant. Suspicious, he inspected the chain and even bit the Star of David with his teeth, then explained to Peter that he could get much more for it if he sold it to a jewelry store. But for that, he explained, he'd have to go to Tel Aviv. Peter replied that he didn't have enough even for a bus ticket to Tel Aviv, and the man kindly agreed to exchange the chain for three Israel liras, a pita bread stuffed with falafel, and a drink.

After Peter had devoured the falafel, which came with a generous splash of pungent red liquid, he suddenly felt as exhilarated as a man of means. With three liras, he could even get to Jerusalem, visit Shani and Marika, and have enough left over to treat them to coffee at a café in celebration of their reunion.

***

Late that night, Peter stood outside Shani's apartment in the Nachlaot neighborhood of Jerusalem and knocked on the door. He heard hushed, startled voices coming from inside, one of which sounded like a woman's. Shani hadn't mentioned having a woman in his life, and he began to worry that he was disturbing him. When the door finally opened to reveal his uncle, dressed in pajamas, he saw a short woman behind him looking very disgruntled. He was so embarrassed, he wanted to turn and run away. It took him just a few days to realize that the woman, his uncle's wife, was impossible to please.

"Peter?!" Shani stared at him for a moment before giving him a big, warm hug that dissolved all his fears. "What a pleasant surprise! I didn't think you'd come so soon!"

"I went to the army base to enlist, but I arrived too late," Peter explained, still feeling uncomfortable under the little woman's petrifying gaze.

"Come in, come in," Shani said invitingly, and Peter walked into a small room filled with the wonderful, familiar aromas of home. "This is my wife, Magda, she's also of Hungarian origin. Magda, this is my beloved nephew, Peter."

"Pleased to meet you," the woman held her hand out to him, but her expression remained stern.

Peter shook her cold hand and said that he too, was pleased to meet her, although he was very confused. He couldn't work out why Shani had hidden that he was married or why his wife seemed so restrained. He wondered if that could be the reason.

"I came with your uncle to Israel on the boat, alone, without any family," she explained, even though he hadn't asked. "My parents and brother were murdered in the camps."

"I see," Peter responded uncomfortably, feeling guilty for the first time in his life for his close family surviving the atrocity.

"Magda, you go back to sleep," Shani pleaded, "I'll make Peter a cup of coffee, and then I'll make up the sofa for him to sleep on."

"So, you're already chasing me away," Magda said sourly and pulled her robe tighter around her body.

"We aren't chasing you away, we'd love you to stay, but you're tired and you need to rest," Shani answered tenderly, then gave her a hug and accompanied her to the bedroom.

"Poor girl," he sighed when he returned to Peter, "her heart is weak, after all she went through."

"How old is she?" Peter wondered about Shani calling her a girl.

"Young, not yet thirty, but with what she's seen in life…"

Peter didn't say a word. He was beginning to understand why Shani had married Magda and why he hadn't mentioned it in his letters. He was too compassionate to withstand her loneliness, and his well-developed socialist sense of justice had been satisfied by providing her with a family.

"But what about you, kid?" Shani laughed again, "I'm so happy to see you here, with us. Marika will also be delighted!"

"Where is she? You wrote that she lives nearby. Who did she marry?"

"Marika married a photographer of Czech origin, and she lives right upstairs," Shani pointed up. "Do you want me to call her down?"

"Now?" Peter hesitated, despite his eagerness to see his cheerful cousin, "Won't we be disturbing her?"

"Quite the opposite," Shani winked at him with a mischievous look that

Peter couldn't recall ever seeing before. "Her husband is photographing a wedding now, as he usually does at night, I know she'll be happy to see you!"

As he spoke, he pulled a wool cardigan on over his pajamas, closed his buttons, and left the apartment with Peter tagging along, still unsure. When he saw Marika standing in the doorway to her home, dressed in a pale dress and looking even more beautiful than he remembered, his heart skipped a beat and he rushed toward her with open arms.

"Peterkum, what a wonderful surprise!" she shouted and fell into his arms. "Ever since Shani Bachi told me that you were in Israel, I've been pestering him to take me to you!"

"Well here I am, in the end I brought myself to you," Peter responded as he inhaled her perfume. It was a refreshing change after the natural odor of kibbutz women he'd become accustomed to.

"Come in," Marika said, "I was planning on going out to meet a few friends, but such a dear visitor such as yourself is an excellent reason to change my plans."

"I think we should go downstairs," Shani said nervously, "in case Magda wakes up and finds us gone. She may go out of her mind with worry."

"What do you think of your new aunt?" Marika asked, putting on a long, elegant leather coat, "Have you met her?"

"Yes," Peter said quickly and glanced worriedly at Shani, concerned he'd be hurt by Marika's mocking tone. He thought that although a chasm separated the two women, that didn't mean that she could be patronizing toward Shani's wife, since thanks to him, she had come to this country where she could afford to wear fashionable clothes.

***

After Peter and Shani finished discussing all that had happened since they'd arrived in Israel, Shani stood up and said it was time to go to sleep. He brought bedding in for Peter and asked him to make up the sofa, but Marika suggested that they go out for a bit. Peter, who was eager to hear more about her new life, especially about her marriage, agreed.

"If so, take a key please," Shani said. He didn't seem particularly pleased with the developments.

Peter took the key from him and promised not to return too late. Then he followed Marika out. To his surprise, she didn't go down the stairs, but instead, she went up, to her apartment.

"We have at least two hours," she told him, "my husband is photographing a wedding in Tel Aviv. He won't be back before two."

Her cheeks were flushed and she was already undressing before she had finished explaining. Peter looked at her in both fascination and alarm. He should have expected his unbridled cousin to behave this way. He was used to hiding his relationship with her and her half-sister, but only because of his mother. Having an affair behind Marika's husband's back was an entirely different matter, and he felt reluctant.

"Well, what are you waiting for?" she said seductively. "Would you like a good cognac?"

Almost completely naked by that point, she walked over to the bar in the wooden cabinet and took out a crystal bottle and two glasses. "To life!" she said as she handed the glass to him. Mesmerized, Peter took a sip.

"But, Marika…why did you get married if this is the way you're living?" he asked eventually, trying hard to slow things down.

"Do you want to discuss that now?" she grumbled, then took the glass from his hand. "I'll give you time for questions later!"

"But—"

"No buts." She began unbuttoning his shirt, planting small kisses along his bare chest. Peter felt the hair on his skin stand and he pulled her toward him.

CHAPTER 19

The next day, Peter took the first bus to Sarafand. This time, he was on time, and he was drafted into the navy. He was stationed in Haifa, after he told the administrative officer that he'd received the highest grades in his high school year in all the technical subjects.

Peter fell in love with the sea the moment he saw it. It reminded him of the Danube River in Baja, where the water was blue and shimmered in the sunlight, unlike in Budapest, where it was gray and dull. The sea was almost infinite and had a volatile nature, as if it were human. During his first storm at sea, he realized that he had an incredibly strong stomach and decided that he and the sea were meant for each other.

Another thing that made him feel at home on the ship was that within no time, they put his technical skills to use. He repaired recalcitrant machines and felt uplifting pleasure whenever he dealt with technical problems.

Also, there were no women serving on the ship. He saw this as a blessing, unlike his fellow sailors who resented the fact. That way, he could concentrate on his important jobs, enjoy the sea, and his new friends, and in the evenings, find solitude on the deck and truly contemplate his life without being disturbed or distracted.

At first, he had a lot to reflect on, all of it revolving around one dilemma: Was he interested in becoming assimilated in Israel or should he live his life like Marika, who seemed to have moved Budapest to Jerusalem?

In the beginning, Peter divided his days off between Jerusalem and Karkur, where Tibby stayed with relatives from his father's side whenever he had leave from the army. A few months after he joined the navy, Jano, Eva ,and Aniko decided to move to Haifa. Jano, who envied Peter's snow-white uniform, also enlisted in the navy and was stationed at the same base, whereas Aniko began attending the Technion. Eva, who didn't want to stay on her own in the kibbutz, moved into a small apartment in the Hadar HaCarmel neighborhood and worked at a café downtown.

Peter was sucked back into the lighthearted and amiable friendship he shared with them, and they never failed to amuse him. He preferred to spend most of his leave at their apartment because it was close to his base and was convenient whenever he had a night off.

His existential questions were slowly forgotten, especially after he received a letter from his mother, who wrote that Sophie was engaged to Alex Molovsky, the senior officer in Budapest. Their engagement raised Martha's suspicions that Peter's induction orders had been no coincidence and there was something behind it.

His mother wrote that she felt betrayed and that she was so furious that she had almost confronted Sophie. In the end, she decided not to cause any fuss because Alex could still find some pretext to persecute them. Peter, too, felt betrayed, but unlike his mother, he had no reason to suppress his anger. He wandered the streets of Haifa for nights on end, unable to find peace of mind, smoking cigarette after cigarette, and thinking about what had happened in those long-ago days in Budapest, and more so, in those nights. He couldn't believe that Sophie, whom he believed to be the most innocent and purest woman in the world, could have tricked him and played him against Alexander Molovsky. On the other hand, the course of events after he fled left little room for other interpretations. Even if Sophie hadn't known about it at first, the fact that Molovsky proposed to her after he fled from Budapest would have aroused the suspicion of even the most naïve of people. How Sophie could have not suspected Molovsky and thrown him down the stairs after he proposed to her, Peter couldn't understand. In any case, he thought that life had shown him which path to choose, after the only time he was serious about his intentions toward a woman and she went and deceived him, or at least allowed herself to fall in love with the man who had plotted to get him out of his way.

Marika agreed. She also thought that their experiences in life had shown them that being too righteous would get them nowhere. "Take Shani and your mother, for instance, they were the only ones from your family to survive," she told him one time when he visited her and mentioned it. "He fought with the partisans, took care of everyone, and was repaid in the form of Magda, who makes his life a misery. And your mother, who took care only of herself and her family, in a somewhat inexplicable and dubious way, if we take into consideration other people's opinions, well, she ended up living with the love of her life."

Peter didn't argue, but he didn't think that his mother's letter gave any indication that she was happy with her life. She wrote that she missed him terribly and that she regretted not insisting she and his father leave Hungary when he did. Peter truly missed his family, especially his mother, and he hoped that one day they would be able to leave Hungary. Meanwhile, he tried to bury his feelings with frequent visits to Jerusalem and by settling down in the Hungarian enclave in the Hadar HaCarmel apartment.

***

His three years of military service passed, and after he was released, he found work as a maintenance manager at the Nesher power plant. Although the army asked him to join the permanent forces and to do the officers' course, he hated the idea of becoming like Alex Molovsky and he refused.

He enrolled at the Technion and took evening classes in engineering. He officially moved in with Eva, Aniko, and Jano. Eva had long been running the café where she used to wait on tables, and they spent many a night there. Although they had money in their pockets, since they were all working, they didn't feel any need for a bigger apartment. They all considered the cramped, joyous commune a refuge from the constant thoughts and memories that filled their minds and appeared without warning, usually at night. None of them wanted to change a thing, and if war had not broken out in Israel in 1956, at the same time as the rebellion against the communists in Hungary, they would probably have continued living like that until they were a ripe old age.

***

When the war broke out, Peter and Jano were called up and sent to be gunners. Peter was bitten by a yellow scorpion and was the only soldier in his regiment to be wounded. He was taken to a hospital in the central of Israel, near Sarafand, where he was hospitalized for a few days. While there, he became friends with a sabra by the name of Avner, who had the bed next to his. Avner had a small transistor radio, and he would listen to the news every hour. It was from him that Peter first learned of the revolt happening in Hungary against the communist rule. He was terribly perturbed by the news, and he became glued to the little transistor, explaining to Avner that it was one and the same to him who won there, provided that his relatives weren't in danger of being hurt.

Avner had been serving in the infantry corps when he was wounded in the stomach and needed surgery. The surgery required donations of blood. Sorely disappointed, Avner told Peter that none of his or his wife's family were prepared to donate blood for him, because they were afraid of not having enough left in their veins. Even the doctors who explained that the body immediately produces however much blood they lack couldn't persuade them.

Peter, who remembered from his school days how the body produces blood, laughed at how primitive the sabras were and told Avner he would donate however much blood he needed. He rejected Avner's offer to pay. The surgery was a success, and they became true soul mates. Avner was different from the other sabras Peter knew from the kibbutz: He was good at chess, loved classical music, and even surprised him with his knowledge of literary classics. After Peter recovered, he continued to visit Avner, and he enjoyed it very much. However, when Avner was released from the hospital, Peter assumed that their friendship would end. Avner and his wife lived in Ra'anana, which was too far from Haifa for them to meet frequently. Although Avner suggested they correspond by letter, Peter found it hard to write in Hebrew and was embarrassed to do so. It was hard enough coping with exams at the Technion, which were returned covered in red marks indicating his spelling mistakes.

He explained to Avner that he was too busy studying and working to write regularly and that sadly, he thought they should part ways. But one day, a letter arrived from Avner announcing that he'd had a son and insisting that Peter come to the bris.

As it turned out, Peter had an important exam on the same date, so he went to the post office to call Avner's office and apologize for not being able to attend.

Avner didn't give up. He told Peter that he'd have to make it up to him by being his guest at home for the weekend. He and his wife wanted to prepare a feast fit for a king for him, to thank him for donating blood and keeping him company while he was in the hospital.

Peter was given no choice but to agree. He also didn't think that spending a weekend with his friend Avner playing chess and listening to music could be all that bad. Although his wife and baby would be there too, certainly no one would ask him to entertain them.

When he got home and told his friends about it, Aniko and Eva looked disappointed. They both had that weekend off, and they'd planned on spending it with Peter and Jano playing cards on the beach.

"Can't you catch a cab back tonight?" Eva asked, snuggling up to him, "We haven't spent a whole day together for such a long time."

"But I promised Avner that I'd spend the weekend with him," Peter hesitated. He didn't want to disappoint Avner.

"Never mind, just tell him that it won't work out," Aniko suggested. "He has his wife and baby to keep him occupied, and we'll be lonesome without you."

"We'll see," Peter answered, thinking that if Avner became too busy with his wife and baby, he'd find a way to avoid staying the night. "I'll do my best, but I can't promise."

Early Friday afternoon, Aniko and Eva walked with him to the bus stop. "Come back soon," they said, hugging him, "and don't become infatuated with your friend's bourgeois life and decide to stay there."

Peter laughed, kissed them both, and boarded the bus. He looked back to see them waving goodbye and thought that no other way of life could please him more. They made life so merry and wonderful. The only concerns they had were for their families in Hungary. The revolution was still in full swing and none of them were receiving mail from their relatives. The burden was much easier to bear together.

***

Peter bought a bunch of flowers at the bus stop in Ra'anana and asked the seller how to get to Avner's address. Then he walked in the direction that the seller had pointed.

He arrived at their apartment, and Avner and his wife Nava gave him a warm welcome. Nava said that she'd heard wonderful things about him from Avner, and she was so happy to finally meet him. They showed Peter into their small but very well-kept home, only to discover that the living room was full of bouquets.

"I see that my bouquet is superfluous," he said awkwardly to Avner. "I'm sure you've run out of vases."

"It certainly is not superfluous! Your intentions were good, and that's the main thing!" Nava said, taking the bouquet from him and arranging the flowers in an empty marmalade jar.

"Sit down, please. Would you like something to drink?" Avner asked. "It'll be an hour before we eat. We're waiting for Yael, Nava's friend."

The casual tone in which he mentioned Nava's friend made Peter suspect they were matchmaking. It would be an understatement to say that he wasn't enthusiastic about the idea. He was perfectly happy with his way of life.

"Thanks, I'll have black coffee, please," he answered politely, looking around the living room. A huge bookcase covered the entire wall opposite him.

"So, Schwartz, what can you tell me?" Avner asked, patting his knee. "How was your exam? The one that prevented you from attending our son's bris?"

"I hope that it went well—" Peter began to say, when he was interrupted by a baby crying in the next room.

"Avner! The baby's crying!" Nava shouted desperately from the kitchen. Avner jumped up and hurried off to the baby. Peter remained sitting, somewhat uncomfortable with the situation and wondering if courtesy required him to join Avner and see his baby, or if he should wait for an invitation.

"Here you are," Nava placed a tray in front of him with a cup of coffee, a bowl of sugar cubes, and a small china milk jug. Then she disappeared into the baby's room. Peter was left alone in the living room, staring at the bookcase and wondering if perhaps Aniko had been right. Avner and Nava would probably be busy with the baby most of the time and leave him to die of boredom or to spend the Sabbath making conversation with Nava's friend, which would probably feel like a job interview. He tried to think of a good excuse to leave after dinner.

Before he could think of one, Avner and Nava returned, with Nava pushing a blue and white baby carriage.

"Here's our little Shai," she announced proudly and pointed at the small bundle in the carriage. "Isn't he delightful?"

Peter leaned over to look at the baby, who was swaddled in diapers, when suddenly a scream erupted from the carriage. Before he could jump away, he managed to detect a tiny, red head, and was amazed at the noise it was able to produce.

Charming littler screamer, he thought to himself, but chose to say, "He'll probably be an opera singer, with those lungs."

"An opera singer?" Nava said, taken aback, picking up the screaming bundle. "What kind of profession is that? I'd rather he become a doctor."

"Or a pilot," Avner said.

Peter, thinking he was joking, was surprised, when in all seriousness, he added, "Look at how intelligent his eyes are."

Peter felt compelled to get up and stand behind Nava so he could look at the baby's face again, only to discover that his eyes were completely glazed over. He couldn't even see the frustration and anger in them that must have been behind his demanding screeches.

"Yes, he really does look intelligent," he said finally, when he noticed that Avner was looking at him as fervently as his son was screaming.

"Could he be hungry?" Avner asked, and Nava quickly took the charming screamer back to the bedroom, presumably to breastfeed him. A few minutes later, Shai's screams of protest died down and the house became blessedly peaceful.

"In Hungary, they say that if you play classical music to babies, they grow up to be calm and quiet children," Peter said, glancing at the new record player in the corner of the bookcase.

"Really?" Avner said, his eyes widening with surprise, and he immediately went to the pile of records and started to look through them, "What kind of classical music? Probably not Beethoven's Ninth."

"Maybe Mozart's Magic Flute," Peter suggested, who had not listened to it for quite some time.

"We'll try." Avner took the record out of its cover and placed it on the record player, but before he could turn it on, they heard the baby crying again and then Nava's anxious calls, "Avner! Come and help me!"

Peter sighed. The prospect of dying of boredom had stopped being the worst of possibilities. The infant's grating screams, along with Nava's irritated reproaches were making his time with them a nightmare. The night will be even worse, he thought. Again, he tried hard to think of a polite excuse to leave later in the evening, but he was finding it hard to focus his thoughts.

The ritual went on and on. Every time the baby's screams subsided, Avner would return to the living room to sit with him. This would be followed by a few moments of silence, which Nava would take advantage of to return to the kitchen, and then, before he and Avner could exchange two whole sentences, the insistent screams would slice through the air, and Nava would match it with a no-less demanding screech of her own: "Avner! The baby!"

Peter felt as if he were participating in a crazy parody, albeit as a spectator. With the few parts of his brain that were still functioning, he thought to himself that if Avner and Nava were planning to matchmake that evening, then neither of them could be considered particularly good planners. If he'd ever considered starting a family in Israel, even fleetingly, the experience he was being subjected to would have made him think otherwise. He didn't believe they would ever sit down to eat their dinner, and he hoped that Nava would at least manage to finish preparing it before breakfast time.

No longer needing an excuse, he blurted out to Avner in one of the quieter intervals, "I don't feel very well. I don't think I should spend the night here."

"It'll pass," Avner promised and patted his shoulder. "You must be hungry. You'll feel better after we eat," and he ran off to the kitchen to bring Peter a tray full of fruit. "Eat, Schwartz, eat," he urged him before disappearing into the baby's room, "it'll help you feel better."

Peter peeled an orange and ate it a segment at a time, thinking that his own living arrangements were so much better, even if one of them were to have a baby. At least four people were needed for a home to function under such conditions.

His thoughts were interrupted by the doorbell ringing.

"Schwartz," Nava called to him from the next room, "could you open the door, please? It must be my friend Yael."

Peter got up and went to open the door, a wicked thought flitting through his mind—to ask Nava's friend to apologize on his behalf and tell the happy couple that he felt so unwell that he had to leave. Then he could simply slip away, never to return. But as soon as he opened the door and saw her standing there, he changed his mind.

***

Yael was pretty, but that's not why he found himself planted in the doorway. She was radiant and seemed full of confidence. Stunned, he asked her, "Are you, Yael?" as if refusing to believe that anyone could assume that she was in need of a match.

"Yes, Yael Davidov, why? Did you think I was Sophia Loren?" she gave him a cheery, bright smile as she held out her hand. "You must be Schwartz, Avner's blood donor. It was very nice of you, by the way," she added warmly.

Only when he shook her small hand did he notice how tiny Yael was, about Eva's height. He looked at her as she sauntered past him straight into the living room, and he thought how similar the two of them were, and yet so different. They were both small, beautiful brunettes. However, Yael lacked the European chic that Eva had in abundance. On the other hand, Yael had a natural grace and unpatronizing self-confidence that made her even more appealing than Eva.

"Where are the happy parents?" Yael asked as she, too, stopped in surprise at the abundance of bouquets in the living room.

"Oh, I forgot to pick flowers," she said with slight embarrassment. "I was in such a hurry to leave…my friends from the kibbutz said that they wouldn't wait for more than fifteen minutes."

"Think nothing of it, they have too many flowers as it is. They didn't even have a proper vase for mine." He took his flowers out of the jar and handed them to her. "Here, take these, I brought them but you can tell the happy parents that they're from you. They're so exhausted by the baby that they won't remember receiving them earlier."

Her laughter reminded him of the bells in Mussorgsky's work. "You're sneaky," she said, holding the flowers up to her nose, "I like it. Why do the flowers smell burnt?"

"It's not the flowers!" he answered in panic, noticing the smell coming from the kitchen. "I think that the food's burning!"

Yael ran toward the kitchen, and he followed. Calmly, she stood before the four steaming pots on the stove. She lifted the lids one by one, turned three flames off, and reduced the heat of the fourth.

"That's it, we've prevented a disaster," she smiled at him again. "The soup can cook a little longer, it'll add flavor, but I reduced the heat."

"Well done," he said, surprised by how naturally she had taken over the family's kitchen, shedding what remained of his reserve. "Where did you learn to work in a kitchen, on the kibbutz? Are you a member?"

"No, I'm employed there as a teacher, so I'm exempt from kitchen duty," she explained to him, much to his relief. He was glad she wasn't a member. "I learned to cook at home, from my mother."

"And what do you teach?"

"Literature and Hebrew grammar," she replied, heading out of the kitchen. She walked straight into Nava, who greeted her with cries of joy.

Avner was standing behind her and he glanced cheekily at Peter, "I see you two have met," he said.

"Yes," Peter nodded, and silently counted the seconds, hoping that when he reached ten, the baby would start crying again and force his parents back into the room, leaving him and Yael on their own. But this time, as if intentionally, the little devil decided to be quiet.

"Well, we better sit down to eat," Avner suggested, and Nava placed a stack of dishes in his hands. Yael, noticing that Peter had been left without a defined job, handed him the glasses and headed back to the stove.

"You seem to be feeling better," Avner said with a wink as they lay the table.

"Absolutely," he admitted, a little embarrassed.

The two women also came to the table, Nava holding the cutlery and Yael carrying the pot of soup. Peter quickly took it from her.

"Thanks," she beamed.

They sat down to eat, and five and a half minutes later, the baby started crying again. Nava and Avner sprang to their feet, but Yael stopped them. "Wait," she said firmly, making them both stop, "I haven't even seen Shai yet. Sit down, you two, and I'll go to him."

"But—" Nava began, but Yael went over to her and put a hand on her arm to calm her, "Sit down, Nava, have a break. You look exhausted. Don't worry, I'm used to taking care of children."

"All right," Nava mumbled, returning to the table. Avner, trying to stifle a sigh of relief, followed suit.

"Not a few seconds passed, and the wails of the charming screamer, as Peter called him in his mind, miraculously subsided. A moment later, Yael appeared in the doorway pushing the blue and white carriage. "He'll be much happier here, with us," she said and sat down, while continuing to rock the carriage.

Peter looked in astonishment from Nava to Avner and from them to Yael, who was eating her soup as she rocked the carriage. He wondered to himself how Avner and Nava hadn't thought of doing that themselves, instead of traipsing repeatedly from the living room to the baby's room in an exhausting, nerve-wracking race.

"The nurses at the nursing home told me that he'd become spoiled if I kept him with me," Nava said defensively, after a few minutes of eating in silence.

"Nonsense," Yael replied dismissively, "a baby needs a sense of security, and you can only give him that if you're nearby at all times, at least for the first few months of his life. Only when he feels more confident in his close environment, can he get used to being left on his own a little, with an adult nearby, of course."

"How do you know so much about babies?" Peter asked interestedly. "You don't have such young students, do you?"

"No, but I have eight siblings, and I took care of most of them when they were babies," she explained easily, as if she was talking about cultivating roses in the garden. Peter was taken aback.

Eight brothers and sisters?! And she took care of most of them as babies? No wonder she seems so sure of herself. He thought that if he would be capable, at his advanced age, of taking care of a single child like the charming screamer, he would award himself the highest mark of excellence.

"Schwartz suggested earlier that we play classical music for the baby," Avner told her, "he said that it was the Hungarian way of calming babies down."

Peter stared at his bowl of soup, afraid that his embarrassment would show and they would all know that he'd made the story up out of thin air, that he was merely trying to get them to listen to music other than the baby's screams.

"Excellent idea," he was surprised to hear Yael's response, "I think that Mozart's work would definitely be worth trying, either "A Little Night Music" or The Magic Flute."

"You two are really suited, don't you think?" Avner sounded amused as he got up and walked over to the record player. The Magic Flute is already waiting, because that's what Schwartz wanted to listen to earlier."

Yael smiled at Peter again, and he looked at her as the music filled the room. He was captivated. A beautiful and radiant girl, who had raised eight younger siblings and also found time to listen to classical music was better than anything he could have imagined. Now he could only hope that his friends had really been planning to introduce them and that they'd checked first that she didn't have a boyfriend.

***

Only when the Sabbath ended, did Peter remember that he'd promised his friends in Haifa to come home as early as possible. That's when he also realized how much he'd enjoyed his time at Avner and Nava's. He looked at Yael, who was sitting at the dining table with Nava, writing down tips that would make taking care of the baby easier. Nava was looking admiringly at her, a feeling that Peter shared. Yael was special, there was no doubt about it. He hoped to see her again, this time on their own. But when they left Avner and Nava's house and walked together to the bus stop, Peter started wondering what that feeling meant. Had he fallen in love with her, he asked himself, making himself panic. Since he'd fled from Hungary and Sophie, he hadn't thought that way about girls.

She simply intrigues me, he tried to calm his nerves, because I've never met girls quite like her. The Hungarians treat life too lightly and avoid problems instead of dealing with them, whereas the Israeli girls are like old ladies and their cultural preferences don't appeal to me. Now, for the first time, I've met an Israeli with European cultural taste, and she didn't mention the word wedding a single time during the twenty-four hours we were together. Clearly, I'd like to get to know her better, that's all. I don't need to be so flustered.

"A lira for your thoughts, Schwartz," he heard her say suddenly, waving the metal coin in her hand.

"What? Oh, they aren't worth that much," he smiled, realizing she was paraphrasing a conversation from the movie Casablanca, and he felt a little less awkward. "Nothing much, I was just thinking to myself that…I'd like to see you again, and I was trying to guess what you'd say, that's all."

"Instead of guessing, you could simply ask," she smiled back, "and then you'd know that I'd like to see you again too."

"When?" he asked quickly, before he lost his nerve.

"At the end of the week, on Thursday, my friends from the kibbutz youth movement can take me to Tel Aviv, when they go visit their families. Would you like to meet me at the Moghrabi Theater at eight, Schwartz, we could catch a movie? I heard that Gone with the Wind is showing."

"Excellent!" he thought he sounded too enthusiastic and hoped that she'd think it was due to the movie she'd suggested. "I haven't seen it yet. So, Davidov, it's a date, then, eight o'clock at the Moghrabi?"

"Yes, eight at the Moghrabi. But why are you calling me by my surname?"

"Because that's what you've been doing all the time."

"Because Avner and Nava do, so I thought it was your first name."

"No," he laughed, "Schwartz is my surname, my first name is Peter."

"Peter?" she rolled his name in her mouth, and he tensed, afraid that as a Hebrew teacher, she'd say that Peter wasn't a Hebrew name, like the sweaty official at Haifa Port had said. "You have a beautiful name, and it really suits you."

"Do you think?" he instantly melted and told her how patronizing the official had been.

"I think it's a shame they send such stupid people to welcome new immigrants," she replied, and looked at him sorrowfully, "Firstly, Peter's not Pinchas in Hebrew, it's actually Simeon, and he was a disciple of Jesus. He was called Petrum in the New Testament. I think the name Peter is perfect for you, because you have a face that evokes images of snowy peaks and green forests, like those in Peter and the Wolf."

"Then will you call me Peter from now on?" his heart expanded.

"Happily, and you'll call me Yael."

"Of course," he replied, "it's a lovely name."

"Do you know who Yael was?"

"Kind of," he shifted from foot to foot, not quite sure of himself, "she's from the Bible, isn't she?"

"Yes," she nodded, "she was the heroine in the Bible who killed Sisera. Well, here's my bus, I have to run."

"I'll see you on Thursday at eight at the Moghrabi," he repeated the details of their date as he walked with her to her bus.

"Yes, on Thursday. Bye for now," she answered and got on the bus. She sat down, then opened the window and waved to him, smiling. Peter watched the bus drive away until it disappeared. Then he ordered himself to erase the silly smile that was glued to his face.

When he arrived home, he tried to hide his excitement from his three friends. He told them that the weekend had been more enjoyable than he'd expected, because a friend of Nava's had taken excellent care of the baby. Since the three of them were busy all week studying and working, they didn't notice how tense and expectant he was as he waited for Thursday to arrive, nor did they see how high above the clouds he was floating. On Monday, Peter found himself humming the words of the song "Yael." "Yael, Yael, all the soldiers called her Yael, Yael" he sang in the mirror as he shaved, unaware that he even knew the song, and in Hebrew, too.

When Thursday arrived, he skipped a lesson at the Technion to catch the five-thirty bus. He tried to curb his enthusiasm on the way, and again he found himself thinking how his life would be turned upside down if he let himself fall in love with Yael. He knew that he'd have to give up the commune that had become his life, and who knows what other far-reaching changes he'd have to make. When the bus stopped in Netanya to pick up passengers, he almost got off to go back to Haifa, but the thought of Yael waiting for him broke his heart. He berated himself for thinking like that—Yael didn't seem to be the kind of girl who would pressure him into making compromises. On the contrary, she looked very happy with her own life, otherwise she wouldn't have been so radiant and confident. Frustrated women didn't look like that. He didn't even know if her feelings for him were as strong as his for her. Although she was very nice to him, and not only out of courtesy, he had no idea how she really felt.

CHAPTER 20

Peter never imagined that Yael was just as excited about their date as he was, perhaps even more. She woke up early in the morning to the sound of birds chirping and tried to decide what to wear. When she told Peter that his face evoked a feeling in her of snowy peaks and green forests, she was actually expressing what she felt the moment she saw him standing in the doorway to Nava and Avner's apartment. He looked different from all the men she'd met before. He had a European appearance and an intelligent, amusing expression, not at all cold or patronizing. This was new and intriguing to her, and very attractive. The more she thought about that weekend, the more she was surprised to realize that he was precisely the kind of man she wanted to marry. This surprised her mainly because she'd never felt that way about any other man. She'd had a serious boyfriend before, whom she dated for two years, but he didn't enthrall her the way Peter did. He was the youngest of three and although she broke up with him after he made it clear that he wouldn't get married before his two older brothers, who seemed in no rush to do so, deep down she knew it wasn't the true reason. At a certain point, Yael had started to find him boring.

She was the second daughter of a Bukharan family of ten, and from a very young age, she'd had to help at home, not only in raising the children but also in other matters. Her father, a respected rabbi and cantor in Bukhara, had to work in Israel as a wagon driver, and since his wages weren't enough to support the large family, Yael started working as soon as she completed her elementary school education. She refused to leave high school, and she attended night school in Tel Aviv.

Yael never perceived her life as difficult. She preferred to see it as interesting. It only made her more assertive. As a teenager, she joined a secular, left-wing socialist youth movement, even though her family was religious, and she even joined the army, which none of her younger sisters did after her.

Her parents respected her choices and put no obstacles in her way, which allowed her to remain very close to her family. Her cultural preferences were, however, very different. When she was twelve, she joined a choir, which exposed her to classical music. She fell in love with it and slowly saved up to buy a small radio so she could listen to her favorite music programs. She couldn't afford to buy a ticket to a concert or opera, but she promised herself that once her siblings grew up and could stand on their own two feet, she would attend as many concerts as she wanted to.

She fell in love with books back in elementary school, and she would read everything she could get her hands on. She was particularly impressed with the European classics, from which she drew her descriptions of landscapes when she saw Peter. None of her many suitors shared her interests. They preferred to talk about their military service, and about what heroes they were, or to tell her how beautiful she was. It was no wonder she became bored with them so quickly. Peter was different. They'd spent more than twenty-four hours together and he didn't say a word about his military service, although she knew that he'd met Avner during the last war. She assumed that he'd also survived the Holocaust, since he immigrated to Israel a few years after the end of the Second World War, but he didn't mention that either. He didn't tell her how beautiful she was, he let his eyes speak for him, following her admiringly whenever he thought she wouldn't notice.

Instead, they'd talked about classical music, books, movies, and theater, and Yael was left with a taste for more.

Eventually, she chose a turquoise dress that she'd sewn herself for her younger sister's wedding. She tried it on but decided she looked too formal, so she removed the lace edging that she'd sewn into the seams. When she looked at herself in the mirror, she was pleased. Her roommate, who wondered why she'd woken up so early, told her that she looked stunning.

Yael took off her dress, put on plainer clothes and went to school, but she found it hard to concentrate on the lessons. The sun, the blue sky, and the blossoming trees outside looked different and inviting, even exciting. She couldn't stop wondering if Peter was looking at the same kind of scenery and if his heart was expanding like hers.

When the school day finally ended, she went to look for the youth movement leaders, who she'd arranged a lift to Tel Aviv with that evening. To her surprise, she found them loading a greasy iron monster on the truck they were taking.

"What's that, have you lost your mind?!" she asked, "Is that what you want me to sit with in the back??

"It's a tractor engine," one of them explained, "and we're taking it to the people building the National Water Carrier, because their tractor has broken down. Do you want to come with?"

"But it's so far," she panicked, "you won't be able to get back in time to take me to Tel Aviv!"

"Trust us, we'll make it. We have half the day to get there, and we don't have to repair it. We're only taking them the engine and coming back."

"Are you sure?"

"Absolutely!"

"All right," she calmed down. The opportunity of a trip on such a spectacular day filled her with energy, "Then I'll have to come with you. What can go wrong?"

Maybe because it was such a beautiful day, Yael didn't think of the possibility of the truck's engine breaking down.

**

Impatient, Peter looked at his watch. It was already eight-thirty and there was no sign of Yael. He was starting to worry. He thought that maybe she'd said the Allenby Theater and not the Moghrabi, but the Moghrabi was showing Gone with the Wind, and that he knew he'd heard well. By nine o'clock he was worried that something awful had happened to her, that maybe she'd had an accident. How would he track her down now and find out what was going on?

He had no way of doing that, and he didn't even have Avner and Nava's phone number on him. Besides, they probably wouldn't be any the wiser.

By ten, he was desperate. He thought that she'd never arrive. Severe disappointment replaced his concern and fears. Maybe she decided he wasn't for her, an old-fashioned, polite European who didn't seem crazy about babies. Maybe she'd sensed somehow that he wasn't planning to get married anytime soon and regretted making a date with him in the first place. The memory of how his date with Noga on the kibbutz had gone wrong suddenly punched him in the stomach. I guess all the Israeli girls are the same, he thought to himself, they all have one goal in mind: to get married. But an inner voice whispered to him that it was impossible. She wasn't like the others. He'd sensed it throughout the day they spent with Nava and Avner. I'll wait for her here until morning, he decided, even though he knew it made no sense since the last bus to Haifa would be leaving at midnight, just let her come. But if she doesn't get here by then, I'll return to Haifa and never try to find her; I'll see it as a sign from above that the life I've been living until now is the best one for me.

He felt a stab in his stomach at the thought of it. And if something has happened to her, an accident, or if she's not well, wouldn't you want to know? he admonished himself and squeezed his eyes shut, trying to erase the horrific images from his mind. No, that's not right, he thought, if you're making such a fixed decision, you should also be deciding what to do if she does arrive; making a decision of the same magnitude.

What decision can I make? he bargained with himself. *I could decide* that if she comes even hours late, I'll take it as a sign from above that we're meant for each other, but isn't that a little beyond reason?

"Peter?!" he suddenly heard her voice, and he thought his imagination was playing tricks on him. He opened his eyes and saw her standing right in front of him, wearing a beautiful turquoise dress. She looked happily surprised, as if she hadn't dared to hope that he'd wait three hours for her. That instant, he realized he was head over heels in love with her.

"I'm so sorry, truly I am," she moved closer and took his hand, "I went on a trip and—"

"Never mind," he replied, "you don't need to tell me what happened, what matters is that you're here now."

They heard a loud honk and she turned around to look at the truck parked on the sidewalk. Two tanned young men were peering at her through the window. "Everything's fine, he waited for me! You can go!" Yael shouted to them. They waved goodbye and drove off. Yael turned back to him. "We missed the film," she said sadly, and he smiled and replied, "Never mind, we'll see it another time."

***

The next day, he told his friends that he'd met the woman who was likely to become his wife. Aniko and Eva were stunned and hurt, but Jano jumped up dramatically and said he was willing to compensate them and marry them both.

The following two weeks were very hard for Peter. Tirelessly, he tried to appease Aniko and Eva and to explain to them what he'd felt deep inside when decided to take such a momentous step. Eva was the first to relent. She gave him a big hug and said that she had no idea he was such a romantic. Aniko, however, whose opinion was more important to him, argued passionately that he was too romantic. "You hardly know the girl. She's Israeli-born, of Eastern origin, and comes from a religious home… how do you think you'll get along if you have nothing in common?"

"We have a lot in common," Peter insisted, "and she's special, she's not stuck in her ways, and she's curious and open-minded."

"Open-minded?" Aniko mocked, "I wonder how she'll react when you tell her about our commune."

"I've already told her that we live together," he replied, "and she saw it as completely natural."

"It'll all end as soon as you get married!" Aniko said, her eyes flashing, "You'll see, soon she'll be insisting that you have nothing to do with us!"

"I don't think so," Peter said, "unless you imply to her that our relationship was more than friendship, which I strongly urge you not to do."

Aniko pursed her lips in anger, and Eva came to Peter's aid. She thought that they should be happy for him and support him. Slowly, Aniko's resistance dissolved, until one evening, she came back from the Technion with a big grin on her face and told them that she'd met an Israeli and he'd asked her out on a date. A week later, she told Jano and Eva that thanks to Peter's influence, they'd also decided to get married. Peter was overjoyed. He imagined them all paired off and living in the Haifa area, just like in Noah's Ark, with them all remaining close friends.

***

A month after their date at the Moghrabi Theater, Peter proposed to Yael. She agreed immediately, without trying to hide her excitement. Then he caught a bus to Jerusalem to tell Shani and Marika the wonderful news. Shani opened the door looking very distressed.

"I received a letter from your mother," he told Peter before he had time to tell him why he was there, "bearing very bad news."

Peter tensed. In the months since the Hungarian Revolution had begun, he'd been in contact with his uncle on an almost daily basis to check if he'd had any news from his parents. Shani constantly reassured him by saying that his parents weren't part of the rebel forces, therefore no harm would come to them. What's more, Sophie was married to that Soviet officer, so she would protect them and their business.

Peter tried to boost his morale by thinking that it may have all been for the better and that fate had seen to it that Sophie could protect his family.

Now, however, Shani was telling him that Sophie had brought disaster on them by joining the students who had started the uprising in Kossuth Square.

Overwhelmed with fear, Peter grabbed the letter from Shani, held it in his trembling hands, and read it.

"Shani, my dear brother," his mother wrote in her neat handwriting, "I hope that by the time you read this letter, you will still be able to save us. The situation is very bad. It seems we should have listened to you and fled from here. When the rebellion began, we believed that nothing bad would happen to us. We stayed home, as the government ordered, and hoped that the situation would become clear within a few days. But just two days later, the soldiers arrested Gizi. When we tried to find out why, we learned the worst. That nightmare I had, which was the reason I agreed to Peter leaving the country, has come true. You don't know about the nightmare because you left before Peter received his induction order, but you can ask him about it, he'll remember. In any case, Gizi's daughter Sophie, who was married to Officer Alexander Molovsky, joined the rebels in Kossuth Square and was killed while trying to stop the Soviet tanks from suppressing the uprising. She threw a Molotov cocktail at a tank before she was shot. Molovsky, her husband, was in the tank. God only knows what pushed that talented and gentle girl to perform such an impulsive and tragic act and bring tragedy on her and her mother. Things everywhere are terrible now. Gizi has been imprisoned, and I'm trying not to think about what she's going through. Our business has been closed under government order, and we are in constant fear that we, too, will be arrested by the soldiers. Yoshka wants to go to Baja to ask for Molnar's protection, but under no circumstances am I prepared to do that. As such, all our hopes are pinned on you and on your ability to get us out. I know that you still have contacts, and I'm asking you, please, use them to save us. Your loving sister, Martha.

"P.S. Please send our love to Peter and don't tell him how bad the situation is. I don't want to worry him."

By the time he looked at Shani, Peter's eyes were wide with fear. "What are we going to do?!" he asked, his voice trembling.

"I'll take care of it," Shani replied, his eyes filled with compassion, "everything will be all right in the end."

"How can you say that? We have to do something, right away!" Peter raised his voice, "Tell me how I can return to Hungary, and I'll go back and rescue my parents!"

"Calm down, Son, there's no need for that. Your mother has asked me to use my contacts, not you. As you read, she asked me not to tell you anything at all."

"Shani, I'm not a child, and I want to help! I spent three years in the army, and I've just fought in the war in Sinai, you can trust me to rescue my parents…"

"Shh, don't wake up Magda. Come, let's go out," Shani said and put on his coat. They went outside to the freezing air in the stairwell. "Go upstairs to Marika and wait for me there," Shani instructed him as he walked down the stairs.

"Wait," Peter called after him, "where are you going?"

"To organize your parent's trip over," Shani whispered and disappeared into the dark night.

***

Peter climbed the stairs, his heart torn between hope and despair. He was just beginning to feel the pain of Sophie's death. His hands still trembling, he knocked on the door, trying to think of what to say to Marika and whether to tell her what he'd learned from Shani.

A few seconds later, she opened the door. She was half asleep. "Peter, my love!" she whispered breathlessly, "I missed you!"

Feeling awkward, Peter just stood there. Under the stressful circumstances, it hadn't occurred to him that Marika might think he'd come to her for quite different reasons.

"You haven't visited me for so long," she prattled on, pulling him into the apartment, "I've missed you terribly. Would you like a drink?"

"Coffee, please," Peter muttered, sinking into an armchair.

"All right," Marika said and went to the kitchen. When she returned, she told him "My husband is in the north, he'll only be back tomorrow. We have all night."

"I don't think that…" Peter began to say, then hesitated. He didn't know whether to tell her the bad news and what Shani was busy arranging. Marika was extremely talkative, and he was afraid she might sabotage the plan.

"What don't you think?" she sat down in his lap and started covering his face with kisses, "Didn't you miss me at all?"

"I missed you, but…I'm getting married! I came here to tell you," Peter was glad he remembered why he was there.

"Congratulations," Marika replied, looking at his face, "and who's the lucky bride?"

"A lovely girl, a literature teacher," he began to answer, but Marika rushed off to the kitchen and returned with a cup of coffee.

"Here you are, drink up," she urged him and took off her robe, "we need to celebrate your news properly." Then she went to the liquor cabinet and took out the ornate crystal bottle of fine cognac, which he had a glass of every time he visited. She poured a glass for him and then for herself.

Peter watched her walk lithely toward him. She was wearing a thin silk nightgown. "Marika, this isn't appropriate, really, I'm getting married, and you're already married. I think it's time to stop…these things."

"Stop? Why?" Marika asked. Unabashed, she sipped her cognac as she looked at him, "You can't be saying that you've lost interest in me."

"No, it's not that, it's just that I love my future wife and I'm not going to be disloyal to her."

"And me? Don't you love me, Peter?" she whispered in his ear, "We've been lovers for so long, I can't believe you want to abandon me for some boring literature teacher."

"She's not boring, she's…well, she's the woman I've decided to share my life with, and I want to do it in the right way."

"You'll do it perfectly, I'm sure of it," Marika nestled up to him.

Peter was already tense from hearing the terrible news about his parents, and Marika wasn't making it easy for him. He felt like he was about to explode. What does it matter if I release a little tension with Marika? he thought to himself. It won't hurt anyone.

As he was about to put his arm around her, there was a loud knock at the door. Marika leaped out of his arms, quickly threw on her robe and tied it. She opened the door to find Shani standing there looking sternly at them. "I hope I'm not disturbing you," he said sardonically, "Peter, I've organized everything! Tomorrow night, they will reach safety!"

"Really?" Peter was overjoyed and jumped to his feet.

Marika held her robe closed and walked over to Shani, "What have you organized?" she asked.

"Matters," Shani snapped, glaring at her, "I don't understand you, Marika, there's a revolution going on in Hungary, your mother is there, and all you care about is…this," he pointed at her night robe, which was visible under her robe, and shook his head vigorously.

"Let's go," he said to Peter.

"Wait!" Marika exclaimed, "What are you hiding from me?! I won't let you leave until you tell me!"

"We're not hiding anything," Shani replied emphatically, "you just don't ask!"

"Well, I'm asking you now," Marika's voice broke, "and I…didn't think I could do anything to help. Tell me, Shani, what has happened to my mother? I beg of you, tell me!"

Shani stopped, thought for a few moments, then finally said, "All right, I'll tell you, but please make me coffee first."

Marika ran to the kitchen again and came back with three steaming cups. Peter noticed that her hands were shaking as she set the tray on the table. His heart went out to her. She suddenly looked like a small, defenseless girl.

"Well," Shani began, after taking a big sip, "your sister Sophie joined the rebels, and…she was killed when she threw a Molotov cocktail at a tank."

Marika, her expression frozen, sat upright and nodded. She reached for the glass of cognac she'd poured for Peter and gulped it down in one shot.

"As a result, your mother was arrested," Shani added, "and Yoshka's business was closed."

Marika's eyes filled with tears. Peter quickly hugged her. "Don't worry, Marika, I'm sure she'll be released soon," he murmured.

"She's already been released," Shani surprised them, "but she doesn't want to leave Hungary. She's afraid she's being watched and that she'll put your parents at risk when they escape."

"I don't understand," Marika whispered.

"I can't tell you more than that," Shani said adamantly, "any information I give you could put Yoshka and Martha in danger until they leave."

"I knew it!" Marika sobbed, "I knew that stupid little Pole would bring disaster upon us, I should have forced Mami to leave with us…I should have insisted!"

"Don't talk about Sophie like that, do you hear me?!" Peter shouted, and wanted to go on and say how much smarter, braver, and better-natured she was than Marika would ever be, even if she were to really try, but Shani, who felt sorry for Marika, held his hand up to stop him.

"Enough, Marika," he said softly, "stop blaming yourself. You had no way of changing the course of events, and your mother will be all right, she's a smart and courageous woman and she has always managed to take care of herself."

"But she's all alone now! Without anyone to protect her!" Marika wailed, burying her face in her hands. Shani, who looked uncomfortable, stood behind her and patted her back.

"I have to go," he said eventually, "if Magda wakes up, she'll die from worry. Are you coming, Peter?"

"I'll stay with Marika," Peter said quickly. Despite his anger at the way she'd spoken about Sophie, he found it difficult to abandon her in such a pitiful state.

"As you wish," Shani said, shrugging and getting to his feet. "You have a key, right?"

"Yes," Peter answered, sitting on the arm of Marika's chair and hugging her.

Shani rushed out, and Marika continued to sob. Peter stayed where he was, muttering words of reassurance in Hungarian and planting kisses now and then on her wet hair. It took her quite some time to stop crying and to fall asleep. Peter carefully stood up, picked her up in his arms, and carried her to the bedroom she shared with her husband. He lay her on the bed and covered her with a blanket. Marika opened her eyes and smiled at him, barely awake, "You'll never leave me, Peter, promise?" she whispered.

"I promise," he reassured her and kissed her forehead. She curled up in the blanket like a content little kitten and fell asleep again.

**

Two weeks after that rough night, Yoshka and Martha arrived in Israel. Peter felt like he could finally be truly happy. His heart was overflowing with joy when he took a cab with Shani to meet his parents at the airport. And indeed, when he fell into his mother's arms, he thought there could be no happier person in the world than he. She burst into tears of relief and held him tight for a good few minutes before letting him go.

"Peter, my beloved son," she whispered, "I've missed you so much."

"I've missed you too, Mami," he said, "but now everything will be fine, you'll live near me and I'll take good care of you."

"What about me, don't I deserve a hug?" Yoshka asked, feeling neglected, and Peter quickly hugged him too.

"Where do you live?" his father asked as they walked arm in arm to the cab station.

"In Haifa," Peter answered, "I wrote to you, I'm studying at the Technion, it has the only engineering faculty in Israel."

"I want to live in a town called Ramat Hasharon," Yoshka surprised him. "Our friends Bila and Shari from Baja live there, as do many of our other friends from Hungary."

"But Papa, Ramat Hasharon is in the middle of nowhere, and it's like a small village," Peter explained, "whereas Haifa is a real city, not like Budapest, but still…there are plenty of places to go out to, and the weather is better than in the center."

"You could also live near me, in Jerusalem," Shani suggested, glancing at his sister, who was looking out the cab window at the view. "It's also a big city, and the weather is more like Europe's than anywhere else in Israel."

"I've made up my mind, I want to live in Ramat Hasharon, nowhere else," his father insisted stubbornly. Peter glanced at his mother and noticed that her lips were pursed. He could feel how nerve-wracked she was. He made an instant decision not to tell them about Yael or about their wedding until they relaxed and rested after the difficult trip.

They arrived at Shani's apartment and met Magda, who had gone to a lot of trouble and prepared a feast in their honor. Marika soon arrived, gave them big, warm hugs, and urged them to tell her how her mother was.

"Gizi's fine," Martha quickly reassured her, "she was interrogated for a few days, but she wasn't tortured, and they eventually released her, when they realized she had nothing to do with poor Sophie's irresponsible behavior."

"They even let her keep the apartment," Yoshka added, "and she asked to send you her love. She didn't want to send a letter with us, in case we were caught and it fell into the hands of the authorities, who would have then known of our plans to leave. But she really is doing well."

Marika nodded and stopped crying. Then she listened to her aunt and uncle as they told them how they'd escaped, glancing playfully at Peter now and then, but he was focused on his parents' stories and didn't notice her glances. That's why he was surprised when she asked, "So, my dear aunt and uncle, what do you think of Peter's wedding plans?"

His parents, Shani, and Magda stared at him in surprise. "Wedding?" his mother said, "Peter, are you getting married?"

"Yes," Peter said awkwardly, wishing he'd told them about it in the cab, and then he told them all about Yael.

"So, they are eight brothers and sisters?" his father said, still surprised, "Does she come from an Orthodox family?"

"No, her family's traditional," Peter replied, his heart sinking at the look on his mother's face. He'd imagined this occasion quite differently.

"Traditional? What is that?" his father asked, an amused glint in his eye.

"It's…they're of Sephardic origin, Bukharin to be precise, and in these families, it's customary to maintain religious practices, but their children are permitted to make their own choices. Yael leads a liberal life, she doesn't follow religious practices, only the high holidays and—"

"Sephardic? You mean one of those primitive people?" his father interrupted him sharply. His mother looked like she was about to burst into tears. Peter felt his blood freeze. He hadn't expected such blatant racism from his father.

"Sephardic, Ashkenazi, what does it matter?" Shani intervened, much to his relief. "We're all Jews here, Yoshka. I think that you're doing Peter a disservice when you attack him like that rather than being happy that he's found a woman he loves."

"Don't talk to me about your socialism now," Yoshka said angrily. "Peter is making a mistake! He doesn't realize that a common cultural background is necessary for a marriage to succeed."

"Like our marriage, Yoshka?" Martha intervened, glaring at her husband.

"Mami, Papa, stop arguing," Peter tried to get them to stop, afraid they would begin their new life in Israel with an argument. "Yael is a wonderful girl, and I fell in love with her after discovering that her cultural preferences are similar to my own. Wait until you meet her, you'll fall in love with her yourselves."

"I'm sure we will, Peterkum," his mother said, embracing him. "You're a smart man, and I know that you wouldn't fall in love with a woman who isn't right for you." As she spoke, she looked at Marika, who blushed. "Congratulations, my son, I can't wait to meet the woman you love."

***

From the moment Martha met Yael, she found her delightful—unlike Yoshka, who looked like he was sitting on pins and needles throughout the time they spent together, three hours to be precise, because Peter had to translate for both sides.

"Is this how you want us to live?" Yoshka questioned him venomously as they were about to say goodbye. "With you translating everything we want to say to your wife? When will you have time to work and study?"

"Papa, stop being so nice," Peter snapped sarcastically, feeling belittled. "In any case, you'll have to learn Hebrew, otherwise how will you live here?"

"That's why I want to live where my friends from Hungary live," his father snapped back obstinately.

Peter felt himself giving in. Suddenly, having his parents living nearby didn't seem like such a good idea. He knew that Yael, who was highly sensitive, would sooner or later notice his father's animosity, and he didn't want her to get hurt.

***

Two weeks later, before he'd had time to make up his mind, Yael surprised him by telling him that she'd found a small, rent-controlled apartment for his parents in Ramat Hasharon.

Reluctantly, Yoshka softened toward Yael when Peter told him she was the one who'd made his wishes come true. Peter now hoped that by the time the wedding took place, his father would have completely forgotten his initial reservations. Later, he thought, after his parents learned Hebrew and felt more self-confident in their new country, he could try to persuade them to move to Haifa to be near him and Yael.

As usual, Peter was overly optimistic. He never imagined that his plans could go awry precisely because Yoshka learned Hebrew so quickly.

***

Peter and Yael's wedding was held just months after his parents immigrated to Israel. Peter was over the moon. He danced a lot, joked around, and was happy to see that Yael's sisters also knew the waltz and tango. They laughed constantly at his jokes, and because he wanted to win over her family and friends, he divided his attention between them and his parents. He didn't notice that Marika was drinking wine at a dizzying pace.

Toward the end of the evening, Marika burst into heartbreaking tears and was dragged away by her distraught husband. However, the remaining guests could hear her shouting outside, bewailing the fact that Peter was now married, and asking herself and God what she would do without him. Peter felt the color drain from his face. Yael had asked him in the past to teach her a few words in Hungarian, and now he prayed that she didn't remember a word. His prayers were answered. Yael ran to him and asked what had happened to his cousin, and why she was crying outside. Peter tried to evade answering, but Yoshka, who was standing next to him, jumped in and explained, his voice mocking, that "Marika is in love with Peter."

"What?" Yael looked stunned. "But, she's…married."

"She has Hungarian marriage," Yoshka said dismissively, "and she said that she wouldn't care if Peter got married to Hungarian but Israelis are tough to do business with."

"What business?" Yael wondered, but Yoshka was now trying to calm Martha down, who was standing there on the verge of tears because of the embarrassing scandal that Marika had caused.

Although Yael stood by Peter's side when they said goodbye to their guests, her eyes told him firmly that he wouldn't be able to avoid a tough discussion that night.

They talked almost until dawn, and it was as difficult as he'd expected. Yael demanded to know what kind of business couldn't be done with Israeli women and wondered if it could be done with his friends from the commune. Peter decided to tell her about all the women in his life, starting with his relationship with Marika in their youth. At some point, he noticed that Yael was on the verge of tears. He hugged her and declared that it was all in the past and that since the day he'd met her, he hadn't even glanced at anyone else.

His words opened Yael's floodgates. "But how," she gasped between sobs, "how can I…trust you?" How can I…be sure that…it won't…happen again…in the future?"

"I promise you, it won't!" Peter answered, holding her close, his heart breaking from the pain she was feeling, "I wouldn't have proposed to you if I wasn't absolutely certain it was all behind me and that you're the woman I want to live the rest of my life with!"

"Only with me?" Yael sniffed.

"Of course, only with you," Peter smiled and kissed her on the lips, "I love you and only you!"

"But…you come from such a different background," she said weakly. "In your culture, it's okay for couples to swap and have extramarital affairs. How will you resist these temptations, when you were brought up to believe that it's actually a good arrangement?"

"That's not true, we aren't all like that," he answered firmly, feeling a stab in his chest as he recalled his parents' relationship. "Here, look at Magda and Shani, my aunt and uncle, they aren't like that, and there are many others who live the way they do."

"Do you promise me?" she asked, her eyes wide. She looked so vulnerable and helpless.

Peter stroked her head and whispered in her ear that he promised. To himself, he made a vow to do all that he could from ever hurting her again.

That's how he ended up deciding to distance himself from his three best friends, and from Marika, too, of course. Although Yael moved in with him in Haifa and never mentioned the talk they had on their wedding night, they saw less and less of Eva, Jano, Aniko, and her boyfriend. He used his work and studies to justify himself, but deep down he knew the truth. Finally, when he graduated, he and Yael decided to move to Ramat Hasharon, to live near his parents.

CHAPTER 21

Dawn was already breaking. Dad sighed as he looked toward the hospital building. "I don't understand why the surgery's not over yet," he said.

"Let's go find out what's happening," I suggested, feeling the worry seeping into my gut.

Dad got to his feet and began to walk heavily toward the entrance. I followed. We found the waiting room empty and froze in fear. "Where is everyone?!" Dad sounded panicky as he took my hand.

"I have no idea," I could barely get the words out. I was trying not to think about the various terrifying explanations behind their disappearance. My legs weak, I walked through the glass doors between the operating rooms and the waiting room, pulling Dad behind me.

A big, young male nurse stopped us immediately. "You can't come in here!" he said in a Russian accent.

"I know, but…we wanted to know what's going on with my sister," I stuttered. "She went in for head surgery hours ago and she…we don't know what happened. My mother and sister have disappeared. They were outside and…"

Just as I was about to burst out crying, I saw his face soften, "You mean the young girl with the abscess on her brain?" he asked.

"A young girl, yes," I replied, confused. "Noa, Noa Schwartz, but she had a tumor on her brain, not an abscess."

"I think it's her," the nurse smiled, "that was the only brain surgery we did tonight. She's fine, she's in the recovery room. You can go to the department head's office if you want more details."

I turned around without even thanking him and ran out. I could hear Dad gasping for air behind me. We were both panting by the time we arrived at the department head's door, which was closed. Without thinking twice, I turned the handle and opened the door.

Mom, Vered, and Gilad were inside with the department head and another three doctors, who were deep in conversation. Mom lifted her head. Tears filled her already red eyes, and they streamed out as soon as we burst into the room.

"Peter, Darya!" she cried out. "It's a miracle! Have you heard?!"

"We haven't heard a thing," I said quietly, leaning against the wall as I felt the blood drain from my body and weakness take over.

"Oh, I'm so sorry!" Vered stood up and rushed over to Dad to hug him. "We were so happy that we forgot to come outside to tell you."

"Tell us what?" Dad mumbled, as pale as the wall behind him.

"That Noa's fine," Vered sniffed, and Mom still sobbing, added, "It wasn't a tumor, it was an abscess."

"That's right, she had a kind of infection," the department head said, whose usual graveness had been replaced with a smile, albeit a hesitant one. "Sit, please, Mr. Schwartz…young lady…we were just explaining."

Gilad stood up, went out, and came back with two chairs. I sat down in one, my heart pounding so hard I was afraid I'd have to be hospitalized in intensive care.

"Noa had a brain infection caused by the streptococcus bacterium," the department head explained, "and because it is so rare—the odds of it developing is barely two percent—it never entered our minds that this could be the problem. The infection spread to the optic nerve area, which appeared to be a tumor, and there was no way to identify and confirm her condition without performing surgery."

"Paradoxically, it was the deterioration in her condition that saved her life," another older doctor continued. I didn't recognize him. "We had to operate immediately, before the abscess burst."

"Yes," the department head nodded, who suddenly seemed uncomfortable, "Professor Bondak is right. If she'd been flown out, it could have led to a deterioration in her condition or even caused the abscess to burst."

"And what now? Will she be okay?" Dad's voice was hoarse with anxiety and emotion.

"She'll be perfectly fine," the department head was beaming again, "we drained the abscess, and now she'll need intravenous antibiotics for two weeks. After that, she'll get well and regain her sight."

"It's too soon to determine if her optic nerves are damaged or not," Professor Bondak added gravely, "but she's young and the abscess had been pressing on the nerves for less than two weeks, so it wouldn't be too optimistic to assume that she'll almost completely regain her sight."

"What do you mean, almost completely?" I asked suspiciously, finding it hard to believe that the danger had passed and that those crazy doctors, who had almost killed my sister because of stupid statistical calculations, knew what they were talking about.

"She'll be able to see, but we have no way of knowing if her eyesight will be perfect," Professor Bondak answered, looking at the papers on his desk. "We'll only know that after she completes her course of antibiotics."

***

A week after her surgery, Noa's vision began to improve and, with it, the entire family's mood. Mom and Dad were floating on air with joy and relief, and Vered and I had to bring them back down to Earth. We barely managed to drag Dad to a lawyer for a notarized letter certifying that he was Martha Schwartz's only heir. Then, when I began to talk about returning to Hungary to handle the sale of Grandma's house, he became even more detached. I wanted him to come with me, because he spoke excellent Hungarian, but he wasn't prepared to leave Noa's side. It was as if he was still having trouble believing that she had truly recovered and that her condition wouldn't deteriorate again.

Otto called me almost every day to update me on developments regarding the sale of the house. He had a few buyers, but they were willing to pay far less than the house was worth. Mom wouldn't hear of it, so she urged me to go on my own, and when I hesitated, Oren offered to accompany me. Unfortunately, Oren was attending that family meeting and when I immediately shot the idea down, using the justified claim that he didn't speak Hungarian and, as such, he would be of no use to me, I noticed the sullen look on his face.

When we got home late that night, he sat down on the sofa and said, "Darya, I think we need to talk."

"About what?" I feigned innocence, mainly because I was tired.

"About us, something bad is happening to us, and I want to know what."

"We're good, Oren" I sighed and sat down beside him, "it's just…Noa's illness…and all the excitement over her recovery…it's all—"

"It's not just that. Ever since you got back from Hungary you've been acting weird. You're so distant I can barely touch you, and now you don't want me to fly over with you. Did something happen with that guy in Hungary? Something that I should know about?"

"Oren, don't talk crap!" I said, annoyed. "What does he have to do with anything? I don't want you to come to Hungary with me because you can't help me in any way there, and also because I haven't been working for a month now. Don't you think that at least you should be working and bringing in a little money?"

"There are more important things than money—our relationship, for instance."

"Our relationship is just fine," I declared, "and if we have a problem, it's not because of anyone else, it's about us, and I don't think that now's the time to discuss it. I can't deal with it now!"

"It has to be now, Darya," he said, taking both my hands in his and looking piercingly into my eyes. "Look me in the eye and tell me that nothing happened with that guy."

I looked into his honest and well-meaning eyes. I could see the desperate longing in them to hear that nothing had happened with Otto, and for that very reason, I could no longer lie.

"Okay, Oren," I sighed, "I'll tell you what happened. It's not what you think, I didn't sleep with him, I just…before I boarded the flight, he kissed me and…it excited me a little, that's all."

"That's all? Really? And now you want to go back on your own to spend another week or two, or who knows how long with him? Why? To carry on where you left off, to take the kiss that excited you so much to the next level?"

"No, not at all!" I defended myself, "You heard me ask my father to come with me. Do you think if I was planning to have an affair with Otto Molnar, I would have asked my father to be there? I don't want you to come and waste time instead of working, and also, I know that you'll be hostile toward him, which would only be natural, but it could make him take back his kind offer or something. He still can, you know."

"Then wait until Noa has completely recovered and go with your father when he's ready, what's the big deal?"

"The big deal is that if we wait, Otto could also go back on the agreement, you heard what my mother said."

"Then take Vered with you."

"I don't get it!" I shouted at him. "What are you trying to say? That I need to be watched? Is that how little you trust me?!"

"How can I trust you after what you told me?"

"Oren, you're blowing this out of proportion, really! What's the big deal? So we kissed, so what?"

"And since that kiss, Darya," he hissed, his lips pursed, "you have hardly let me anywhere near you. Can you tell me, with your hand on your heart, that the two aren't connected?"

I didn't respond. Suddenly, I felt deeply sad, when I realized he was right. I did think I had a crush of some sort, an inexplicable wave of chemicals that passes as quickly as it comes, but of course I couldn't tell Oren that.

"Maybe you're right, Oren," I finally answered gloomily, placing my hand on his knee, which was twitching nervously, "but let's say we run away from these issues, and I never see Otto Molnar again, it may happen again, with someone else. This is about our issues, and we have to deal with them, not avoid them."

"What are you really saying, Darya," his eyes flashed with anger, "that you want me to give you permission to see if you've fallen in love with someone else?!"

"I haven't fallen in love with him! Don't overreact! Maybe I was just…a little attracted to him or something…and I'm convinced I'll feel nothing the next time I see him. Look, Oren, I was in a terrible emotional state that night when Vered called and told me that Noa's condition had deteriorated, and he was so kind and considerate. And that, with all of those stories about my grandmother, I don't know, it's just a phase, I'm sure, it… nothing can happen with him now."

"I heard you on the phone with him," he grimaced, "and you sounded really into him. It hurts me to say this, Darya, but I'm not prepared for you to go there!"

"Excuse me?!" I challenged him. "What right do you have to stop me from going?! It's a family matter, my family's financial matter, and I have to take care of it, and you shouldn't be interfering at all! I've never given you any reason not to believe me before, and even now you have no good reason. I told you everything when I could have chosen not to, right?"

"Tell me, do you understand what you're asking of me? To sit here like an idiot waiting to see if the crush you have on another man is going to pass…so kind and considerate," he mimicked me. "What is this crap, Darya? You've completely lost your balance!"

"Well, what do you suggest?" my voice tremored as I asked. I knew what his response would be, and as much as I feared the possibility of breaking up, a part of me seemed to want to.

"No, what do you suggest?!" Oren asked aggressively, even though he looked like his world was in ruins. "That I step aside and free the way for you to examine what you feel for a man you met just a week ago?!"

"I don't know," I mumbled. I wanted to cry, but strangely the tears refused to come and release the heavy lump of grief inside me.

"You don't know, that's all you have to say to me after twelve years? Years in which you allowed me to believe that you were refusing to marry me for technical reasons? Years in which you let me believe that you truly love me? And all this time, you've just been looking for someone who you would feel strongly enough about to cut yourself free of…of…what was it, Darya?! What feelings do you have for me? Of dependence? Security? Are you, too, one of those girls who can't define themselves as women if they don't have a man to latch onto?!"

"That's not true, Oren," I said, my voice breaking. Finally, someone up there had decided to take pity on me and release the floodgate holding back my tears.

"What's not true?!" his voice rose to a shout, and he stood up and kicked the table so hard that the vase of flowers fell to the floor and broke. "What's not true?! That you've been messing me around? That you've never loved me? Tell me what's not true in what I said!"

"Be careful! You'll cut yourself!" I shouted as I watched him walking barefoot around the glass shards.

"Now you remember to be concerned about me?" He went to the laundry corner and returned with a broom and dustpan but didn't bother to put on shoes. "Are you kidding me? What do a few glass cuts matter? Do you understand anything of what I feel?!"

"I do, I totally understand," I said and went over to help him pick up the shards, "but…I do think you're overreacting. I've loved you all these years and I still believe I feel something…strong…for you. It's just that I panicked when I realized that…" I continued to defend myself. One of the shards penetrated my finger, and I started to bleed. Oren looked at me in despair. Then he straightened up and pulled me to the bathroom. He turned the faucet and let the stream of water wash the blood from my finger. Then he took a bandage from the closet and carefully wrapped my injured finger.

"Damn it, Darya," he said eventually, "I can't hate you even at moments like these. Enough! I can't take any more! This is it! I want you out of my life! Do you hear me?! It's over, I don't want to hear from you ever again! Do you understand? Don't call to ask me how I am and certainly not to tell me how you are! I'm tired, Darya, you've managed to wear me down. I never again want to feel as bad as I feel now!"

"But," I whined in shock, "I don't really want…to break up…I thought, maybe we'd…take a break."

"No break, no nothing!" he said decisively. "As far as I'm concerned, there is no such option. Either we stay together and you forget about this Otto person, I have no idea how—as far as I'm concerned, you can see a psychologist, a psychiatrist—or I don't know what. God!" He stopped talking and looked at me. I'm sure he could see the desperate shock and fear in my face, "You can't forget about him, can you? Even digging him out of your brain with a shovel wouldn't help!"

I lowered my teary eyes and looked at the floor. "Don't talk nonsense, I can forget him, and I will, as soon as I get back from Hungary!"

"And that's what I don't get, Darya. If you go, you have nowhere to come back to!"

"You can't be serious," I looked up and tried to catch his eye, but he turned away in disgust.

"I'm dead serious, more than I've ever been!" he replied quietly. "If you go now, don't even think of coming back."

"But why?" I felt intense fear creeping through my body. Oren had never given me an ultimatum before. I was suddenly afraid that he knew he was giving me no choice but to leave and that he no longer cared that much.

"Because I'm sick of your games," he said, confirming my fears.

CHAPTER 22

Early the following morning, I trudged off to my parents' home with two large bags and one suitcase. Much to my relief, there was no one there. They had probably stayed at the hospital all night to keep an eye on Noa, leaving no one to see me at my worst and force me to tell them what I was still having trouble digesting myself. Oren and I had broken up.

I tried to get those words out of my mind, where they kept repeating themselves like a broken record, and to concentrate on my trip to Hungary. I felt that it was the only thing I could do to improve my mood and that I needed to go as soon as possible. I tried to stuff the bag and suitcase that I wasn't planning to take into a corner of Dad's office, which used to be my room. I didn't want anyone noticing them and trying to figure out what they were doing there. Eventually, I stuffed them into the storage box under my old bed and sighed in relief. Performing such a complicated technical task was a sign that I still had some strength left. Then I called the airport and booked a ticket for the eleven-a.m. flight to Budapest. I now had two points to my credit, after successfully accomplishing another task. Somehow, I was managing to function, despite feeling like a vital part of my body had been removed as a result of my breakup from Oren.

Before leaving the apartment, I called my mother's cell phone to tell her that I was leaving for Budapest and to ask how Noa was. Mom told me that Noa was fine, she was progressing nicely, and wished me good luck on my mission. I hoped her wishes would apply to another area of my life, which was the reason I was embarking on this meandering path.

In the cab on the way to the airport, I prayed I would be able to sleep on the flight, if only to stop me from thinking about what had happened the night before. That, however, is not what happened. Throughout the three-hour flight, I kept turning the events over in my aching mind, rehashing all the harsh turns in our conversation, trying to find a thread to hold on to, a lifeline. It's impossible that Oren doesn't want to see me again, I panicked repeatedly, it'll pass. He'll think it over and realize what a mistake he's made. After all, he's loved me and only me for twelve years now, so how can he suddenly throw those years away and ignore them?

Naturally, I could have asked myself the same questions, but I preferred not to. Instead, I thought about how Oren had suddenly put pressure on me to get into serious mode, just when it was impossible, and I wondered if he'd done so intentionally. Could he, too, want a little freedom? The thought surprised me. He was also eighteen when we met and that big act of his— that no one else interests him—well, maybe he's feeling a sudden need to reexamine that himself? Just the thought of it was painful, so much so I could feel the pressure building up in my temples, but then I heard the crew announce that we'd be landing soon, and I realized it was due to the drop in the plane's altitude.

I hoped that Otto would be waiting for me at the airport, even though we hadn't discussed it in our last call. More so, I was praying that spending time with him would suppress all thoughts of Oren.

Otto was there waiting. When I saw him standing at the end of the passenger hall, wearing jeans and a black turtleneck sweater, my vision blurred. I had to stop for a moment, catch my breath, and slow down to hide my excitement from him.

I walked slowly toward him, and he gave me a light hug and a peck on the cheek. His smile made it clear that he remembered our goodbye kiss and particularly what I said to him afterward.

"You look wonderful," he said and took the suitcase from me. "I can see that you caught up on sleep at home."

"Yes," I nodded, just standing there, hoping he'd get the hint and sweep me up in his arms and kiss me passionately. Instead, he started walking toward the exit.

"Did you bring all the documents?" he asked as we got into his car.

"Yes."

"What's the matter, Darya, have you forgotten your English?" He leaned toward me and looked at my face, "The last time you were here, you had a lot more to say."

"I'm a little confused," I confessed shyly, "your behavior, all the goodwill and kindness you've shown me.... Tell me, what will you do after you transfer the house to me? Where will you live?"

"Me?" he looked surprised, "I can live anywhere I please. Hungary is a big country, and now that we're joining the European Union, half the world is opening up for me."

"How old are you anyway?" I asked. In Israel, only youngsters who have just completed their army duty answer in that way.

"I'll be thirty-five in May," he replied as he started the car. "Why? Do you think I'm too old to turn over a new page in life?"

"No, on the contrary!"

"What do you mean, on the contrary?" he smiled.

"Your positive attitude makes you seem much younger."

"Look," his face grew serious, "I'm an electronics engineer. My profession is in demand all over the world. In fact, my grandfather's will pretty much prevented me from leaving Baja. Now I feel free to start a new life wherever I want, even in Israel."

"Israel doesn't belong to the European Union," I answered, trying to hide my excitement that the idea had crossed his mind, even as a joke, "besides, you can't live there if you aren't Jewish."

"I could convert."

"Otto, you can't be serious!" I said, startled by fleeting images of us living in a rented apartment near the beach in Tel Aviv.

"Right now, not really," he laughed and patted my thigh lightly, a gesture that was intended to calm me down but that had the opposite effect, "but if you didn't have a boyfriend, I would seriously consider it."

"I don't have a boyfriend. We broke up," I blurted the words out as if they'd been waiting for the opportunity on the tip of my tongue.

"Really?" he looked at me and slowed down. "What happened?"

"A lot, it's a long story," I sighed. The memory of our upsetting separation brought me down again, and I didn't want to discuss it.

"Then can I kiss you properly now?" he asked and pulled over to the side of the road.

"To be honest, I was wondering when you'd ask," I answered with relief. He wrapped me in his arms and moaned as his lips touched mine. We kissed passionately for what felt like forever, until I felt his warm hand crawl under my sweater. I started feeling guilty and anxious.

"Otto," I pulled away from him, "I—"

"I understand," he said, pulling his hand away and starting the car. After he started driving, he put his arm around me again, this time over my sweater.

***

We arrived in Baja at dusk. The trip took twice as long as expected because Otto insisted on keeping his arm around me and kissing my head and face every three minutes or so.

"You're so adorable and sweet," he said, "I just can't stop kissing you."

"In the end, someone will murder you," I remarked in response to another angry honker protesting how slowly we were moving on the freeway.

"What do they know?" he answered dreamily, stroking my hair. "Nothing like this has ever happened to them."

"What is happening?" I prompted him.

"Don't you see? Darya, I fell in love with you before we even met. I fell in love with the image in your grandmother's picture and in the stories about her, and then you suddenly showed up, and the resemblance was incredible, as if it was our destiny."

I shied away in response to his confession so I could organize my confused thoughts. It hadn't occurred to me that it was my grandmother he'd really fallen in love with and that he was only projecting his feelings onto me. I, on the other hand, was head over heels in love with him, Otto Molnar, there was no other explanation for my crazy behavior. My stomach contracted in panic. Dad's warning was reverberating in my mind, refusing to stop…He's from a different culture, too romantic.

"Otto, that's just a romantic illusion," I eventually responded, almost whispering, a sharp pain spreading through my gut, "get it together, try to see me as I am. I'm nothing like my grandmother. Sure, I resemble her outwardly, but that's all. I'm not strong and brave like she was, not at all. When I try to imagine what I would have done in her place, I don't think I know. I probably would have shriveled up in a corner and died from despair."

"No way," he said and pulled me to him, "look how you functioned after your sister became ill. You traveled across the globe looking for money to save her. You wouldn't have been capable of dying quietly in the corner, knowing that the people you love are in danger. You would have acted precisely as your grandmother did!"

"Do you think?" The compliment thrilled me and I nestled up to him again.

"Definitely! You're an amazing woman. You're unbelievably strong and courageous—and you're beautiful and sexy to boot!"

"Maybe, but I can't cook," I warned him, "and at thirty, I still don't know what I want to do with my life, and in the meanwhile, I'm working as a flying waiter and I've been stuck on my master's thesis in history for five years."

"To the best of my knowledge, your grandmother also couldn't cook," he responded with a smile, "and I think your profession is wonderful. That way, you get to travel the world and learn so many new things, and as for your thesis, what's the hurry? Who cares if you do your doctorate at forty? What's wrong with that?"

"Where have you been all my life?" I sighed, firmly suppressing the tiny voice whispering in the back of my mind that Oren, too, thought just the same—that there was no fire to put out and that we could live life at our leisure without agonizing over it.

We arrived at the house and found a surprise waiting for me. Otto, who had probably guessed without me telling him that I lacked cooking skills, had prepared chicken paprikash and dumplings.

When I asked him how he'd guessed what my favorite Hungarian meal was, he smiled mysteriously and said, "You see? I know you better than you think."

We had a bottle of Hungarian red wine with the meal, and after we'd eaten, we both fell exhausted on the sofa, opposite the picture of Angelika and Adrianus.

"It's incredible how sad that picture is," I said, looking at it, "as if they both knew what would happen."

"What do you mean?" Otto asked, curious.

"I mean what happened to Adrianus shortly after the painting was completed. Didn't you know he was killed by some bastard who tried to rape the nun?"

"No, I don't know much about the painting, but it has a tragic feel to it. When I asked my grandfather, he was surprised and said that he thought only people who've experienced unfulfilled love can detect the sadness emanating from it."

"And hadn't you experienced that kind of love?"

"Me?" he smiled, "I was fifteen at the time, and I hadn't experienced any kind of love yet."

"And since then?"

"I don't know…" He sounded embarrassed.

"You don't know? That sounds evasive," I reached out and stroked his pale hair, "has nobody ever broken your heart?"

"Not really. I don't view love as something that should hurt me. If I don't enjoy it, then what's it worth?"

"Are you serious?" I asked, my interest piqued. He had an attitude to life that distinctly reminded me of my father's, or at least of the attitude he used to have.

"Absolutely. Don't you think so?"

"I don't know if we can always control it," I tried to remember having my heart broken, but I couldn't. Episodes from my dumb teen years, and even from my trip to South America after the army, when I thought that my heart was breaking, seemed ridiculous to me in retrospect.

"What would you do if, for instance, I wasn't interested in you?" I was posing a tricky question, but he didn't fall into the trap.

"You're something else entirely," he sat up on the sofa and took me in his arms. "Clearly my heart would shatter into smithereens, and no glazier could ever fix it."

"You are kidding, right?"

"A little," he kissed the tip of my nose, "but why should we occupy ourselves with hypothetical questions when we can occupy ourselves with practical love instead?"

"Do you think you could?" I played along, trying to buy myself a little time. The more enticed I was by the thought of sleeping with Otto, the more I was afraid of doing it.

"To me, it seems like ages ago," he paused, his face serious, "but if it's not right for you yet then I'll wait for however long it takes."

"And for now? Do I sleep on the sofa?" I suddenly noticed that we were already in the bedroom. An involuntary shiver of eager anticipation spread through my body.

"Are you crazy? I'm not that bad a host," he smiled, lowering me onto the wide bed, "you'll sleep here, and I—I'll find myself another bed."

"Where?" I asked as I pulled on his shirt, urging him to sit down next to me.

"Do you know how many rooms and beds there are in this house? He answered with a question, his eyes gleaming mischievously.

"Fine," I answered with a sigh, "but because you're such a generous host, I'll allow you to sleep here beside me, but only to sleep."

"Awesome, thanks," he lay down beside me, supporting his head with his hand. He looked amused. "Is this your way of testing me?"

"I just don't know what I want yet," I confessed in all honesty. I was hoping he'd do something, anything, to help me shake off the paralysis I was experiencing. It was so long since I'd flirted with a man, I'd forgotten how to.

"And? Would you like me to decide what you want?" He gently ran his hand over my face and then proceeded to my neck and the hollow between my breasts.

I tremored.

"Do you want me to continue?" His expression was still amused, but tender, and I knew that if I told him to stop, he would.

Maybe, just once in your life, do what you really want? I heard a tiny voice whispering from the back of my mind. I nodded, rising up on my knees and leaning over Otto, "I think I'll take it from here," I said and kissed him long on the lips.

***

The following morning, we went to meet Otto's lawyer in his office in the town center. The meeting was long and exhausting. I had to struggle to read all the small print on the documents that had been translated into English, even though I trusted Otto completely. Mom told me repeatedly before I left that even if he seemed as pure as an angel, white wings and all, I still had to be wary of his lawyer's wording. "Sometimes they trick people, even in ways that their clients are unaware of," she explained. And when Dad smiled skeptically, she went on to say, "Don't be naïve like Dad."

When the meeting was over, Otto asked if I wanted to have breakfast.

"Yes," I agreed, thinking we'd eat at home, but Otto pulled me into a friendly, homey café.

We sat down at a side table by the big window facing the street and Otto ordered coffee and crêpe-like pancakes with cheese and raisins, palacsintak they were called. This time, he asked me what I wanted before ordering.

The palacsintak tasted like home and reminded me of the pancakes that Grandpa Yoshka used to make for me and Vered when we visited him on our own. When Mom was around, she wouldn't allow us to eat rich or fried food, except on special occasions.

"How long do you think it'll take to sell the house for the appraised amount?" I asked.

"Quite some time," he replied pensively, "two hundred thousand dollars is relatively expensive for our market."

"Are you serious? For such a big house?" I said, surprised, "For that price, you can barely buy a two-bedroom apartment in Tel Aviv."

"Well, Israel is the Holy Land, so homes there are expensive," he chuckled, just as a beautiful, elegantly-dressed brunette stopped outside the window and looked at him in surprise. Otto's smile broadened and he waved hello to her, but she grimaced and stormed into the café.

"Who is she?" I asked nervously, but before he could answer, she came over to our table and started barking a hundred words a second in Hungarian at him. At the end of her speech, she opened her elegant purse and took out a bunch of keys, which she threw on the table before turning around and storming out.

Otto watched her leave and then looked apologetically at me.

"Who was that?!" I demanded to know, although it seemed pretty clear.

"That was Greta, my ex-girlfriend," he answered, his voice touched with amusement, "and as you could see, she has a very Hungarian temperament."

"What do you mean ex? When did you break up? Her anger seemed very fresh!" Again, Dad's warnings raised the alarms in my mind and I felt my stomach contract, or maybe it was Otto's amused reaction that was making me feel that way.

"We were together for…let me think." He furrowed his brow and I waited, afraid to hear that they broke up yesterday, "A year, yes, until last February, I remember it was snowing when we broke up."

"February? Two months have passed," I noted with relief, "so why is she still so angry?"

"I guess because of my keys," he explained, and after seeing the puzzlement in my eyes, he continued. "She kept ringing and asking me to come and get them, and somehow I never got around to it, so she probably thought there was still some chance of us getting back together, and now, after me with you, she must have realized that it wasn't going to happen."

"Oh," I said, although the story sounded a little lame to me, "and why did it end?"

"Oh, she was starting to bore me."

"She's very pretty."

"Yes, and she is just as superficial. All that she cares about is money and clothes."

"So why were you with her for a year?"

"Daryakum, what are you asking?" he smiled awkwardly. "You don't really want to hear the answer, I hope."

"Actually, I do," I insisted, feeling masochistic.

"Why, what will it give you? She's been history to me for ages," he took my hand and squeezed it. "What matters is you and me."

"True, but in order to know what will happen between us, I have to know a little about your history."

"Fine," he sighed, "if you insist. It's not that we were together for the entire year, we kept on breaking up and getting back together, until one day, she asked me to pick her up from her office and I caught her messing around with a colleague. She probably thought it would make me jealous or something and that I would never leave her again, but it had the opposite effect, and I wouldn't go near her after that."

"Because you were angry?"

"Not really," he stared, puzzled, "what was there to be angry about? I was just becoming bored by her idiosyncrasies and the scenes she caused."

***

The next morning, Otto went to work and I slept until noon. When I woke up, I walked around the big house, thinking about the things I didn't want to get into when Otto was around. I went down to the damp and dim basement that had plastic bags piled in the corners, and I tried to imagine how Grandma Martha's parents must have felt when they had to hide there, in their own home, from fear of the Arrow Cross and the Nazis. After a few minutes, the gloomy walls began to close in on me, so I went back upstairs. I looked for a flashlight in the kitchen drawers, and after finding one, I went back down.

The light of the flashlight made the basement look bigger, and in one corner, which had been in complete darkness before, I found a bunk with a thin mattress and a few folded woolen blankets on it. Could they have left the bed that my great-grandparents had slept on like this? I wondered, *or was it a penal colony where Otto was sent to sleep when he was a bad boy?* I kneeled carefully on the bunk, which stank of mold. Then I shone the flashlight on the adjacent wall to see if anyone had written something to shed light on the mystery. When I couldn't find anything, I began to rummage through the plastic bags piled up beside the bunk, where I found plenty of spoils: Mysterious images looked at me from faded pictures—men in suits and women in dresses stood facing the camera, their posture somewhat stiff, indicating that having their picture taken didn't come naturally to them. There were a few portraits, and I looked through them for familiar faces, but I didn't recognize anyone. In the end, the picture of a beautiful, blonde woman with her hair up caught my attention. Her eyes were deeply sad, even though her lips were smiling. Her face seemed oddly familiar to me. I didn't believe she was related to Grandma Martha, because as far as I knew, none of them had blonde hair. Then I realized why I thought I recognized her: Her smile resembled Otto's. She must have been his grandmother, Paul Molnar's poor wife, who'd had to live all her life with a man who loved another woman. That must have been why her eyes expressed so much sadness.

I rummaged through the bag and found letters, two of which were bound together with a rubber band. For some reason, I decided they were interesting, and I opened one. In the light of the flashlight, I scanned the faded letter, which had been written with a fountain pen in an unfamiliar language. I almost put the letter aside to return to the photographs, when my eye caught the signature, which was in Latin letters, and I shuddered. The name was Angelika. Excited, I opened the second letter, and again my eyes were met by cramped, unfamiliar words. When I looked at the bottom, I discovered a different signature. The name was Aggie or Agnam. I compared the two letters and saw that the handwriting was different. Someone who lived here, maybe Otto's grandmother, had corresponded with Angelika. That was very interesting. I checked the rest of the letters, but none of them contained Angelika's signature.

Otto, who seemed to be searching the house for me, called out and startled me. I ran up the stairs, still holding the photo and the two letters.

"Hi," he hugged me when I reached him, "where did you disappear to?"

"I was in the basement," I explained, "and I found this photo. It's your grandmother, right?"

Otto took the photo for me and looked at it for a while. "Yes, that's my grandmother Aggie when she was young. How beautiful she was!"

"And sad," I added. Otto looked at me blankly, then looked at the photo again.

"Do you think?" he asked.

"She looks sad, at least in the photo. Her eyes are terribly sad. And in my opinion, she had good reason to be—it couldn't have been easy living with a man who didn't love her."

"Well, I'm not convinced she knew that. I actually remember her as a very active and sociable woman. She was always having friends over, and my grandfather was the one who was quiet and introverted, I was the only one he talked much with."

"Well, clearly he was thinking about Martha all the time, and she compensated herself with social activities, surrounding herself with people so that she wouldn't have to stay alone with him and deal with his lack of love for her."

"Perhaps," Otto answered, his tone amused, indicating, to my disappointment, that his grandmother's pain didn't touch him at all. "I'm sure she compensated herself in other ways, too. As you can see, she was a very beautiful woman."

"Otto, you really are heartless," I complained, "how can you be so nonchalant about your grandmother's suffering?"

"Because she's already dead, sweetie, and I know that she wouldn't want me to torment myself with what happened to her sixty years ago. I'm certain that if the afterworld exists, then the four of them are finished arguing over what happened and are busy playing cards. Who knows, maybe my grandfather managed to beat yours for once."

This time, I burst out laughing, imagining the scene in my mind. At that moment, I also understood how Otto could live in the house without sinking into depression. He was undoubtedly a specialist in exorcising evil spirits. But somewhere deep inside, I made a footnote, once again confirming what my father had claimed: Otto and I had radically different attitudes to life.

"Look," I said, waving the envelopes at him, "there are letters, too. Your grandmother, it turns out, was corresponding with Angelika, the nun in the painting. Read it and the other letter, maybe your grandmother was sharing her feelings with Angelika."

Otto took the letters from me and took Angelika's out of its envelope first. He stared at it for a few seconds and said, "That's not Hungarian or English, I don't understand a word."

"It must be Latin," I said disappointedly, "do you think your lawyer can read Latin?"

"Maybe," he smiled and took the second letter out of its envelope, "but why is it so important to you?"

"Because…I don't know. It's strange that Angelika was corresponding with someone from here. Whose name is at the bottom of the second letter? Your grandmother's?"

"Yes," he replied, "do you want me to ask my lawyer now? He'll probably want to be paid for this too."

"That's fine," I said, "we'll pay him. It's important."

Again, Otto smiled forgivingly at me and went to the phone. A few minutes later he put down the receiver and said to me, "Sorry, he says he only knows a few words, not enough to read a whole letter."

***

Early on Saturday afternoon, when we got out of bed, Otto asked me if I wanted to join his friends for a picnic on the banks of the Danube. I agreed happily. I'd been wondering all week if he had any friends, although judging by the number of people who called him in the evenings, he seemed to have plenty.

The weather was wonderful. The strong shades of the blue Danube shimmered under the sun's merciful rays, the kind of which we almost never saw in Israel. A breeze teased our clothes and hair when we arrived at the gazebo where we were meeting his friends. We found two identical blondes there, who were busy setting the table. Otto kissed them both on the cheek and asked them something in Hungarian. They pointed at a long rowboat. There were eight on the boat, men and women, and they could easily have been taken from a movie from the 1940s, had they not been wearing Gap jeans and shirts.

Otto introduced me to the blonde twins, Ili and Kata and explained that I didn't have to remember their names, because they all just called them the blonde twins. I shook hands with them and they smiled politely. Then, when they thought we were looking at the boat, I noticed them whispering and giggling as they glanced at us.

"Were they also your girlfriends?" I couldn't stop myself from whispering to Otto.

"Who?" he looked at me, uncomprehending. When he saw me glance in their direction, he raised an eyebrow. "Oh, you mean the blonde twins. We've had a short fling here and there, nothing serious."

"With each individually or with both of them together?" I joked sarcastically, and Otto responded with a smile, but then he put his arm around my shoulder and said softly, "Daryakum, what are you worrying about? Baja is a small town, and these are my childhood friends. Obviously, I've had relationships of some kind or other with most of the girls. But that's in the past, really."

Just as he finished his last sentence, the group from the boat joined us. They were introduced to me with smiles, hugs, and a lot of noise. There were five men and three women, and they were amiable and easygoing with me, even taking the trouble to speak in English. When the last man and woman were introduced to me, as Diana and Latsi, I breathed a sigh of relief.

The picnic consisted of cold meats, cheeses, and heavy bread that looked home-baked. They all drank Czech beer and spoke a mixture of Hungarian and English.

"So, then," Latsi patted Otto on the shoulder, "do you still have your heart set on leaving us soon?"

"Very much so," Otto answered and winked at me, "as soon as I sell the house, I'm moving to Budapest. I've sent my CV to a few high-tech companies there, and I've already received an answer from one. I have an interview with them."

"Otto?" I whispered to him in surprise. "Why didn't you tell me about it?"

"I wanted to surprise you," he whispered back and kissed me. From the corner of my eye, I noticed the twins again, who for some reason were constantly in my field of vision. They were giggling and elbowing each other like silly teenagers. I decided that I really didn't like them.

"You must rent a big apartment in Budapest, so we can all stay with you," Diana said and put her arm around Otto's shoulder. Her husband winked at me and added, "We've suffered him for thirty years now, it's hard to give him up all at once."

"If that's how it is, I'll rent a room in an apartment hotel," Otto laughed in response, "and if you dare to come and visit me, you'll have to sleep in a cardboard box on the street."

"Ye, ye," a woman by the name of Klara joined in the banter, "you aren't even capable of leaving a cat out on the street."

With that, I definitely agreed. Otto really was one of the most generous and compassionate people I'd ever met. I laughed with them and took a big slug of beer from the bottle, which was a little too heavy for my taste. I felt much better with the new direction the conversation was taking. I felt warm inside when I thought about Otto moving to Budapest, where we could meet more easily. Although my flights to Budapest didn't usually include a layover, sometimes we received surprising bonuses. Besides, Budapest was much easier than Baja to get to from other European capitals.

Another couple, emerging from behind a hedge, caught my eye. The beer caught in my throat and I started to cough. From afar, the woman looked very similar to Greta, Otto's ex. He patted me on the back to help me stop coughing, and everyone else looked to see what I was looking at. The couple came closer, and unfortunately, the woman was indeed Greta. She waved smilingly at them from afar and tightened her grip on the man's waist. He turned to her and gave her a long kiss on the lips. One of the twins said something in Hungarian and they all laughed.

Greta and the man, who was extremely handsome and looked somewhere around twenty, finally came over to us. They all hugged and kissed her, and the annoying twins fawned over her. She introduced everyone to the dark, young man, whose features seemed slightly Mongolian, and I watched Otto's reaction. When his turn came to shake the man's hand, I thought I saw his face twitch nervously, but for just a blink of the eye.

Then he pulled at my hand and said in English, "This is Darya, my girlfriend. Darya, this is Greta, whom you've seen but not actually met."

Greta, smiling radiantly, held out her hand and shook mine. "I'm very pleased to meet you, Darya, your name is beautiful. You must be Italian."

"No," I replied, "actually, I'm Israeli."

"Israeli?" she sounded surprised, and she glanced quickly at Otto, obviously to provoke him. "Now I understand everything, so you must be Jewish, then."

"I certainly am!" I declared defiantly and asked, "Why? Is that a problem?"

"No, on the contrary, it's nice, because my Frantz is also Jewish," she answered and pointed at the dark man, who held his hand warmly out to me. "You must have things in common to talk about, and at least that way, he won't be bored."

Still talking, she turned her back on me and walked over to the table, where the women were now sitting. They all started talking to her in Hungarian, whereas the men, who were sitting on the blanket to the side, began a game of poker. Franz, who looked uncomfortable, stayed with me on the blanket, as if he didn't know what to do with himself. I felt sorry for him, and I offered him a bottle of beer. He smiled gratefully, leaned against the side of the gazebo, and asked, "Tell me, are you really from Israel? Were you born there?"

"Yes," I replied, "and where are you from?" He seemed shy and looked much younger than the rest, leaving me to understand that he hadn't grown up with this crowd.

"I'm from Budapest, I grew up there, and unfortunately, I've never visited Israel."

"Well, you're still young," I encouraged him.

"I wanted to come and join your army when I was eighteen," he continued talking to me but his eyes were on Greta, who had moved to sit with the men and had shoved in between Otto and Latsi," but my parents refused and I'm an only child, so I gave in to them."

"I can understand them," I said, just as Greta put her arm around Otto and whispered something in his ear. With extreme difficulty, I continued talking, "They probably wouldn't mind you going to Israel just for a visit."

"No way, they barely agreed to me coming to Baja, even though I'm here to work," he responded. "My mother calls me every day and cries over the phone that she misses me."

"Really?" I asked distractedly, fully focused on Otto and on the hope that he'd shake off the witch already and move away.

"Yes, but Greta doesn't want me to leave," Frantz said, his face forlorn.

Otto finally stood up and came to join us. He asked Frantz to take his place in the poker game and invited me for a walk along the river.

"Do you want to go home?" he asked, holding my arm.

"No, why now? Just when things are getting interesting?" I challenged him.

"Darya, my gorgeous," he hugged me, "don't take Greta seriously, she's just putting on an act to make me jealous, and you."

"In my case, she's doing quite a good job."

"Stop, really, I've already explained to you that I'm not interested in her. And I'm planning to move to Budapest soon anyway."

"She could always follow you there. Her boyfriend, Frantz, is also from Budapest."

"Oh, did he tell you his whole life story?"

"Just about, and if we're on the subject of stories, what was she whispering in your ear?"

"Oh, that you're delightful and that I shouldn't leave you alone with Frantz for too long," he smiled apologetically. "You see? That's her style; infantile, stupid, and as transparent as a little girl's."

"So why were you with her for so long?" I asked again. "Okay, I get it, you split up and got back together all the time, but why? What made you go back to her?"

"Is that what's important to you now?" he bent over, picked up a small stone, and threw it at the river. The stone skimmed the water a few times before sinking.

"It's important to me to know, because I want to be sure that it won't happen again."

"Darya, listen to me," he stopped and looked deeply into my eyes, "I love you! There is no way in the world that someone like Greta will make me give you up! Look at me," he turned around, and I did the same; Greta was sitting surrounded by the men, who had stopped playing, and she was flirting with them and giggling. "That's what she lives for—to feel like she's the center of the universe, that all the guys want her, that's her whole story. That's why I said that she's superficial. And that's why she chases me a little more than the others, because I refuse to play along with her anymore."

"Are you certain?" I turned to look into his eyes. Otto looked back candidly, his blue eyes that I had grown to know and love shining, and said, "I'm a million percent sure."

"I love you!" I said, and hugged him closely.

"Wow, that's the first time you're telling me that, you know that? You're such a little miser!" he laughed and kissed me. The heavy stone weighing on me slowly began to crumble. I kissed him back, allowing myself to be swept away with passion, and I didn't care that they were all watching from afar.

***

That night, when we were lying in each other's arms after a few hot rounds of lovemaking, I suddenly remembered to ask, "Say, Otto, how come none of the women in your clique are angry at Greta?"

"Why should they be?"

"Because of the way she behaves, because she flirts with all the men and gets all the attention. I, for instance, would get extremely irritated, especially if I was in Diana's place. Did you see how her husband was devouring Greta with his eyes, as if he were imagining the two of them in bed?"

"He has no need to imagine it, they've already slept together," Otto laughed. "Latsi was Greta's boyfriend for three years, and they also broke up and got back together all the time until he had enough of her and chose Diana, who was always very stable and much smarter than Greta. What does she have to be concerned about, I don't understand?"

"And I don't understand how you all live like this, with all the drama,"

I sighed. "All the men have dated Greta, and everyone's friends with everyone. It sounds like both heaven and hell."

"That's life, isn't it? Both heaven and hell," he said and leaned over me, pulling the sheet from between us. I surrendered my body to his kisses, trying to focus on the wonderful sensations, trying to avoid thinking about how a person with such a light-hearted and hedonistic worldview could ever get used to my own.

***

We spent Sunday at home, making plans and packing. I had to fly back to Israel the next day, and Otto wanted me to take the painting of the nun and the bear back to Israel with me, as well as Grandma Martha's portrait. "Unless you want us to go to the art museum in Budapest and ask them to evaluate them first," he said. "You should probably insure them before they're thrown about on the plane," he added.

His suggestion required me to call my parents. I really didn't want to be met with Mom's angry looks afterward, after she discovered that I'd dumped the valuable paintings in the cargo hold and put them both at risk.

My mother didn't let me down. She immediately said that Otto was right and that I should do as he said. Dad, of course, quickly agreed with her—he also wasn't looking for trouble.

"How are you otherwise?" he asked me, after we'd agreed upon the practical matters, "Are you enjoying your time with Molnar's grandson?"

"Very much," I answered tersely.

"Well," he grumbled, "just come back already, we miss you terribly."

I wanted to ask him who "we" referred to and to find out if Oren had visited them or called and told him that we'd separated. On second thought, I changed my mind, assuming that I'd be giving Dad an opening to cross-examine me.

***

At dinner, Otto was deep in thought and quieter than usual. When I asked what the matter was, he answered simply, "I'm sad because you're leaving tomorrow, and I have no idea when we'll see each other again."

"Oh, Otto, you're so sweet," I stroked his arm and put my head on his chest, "we'll see each other very soon, I promise. I have plenty of free tickets that I haven't used yet, and I can come whenever I have a few days free between flights."

"When do you think that will be?" he grumbled. "You haven't told me."

"I don't know exactly when, but tomorrow, when I land in Israel, I'll go straight to our dispatch desk, pick up my flight plan for the month and call you and let you know, okay?"

"Okay," he seemed a little happier, and I made a note to myself that I had nothing to worry about. By the look of him at dinner, he'd be counting down the days until he saw me again.

CHAPTER 23

Dad surprised me by being at the airport to pick me up. I asked him to wait while I ran over to the dispatch desk for the coming month's flight plan. I was thrilled to see I had four days off the following week, which meant that I could visit Otto. I called him right away and told him. He sounded over the moon and I left the office with a grin on my face.

Dad, who'd been waiting for me in the car, looked at me for a minute before finally saying, "You look happy."

"You make that sound like a bad thing."

"Not at all. I think it's great, I'm always pleased to see you like this. How was it in Baja?"

"Awesome, it's a beautiful place. But Otto doesn't want to stay there for some reason, he's planning to move to Budapest after he sells Grandma's house."

"He's already shared his plans with you, has he?"

"Yes. I asked him what he plans to do. I felt a little uncomfortable at the thought of him being homeless because of us."

"And did you tell him about your own plans?"

"What do you mean?" I asked in surprise, then I noticed a hint of concern in his face, even though he was trying to keep his face expressionless. "I see that Oren told you we broke up."

"Yes," he replied and looked at me. "Do you want to tell me about it, perhaps over coffee? We could go to a café."

"Okay," I sighed, "we probably should talk, just the two of us before everyone starts badgering me with irritating questions."

Dad tried his best to be considerate and tread carefully, and he didn't interrupt me with questions, waiting for me to finish telling him the story behind our breakup. After I was done, he sighed and asked, "How did you get into such a tangle, Darya? I did warn you about that man and his romantic charm."

"He has nothing to do with it, Dad, really. Things between me and Oren were coming apart at the seams before I even met him. Maybe he was a catalyst and he put us on the spot so that we'd have to take a better look at the problems we were experiencing. And Oren, instead of addressing the issues, chose to give me an ultimatum, which was what lead us to break up."

"Then he's to blame now?"

"He…I don't know…in any case, maybe it's good that it happened now and not later, when we were already married with two kids."

"I'm not sure that it had to happen at all. Don't you think it's a little unfair to compare a man who you lived with for twelve years, with all the burnout involved in that, to a man who you've only just met?"

"I've never compared them to each other, Dad, it's just that…I don't know what happened to me. Otto is so special that you just can't help falling in love with him."

"Precisely, special because you're from such different cultural backgrounds."

"Dad, that's enough, stop it. You're making me feel like a moron."

"Heaven forbid, Daryakum, I simply think that you're a bit naïve. But you know I respect your choices. Just promise me that you won't pin too many hopes on him."

"Okay, okay," I grumbled, "I promise. How much longer do you think you can protect me, Dad? I'm a big girl, you know."

"You'll always be my little girl," he smiled and stroked my hair. "Tell me, what are you going to do now? For instance, where are you planning to live?"

I didn't respond. The truth was, I'd tried all week not to think about it. With all the excitement of a new relationship, any thought of life back home without Oren made my heart contract.

"Darya, don't get me wrong. Mom and I would be tickled pink if you moved back home."

"I know," I said, feeling the tears well in my eyes, "Tell me, did Oren come over or did he just call?"

"He came over, and he looked fine."

"Good," I said, my throat constricting, "I'm happy he's okay. I…I…" Against my will, I burst into tears. Dad put his hand on my shoulder, looking at me with obvious concern.

"Now, now, Daryakum, why are you crying? Because of Oren? I'm convinced that you two could still get back together, if only you'd go to him and talk—"

"—It's not because of that, it's just that…" In fact, I was having trouble explaining even to myself why I was crying. Maybe I was releasing all the emotion I'd been feeling after all that had happened, after all the intense developments, which I hadn't had time to stop and really think about. It wasn't easy saying goodbye to the person I'd shared twelve years of my life with, and it was terrifying and disconcerting to then immediately find myself head over heels in love with someone else.

"Dad, don't worry," I continued, "I'll be fine," I assured him weakly, as soon as the tears subsided. I picked up a cloth napkin from the table and wiped my face with it. "I do intend to hang out at your place, but just for a month or two until I find my feet again. Is that okay?"

"You can hang out for as long as you want. Vered and Gilad are back in Haifa, so it won't be too crowded."

"Tell me, what's with Noiki?" I asked, embarrassed that I hadn't thought of asking about her before.

"She's totally fine. She can see perfectly now, even the things she shouldn't see at all."

"What do you mean?"

"That a few minutes after Oren came to visit her, she was already asking him if you'd broken up and why, and before he could answer, she told him that she'd be happy to take your place as his girlfriend."

"Cheeky!" I smiled, "And what did he say?"

"He said that yes, you'd broken up and that her offer was very tempting, and then she asked him if he'd also be willing to take Mickey, and to that he replied that he'd have to think about it."

"You don't say."

"Yes," Dad looked at me carefully, "I hope that you realize that a guy like Oren probably won't be on his own for very long. Before you know it, someone else will snatch him up."

"Do you want me to start crying again?" I asked, feeling a giant pit growing inside me at the thought.

"No, but I think that you have to open your eyes and face facts, to weigh whether you really want to lose Oren to an illusion."

"Dad," I sighed, "Otto is not an illusion, you don't realize how much he loves me. In fact, he loved me even before we met."

"What?!"

"Yes, he told me that he fell in love with Grandma's painting and with the stories about her, and when he met me and saw how much I was like her, he realized that he'd been waiting for me all his life."

"Darya, Darya," Dad put his arm around me and shook his head, as if he thought that Otto and I were hopeless cases, "did you forget what I told you about the romantic side of Hungarians?"

"No, I didn't forget, I even told him that it sounded too romantic and totally insane. But he convinced me that I really am like Grandma, even in character. Don't you agree?"

"Me? I always thought that of all my girls you're the most Hungarian, and yes, you're also a lot like Grandma," he sighed, "but I'm not so sure I'd want you to have a life like hers."

That's when I remembered that I had Angelika's letter with me, in my purse. "Dad, you can read Latin, right?" I asked.

"Yes," he replied, "why?"

"Because I have two letters here that I'd like you to read. One is from Angelika to Aggie, Otto's grandmother. The second seems to be from Aggie to Angelika." I took the two letters out of my purse and handed them to him.

Dad put on his glasses, opened one, and began to read. "Interesting," he said, "basically, Angelika sent a letter to Molnar asking him for the painting of the nun and the bear. Hold on, when is this letter from?" he asked suddenly and grabbed the envelope on the table. He examined the postmark and then exclaimed, "No way, it's impossible!"

"What?!" I almost shouted, no less excited than he.

"The stamp is from May 1945, and the letter was sent from Paris! That's incredible! We always thought that Angelika went missing in Hungary!"

"What?!" I was stunned. It had never entered my mind that Angelika could have disappeared. For some reason, I believed that God would have rewarded such a wonderful, pious woman with a long and peaceful life.

"Yes," Dad said excitedly, "Angelika never reached Imre! He waited for her in Menton and wrote to us and to Shandor only a few months later to ask what had happened to her. Naturally, we began to look for her, but no one had seen her since she left our house in the spring of '45. A few months went by and we stopped the search since we had nothing to go on. Heavyhearted, we assumed that she'd tried to find Molnar in the camp where he was being detained to ask him for the painting and that she'd probably run into Russian soldiers who'd murdered her and hidden her body; which is what we thought had happened to Raoul Wallenberg, another man with a pure soul who saved many, including me, just to mysteriously disappear."

"But what do you think happened to her?" I asked, now in suspense. "Maybe she decided to return to the convent where she grew up and to live a life of seclusion."

"I don't know, let me read it again," Dad responded and returned his attention to the letter. I waited in anticipation, as if my future depended on it, until again Dad exclaimed, "Here it is! She's asking them to send the painting to the San Florence Abbey near Saint-Jean-de-Luz in the French Basque region. It's unbelievable! It seems that she really did decide to go back. But why didn't she at least let one of us know? We were all so worried! Poor Imre couldn't live without her and died of a broken heart a few years after she disappeared!"

"I also don't get it," I replied thoughtfully, "but I have to find out what happened!"

***

Psychologists claim that the ability to adapt rapidly to change indicates high intelligence. In light of this fact, and the speed with which I adapted to living with my parents again at the age of thirty, a week later, I found myself wondering why I'd never been recognized as gifted. Although my old room, which had been turned into Dad's office, was a constant mess, and I had to jump over two bags and an open suitcase to get in and out, it didn't stop my mood from soaring to new heights every day, especially after flights, when I would sit at Dad's computer and read Otto's messages telling my how much he missed me.

As Dad had predicted, Noa's rapid recovery had a radical effect, even on my mother, and she gallantly ignored the mess I was making of their home. Either that or she couldn't see it under the mess that Mickey left in his wake as he bounced around.

Noa was dismissed from the hospital a week after I moved in, and she filled our home with light, joy, and complaints. Still, even living in a two-and-a-half-bedroom apartment with Mom, Dad, Noa, and the dog couldn't dampen my happiness, especially when every passing day brought me closer to my next trip to Hungary.

I got together with Oren only once, to sign the form removing me from his bank account. Although he offered to transfer some of our joint savings to my account, I adamantly refused, knowing full well that the term "joint" used to describe the account was only a kind figment of his imagination. Basically, all the money was his.

He seemed distant and reserved, and when we left the bank and I suggested having coffee together, he quickly refused. "I have a few more errands to run, and I'm flying to New York tonight for a week," he said, avoiding my eyes and smashing my heart into smithereens again. But a minute later, I received a text from Otto, reminding me that we'd be seeing each other that night, and my heart healed with surprising speed.

***

When I arrived in Baja, Otto told me he had serious buyers for the house. The next day, they came over to meet me and put in an offer of a hundred and eighty thousand dollars. They were a very nice, Hungarian couple in their thirties, and they were planning to move to Baja from Debrecen to open a rowing club on the Danube. They had three nice children, who were polite and quiet until they were allowed to go outside to the yard, where they played around and screeched loudly like normal children.

I watched them through the window, then realized with surprise that it was the first time I'd seen a family with three children here. Otto looked at me as if reading my mind, and after they left, he told me how rare young couples with three children were in this part of the world. "But luckily we found them," he added, "no person on their own or even a couple would go for such a large and expensive home in a place like Baja."

In the evening, I consulted with the family on the phone, and together with Vered and our parents, we decided to sell the house to the nice couple at the offered price. Although Mom thought we could bargain a little, when I told her to come and do it herself, she backed down and agreed to close the deal.

We met with them again the next day, this time at Otto's lawyer. We signed a few papers, determined the payment terms, and I transferred the ownership of the house to them. The lawyer concluded the meeting by saying, "Wonderful, now shake hands. The money will be in your bank account in Israel within a week."

When we got back to the house, Otto gave me the exciting news: He'd been hired by IBM in Budapest, and he would be starting there the following month.

"Next month is May," he added, "which is when I celebrate my birthday, so it's a little symbolic, don't you think?"

"I do, I sure do," I hugged him enthusiastically, thinking about the best thing of all—in Budapest, the threatening shadows of Greta and the irritating twins would no longer be hanging over us.

Otto decided that we had a lot to celebrate and suggested meeting up with his friends at a bar, but I said no, I was too tired and I'd rather celebrate at home on our own. He didn't object, and he went to the kitchen to prepare dinner, which we had with a bottle of champagne and the same fine cognac we had the first night we met.

Then we moved to the bedroom and made the walls blush at the indecent acts we performed on each other. I fell asleep in his arms at dawn, feeling like I was the happiest woman in the world.

***

The next time I was in Hungary, I met up with Otto in Budapest. He was staying at a hotel and looking for an apartment, and I went along on his search. On the second afternoon, we went to look at an apartment on the Heroes' Square, near Andrassy Avenue, just across the road from where Gizi lived. The moment we walked into the apartment, which had huge windows, high ceilings, and was bathed in bright natural light, Otto stated, "This will be our apartment."

I thought it was a good choice, because the other apartments we'd looked at were dark and depressing, but mainly because I was happy that he said "our." Otto stayed in the kitchen to discuss matters with the realtor while I wandered around the apartment, imagining it after we furnished it.

It wasn't particularly big, especially compared to the house in Baja. It had two small bedrooms, a living room, a small kitchen, and a tiny bathroom. However, it was so bright it looked bigger, and I immediately felt at home.

In the evening, we had dinner at a restaurant called Getto Gulyas, which had an old-fashioned, European style to it. Otto ordered us red Hungarian wine and veal goulash, which he insisted was the best dish on the menu. After we drank to finding an apartment, he suddenly took my hand and asked, "What do you think of the apartment? Do you like it?"

"It's awesome! Really!" I answered, taking a sip of wine, which was a little heavy for my taste, but smooth and pleasant.

"Awesome enough to move in together on a permanent basis?" he continued to stare into my eyes. I was speechless with confusion. Otto burst out laughing.

"What's the matter, Darya? Did the cat get your tongue?"

"No," I said, feeling myself blush, "it's just that I haven't thought about it."

"What do you mean? We're a couple now, aren't we?"

"Yes, but my job is in Israel."

"Can't you ask to fly out from here instead?"

"No, I don't think so," I muttered, "I don't know of anyone with an arrangement like that."

"Will you find out? Maybe there's the option and you just don't know."

"Okay, but don't count on it too much."

"Fine, but promise me that you'll come here often," he asked.

"I'll come at every opportunity," I replied and kissed him. "Do you think that I can bear being away from you for more than a few days?"

"I hope not." Otto took my hand again and looked deep into my eyes, "By the way, what does your family think about our relationship?"

Our meal arrived, saving me from squirming in an attempt to come up with an answer. As I tasted the goulash, which was heavenly and shot right to the top of my list of favorite Hungarian dishes, Otto winked and said, "From your reaction, I understand that they aren't very enthusiastic about me."

"Who?" I tried to feign innocence.

"Your family."

"Not enthusiastic?" I repeated, trying to buy time and find a nicer way of putting it. "Well, that's not quite accurate. Firstly, they don't know you yet, and secondly, they trust me not to fall in love with some…monster."

"Thanks for the compliment," Otto smiled sardonically, "and when do you plan on introducing us, so they can see for themselves that I'm not a monster?"

"Otto, to be honest, do you know when we introduce our partners to our parents in Israel? When we want to get married," I stared cheekily at him, hoping that would scare him off and make him leave me alone. The idea of introducing him to my father and then hearing his fixed opinion on Otto's worldview on monogamy frightened me. I still didn't know if he was wrong about Otto being an old-fashioned European romantic.

"Are you trying to scare me?" He leaned his head closer to mine,

"Because you really aren't. If you say you want to marry me, we can go tomorrow to choose a ring."

"Otto," I gasped against my will, overwhelmed with unimaginable happiness, "are you being serious?"

"Yes," he answered simply.

"You hardly know me, we aren't even living together yet, how can you want to get married so soon?"

"I love you, Darya, I told you a long time ago. I feel like I've known you all my life."

"I love you too, Otto," I tried to speak calmly, panicking from the intense emotion I was feeling. A minute ago, he'd been talking about buying a ring, and I was almost tempted to say yes.

"But?"

"But what?"

"From your tone of voice, a but should come next."

"Okay," I smiled, "there is a but. Don't you think we're moving too fast? A wedding is something you do after you've lived together and your plans are in sync. What will our life be like if we get married tomorrow morning? Precisely the same—you'll be living here, and I'll be in Israel, and I'll fly over to visit every opportunity I get, just as I promised."

"That's right," he confirmed, "and what's wrong with that?"

"Nothing, but if that's the way it is, I don't see the point of having to get married."

"I didn't say we had to, you were the one who brought up marriage."

"Because you want to meet my parents."

"So that we can have some kind of future together."

"Otto, really. Do you think that if my parents don't like you, even though I can't imagine it, that it'll make me end our relationship? What is this, the Middle Ages? They can't force their will on me, and nor would they want to."

"I know, sweetie, but still—I don't understand why you're so opposed to the idea."

"I'm not opposed to it, Otto, it's just…you see, that ex-boyfriend of mine, the one I told you about, we were together for twelve years. And my parents were very fond of him, and it was really hard for them when we broke up, so I want to give them time to get used to the idea that we're no longer together and that my new boyfriend's not Jewish and is also the grandson of my grandmother's lover."

"You were together for twelve years?" he seemed stunned. "That's a long time. It's almost like being married. Why, then, did you break up?"

"Because he was pressuring me into getting married," I mumbled half of the truth. I couldn't tell him that he'd played a big part in the breakup.

"Oh no!" he replied, his face startled. "If so, I've made a fatal mistake, proposing to you! I beg you, please erase it from the record."

"Stop it," I kicked him lightly under the table, "stop laughing at me!"

"I'm not laughing at you, Darya, I'm really frightened. I had no idea that you're one of those women who don't ever want to get married."

"You see?" I smiled triumphantly. "I told you that you don't know me yet. Go figure what else you may discover."

"Darya, my love, nothing I find out about you will change the fact that I'm madly in love with you." Then he hugged me and whispered softly in my ear, "I will love you even if you never want to get married, and I don't care if we live this way forever, with you running around the globe and landing in my arms to rest from your travels. That would also be just fine."

***

The next day, we went to the art museum and Otto left Imre's two paintings with them to be appraised for me. An older woman saw us in her office and introduced herself as Margot Kellner, the museum curator. She smiled kindly and even offered us coffee and cookies, but she didn't speak much English, so she and Otto did most of the talking.

"All right," he finally said to me, "she says that they're willing to buy the painting of the nun and the bear for twenty million forints, and you—"

"What?!" I interrupted him with a shout that reverberated through the museum, and I knew that I'd made a few birds on the street fly over the trees in panic. "How can it be twenty million?!"

"Calm down," he smiled, looking apologetically at Madam Kellner, who was completely taken aback. "Twenty million forints is…that's just under half a million dollars." Then he took his phone out of his pocket and tapped away, "In fact, it's exactly four hundred and eighty-three thousand dollars. She says that Imre Schwartz's paintings are very rare, and this painting is particularly impressive. On the other hand, for your grandmother's portrait, she's offering only twenty thousand dollars."

"You're kidding!" I could barely get the words out. Even in dollars, the amounts sounded insanely high, "That's unbelievable!"

"You're right," Otto nodded and with an official, businesslike tone, he continued, "She was also honest enough to explain to me that if you put it up for auction at a place like Sotheby's you can get a lot more for it."

"Okay," I said, "please thank her for me. I have to call my parents. This really requires a family discussion."

***

My parents were thrilled by the news, but they were on the same page when it came to not selling the paintings to the museum. "We'll keep Grandma's portrait," Dad said, "and as for the nun and the bear, send the painting here for now. We'll think about it later."

"I don't think I want a painting of a nun hanging on the living room wall," Mom said, who was talking from the other phone. "In my opinion, we should put it up for auction, as the museum curator suggested."

"Yael, you've never even seen the painting," Dad argued, "why not see it first and then decide if you want it on the wall or not?"

"Dad's right," I said, "and anyway, I'm planning to find out where Angelika disappeared to. Who knows, I may find out she's still alive and living in a convent. I'm sure she'd want the painting back, or at least see it. We owe her at least that, right?"

"What are you now, Darya, a detective? I don't like it," Mom sighed, but in the end, she said, "All right, send them both here."

Only after we hung up did I allow myself to burst out laughing at the thought of my mother refusing to hang a painting worth half a million dollars in the living room, just because it depicted a nun. Otto asked me what was so funny and I told him about the conversation. To my surprise, he didn't find it at all funny.

"I can smell that your mother's going to give us trouble over our relationship too," he said, his face sad.

"No way, Otto, it's all in your mind," I quickly reassured him. "In fact, she knows that I'm here with you now and she didn't say a word about it."

"Really?" he tried to smile, "That's good."

"It's excellent," I assured him, "my mother isn't one to keep her criticism to herself."

Actually, I had no idea if Mom even knew what kind of relationship I had with Otto. For understandable reasons, I'd only told Dad. Although I didn't swear him to secrecy, I knew that he would spare her the grief until he was certain that he had no other choice.

***

In the evening, I called Gizi and told her I was in Budapest. I asked if I could visit her with Paul Molnar's grandson. Gizi replied that she'd welcome a visit.

"Come," I told Otto, who looked at me in surprise, "you wanted to meet my family, right? Well, we can start with my father's aunt."

"Do you think that's a good idea?" he appeared hesitant.

"For sure," I said.

Gizi looked very happy when we arrived. She'd even prepared what she described as a modest dinner, which included meat dumpling soup and stuffed cabbage. She asked after my family, and when I told her about Noa's surprising recuperation, she looked happy. "I'm thrilled that it all ended well," she said, her eyes shining, "and that you've also received a little money, it can never hurt."

"True," I nodded and cuddled up to Otto, who then enthusiastically told her how well Imre's paintings were received at the Museum of Fine Arts.

"That doesn't surprise me," Gizi remarked, "Imre was a gifted artist, it was very unfortunate that he died so soon after the war. If he'd lived, he would have achieved great international success."

"You know, Gizi," I remembered the investigative mission I was on, "Angelika didn't disappear in Budapest after the war. She returned to France."

"What?!" Gizi appeared stunned, just like Dad when he was reading the letter, "How do you know? That can't be!"

"It's a fact," I said. I handed her the letter and pointed at the postmark, which proved that it had been sent from Paris in May 1945. "She sent this letter to Paul Molnar."

Gizi looked at the postmark, opened the letter with trembling hands, and started to read, muttering constantly, "This is incredible, it's incredible."

"It's incredible," she added again when she was done. "How could she do such a thing? She was such an honest, courageous, and kind woman—how could she abandon the people who loved her? Imre went insane with the worry and sorrow, that's why he died. She could have at least let him know she was alive."

"That's why I want to look for her at that convent," I explained. "It makes no sense to me either. And if I find her alive, it'll be interesting to hear why she did it."

"When are you planning to go?" Gizi asked, so excited I was afraid she'd offer to come with me.

"I don't know," I replied, "I asked to work on a flight to Paris with a long-enough stopover so that I could go to that town, Saint-Jean-de-Luz. It's in the southwest of France. When I get back to Israel, I'll see if I've been scheduled on a suitable flight. If not, I'll have to take more vacation days. We'll see. Either way, I'll let you know when I get back."

"Do, please!" Gizi said and hugged me. "It's very important to me to know what happened to Angelika. She was very dear to me!"

***

The next few days in Budapest were hectic. Otto and I went to Ikea and to the colorful Sunday markets looking for furniture for the new apartment.

Before I left, Otto asked me to promise I'd be there on the thirtieth of May for his birthday, so we could celebrate the beginning of the new chapter in his life, he explained. And, naturally, I promised.

I took the paintings home, where we argued over what to do with them. Dad agreed that we should keep the painting at home until we found out what happened to Angelika. We owed it to her. Mom, whose breath caught when she saw the painting, muttered again that she didn't like the adventure I was having tracking down the family stories. In the end, she suggested a compromise, which included using the money that was transferred to us from Hungary to buy a larger, more spacious apartment, where we could hang the pictures on a dedicated wall.

I received the May flight plan the next day, and I was pleased to see that I had a flight to Paris scheduled with a four-day layover, so I would have enough time to go to Saint-Jean-de-Luz to trace Angelika's footsteps. The only problem was that my next flight was to New York, with another four-day layover, and the return flight to Israel was on the twenty-ninth of the month, the day before Otto's birthday. I really hoped that I'd be able to keep my promise with such a tight schedule. Just to make sure, I booked a seat on the flight to Budapest on the morning of the thirtieth.

***

Meanwhile, I tried to get back into my routine, and I even had a meeting with my thesis supervisor and asked to complete it with an in-depth and comprehensive interview of Shandor Bachi, who I believed to be the only person in the world who could provide first-hand answers to the questions she'd raised. Much to my surprise and delight, the professor agreed, which I saw as the first sign that my life was on a better track. Not wanting to ruin my achievement by procrastinating as usual, I rang Shandor Bachi immediately after the meeting and asked Angela to ask him if I could visit soon to interview him. Angela surprised me by handing the phone to him, and Shandor said that he'd be very happy to be interviewed for my thesis.

I didn't say a word about the surprising news regarding Angelika. I preferred to tell him face to face. I was hoping to have more information by then and that I may even be able to arrange for them to see each other.

***

The only question still weighing on me was where I would live in Israel. My parents, who usually didn't interfere in such matters, were doing all they could to make me feel wanted at home, especially after they decided to move to a bigger place. It shouldn't have surprised me that Mom wanted me to stay. It was Dad, however, whose face fell whenever he saw me looking at apartment listings, who really made me anxious.

"Daryakum, I don't understand why you're in such a hurry to leave home," he responded when I tried to ask him why he was behaving that way. "You just broke up with Oren. Why not wait until you have enough money for a full year's rent?"

"Why wouldn't I have enough for the rent?" I asked. "No one's told me that I'm going to be fired anytime soon, and I'm making enough to rent an apartment. I think you're still hoping I'll go back to Oren. Am I right?"

"No, really I'm not," he replied quickly, but when I looked piercingly at him, he broke and smiled, then admitted that he'll always hope for that to happen. "You know what I think about it, I've never hidden it from you. I'd feel much more at ease if you were living with someone you can trust."

"Dad," I sighed, "I can trust Otto too. He even asked me when he can meet you all."

"That doesn't mean anything," he sighed in response, "and in any case, that's not why I'm asking you to postpone looking for your own apartment. I just want you with us for a while, and maybe you can help me and Mom find a new apartment. There have been so many changes in our lives lately. I would love you to stay and help us get used to them."

"I don't think that Noa feels the need to find a direction in life right now," I replied, when suddenly I realized what he was thinking. "I think you want me to help you deal with Mom, who will probably lose it completely by the time you find a place that meets her expectations."

"Do you think I need your help in dealing with Mom?!" Dad protested, but when I gave him a challenging smile, he smiled back and admitted with a sigh, "Okay, Darya, okay, you're right. Mom may drive us all crazy while we're looking, and it would be easier if it was divided up between a few of us so that we can all stay sane during this difficult period."

"Then I'll stay, Dad, for as long as you need me," I said, hugging him.

CHAPTER 24

I was all psyched up on the flight to Paris, constantly thinking about how I was about to meet Angelika and hear all the stories directly from her, firsthand this time. Although I wasn't at all sure she was still alive, my imagination ran wild as I envisioned all kinds of scenes in my mind. When we landed, I asked the steward for permission to stay there so I could book a flight to the area where Saint-Jean-de-Luz was located. I thought it would be too complicated to take care of it over the phone, especially since the French clerks had no patience for anyone who didn't speak their aristocratic language.

When I left the airport with two tickets in my purse for flights to Toulouse and Biarritz, with only three hours between them, I knew I'd done the right thing. I would never have been able to arrange all that on the phone, pacing the floor in my hotel room. When I walked into the lobby, enthused by how well I had done, I realized I was hungry, and then I ran straight into Rona and Shira, two longtime flight attendants I was friendly with. They had just returned from a shopping spree and suggested we eat together at Andre, a nice restaurant on the Champs-Élysées that was very popular with the El Al staff.

First, I ordered a huge bowl of black mussels and a glass of white wine, then I asked them to fill me in on what's new in Paris shopping-wise. I hadn't been in Paris for close to a year.

"Hold on," Rona replied with a wink, "I think there are more important things to discuss, such as what's going on with you and Oren Russo? Is it true that you've broken up?"

"Why do you think that?" I said defensively. For some reason, until that moment, I hadn't considered how quickly the news of our breakup could spread through our gossip-craving airline. In any case, I had no desire to discuss the matter with those two yentas.

"Because we saw him hanging out with a spring chicken, one of the attendants from the new courses," Shira replied enthusiastically. "In fact, we flew here with them, and she didn't stop talking about him the whole flight."

"No way!" The mussels stuck in my throat and I started to cough. It was hard enough coping with the fact that Oren was now in Paris, maybe even on his way to Andre, but no way could I deal with him being joint by the hip to some babe.

Shira patted me on the back, trying to help me stop coughing. Rona, on the other hand, just stared at me annoyingly. When I could finally breathe and tried to take a deep breath, she tilted her head toward the door and whispered, "Here they are, as large as life."

Now I really felt like I was on the verge of choking, looking at Oren in the doorway with that young, irritating attendant who'd invited him to a club in New York and then bombarded me with annoying questions about the nature of our relationship. This was more than I could take. I cringed in my chair and prayed for the earth to swallow me up and transfer me directly to the other side of the globe. Shira and Rona didn't notice how distraught I was, or maybe it just didn't interest them. They were debating whether to call the two of them over to join us or to wait and see if they'd come over of their own free will.

"Don't you dare!" I snapped at them when I found my voice again.

"What do you want us to do?" Shira asked. "Just carry on eating and pretend we haven't seen them? That'll look a bit strange, won't it?"

I was starting to feel nauseous, really nauseous. I took a long sip of wine, hoping it would help me feel better, but it didn't. Meanwhile, I watched them, as if compelled by a demon. I couldn't take my eyes off Oren and the babe, and I watched them walk toward the bar and sit down. She was all over him, smiling glowingly and looking head over heels in love with him. He, on the other hand, was reserved and distant with her, but that didn't make me feel better, because I knew that he always behaved that way in public places. I realized that, luckily, they still hadn't noticed us, so I immediately devised a quick getaway plan.

"You two, go over to them now," I hissed to Shira and Rona, startling them. They were still staring at the couple. "Go chat with them, but stand so that you're blocking their field of vision. I, meanwhile, will get the hell out of here."

"Where will you go?" Rona asked. She must have been a bit slow on the uptake.

"To the hotel! Move it, go over to them already, and don't you dare even hint that I was here, got it?"

"Got it, but why..." Rona said, still trying to understand, when Shira pulled her behind her, "Stop asking so many questions, Rona! What are you, two?"

I waited until they reached the bar and the royal couple, and then I took advantage of the fact that Oren was choosing to focus his blatant friendliness on them and to kiss them both, and I quickly escaped under cover of the restaurant's dim lighting. Once outside, I breathed a sigh of relief, inhaling the freezing evening air, and hailed a cab to take me to the hotel. Once in my room, I rushed to the bathroom and puked.

I was feeling like a ragdoll by the time I got into the tub, violating my number one rule when it comes to hotel rooms—only to use the shower. I filled the tub with warm water, then sat and stared at the white towels hanging on the hooks in front of me. *I hope that you realize that a guy like Oren probably won't be on his own for very long*, Dad's warning ran through my mind. *Okay*, I snapped back at him in my mind, *but why does he have to be with that stupid bimbo, who's all over him like I don't know what?*

I stayed in the tub for ages, arguing with Dad and with myself. In the end, I decided I had to get out before I caught pneumonia. The water had cooled down, as had my anger. After all, I didn't wish for Oren to stay on his own forever eating his heart out over me. I wanted him to be happy, to move on with his life, as I had.

I left the bathroom filled with sickening emptiness. I walked over to the minibar and took out a can of Diet Coke and a small packet of almonds, nibbling them as I stared out the window facing the street, hoping to see Oren returning all alone to the hotel.

***

At one in the morning, after eliminating half the minibar, including four little bottles of vodka, I saw Oren and the attendant step out of a cab. She was clinging to him and he had his arm over her shoulder as they walked toward the hotel entrance. I burst into tears on the bed, cursing stupid Rona and Shira who had done as I asked and not told him I was at the restaurant and that I'd run away because of him. I believed that if he'd known about it, he would have rushed after me to the hotel to talk.

And what would that have given you? I asked myself, trying desperately to calm down. The chance to eat each other's hearts out again? Oren wouldn't have missed the opportunity to remind me time and again that I was the one who initiated the breakup, because I'd never really loved him, and I would reply that he was the one who'd consoled himself so quickly in the arms of some silly bimbo, just to prove that he didn't love me all that much. I thought that crying would at least exhaust me enough to fall asleep, but after that miracle didn't happen either, I called Otto in desperation.

"Hello," I heard his sleepy voice on the other side of the line, which sounded startled when he heard me, "Darya, is that you? What's the matter?!"

"Nothing, I'm in Paris and…I missed you," I tried to steady my voice to hide any trace of tears.

"You're in Paris?!" he sounded happy. "That's wonderful. So how about coming here tomorrow?"

"No, I don't think so. I'm planning on going to Saint-Jean tomorrow to look for Angelika," I said despondently. A warm hug from him could have been an excellent cure for my low mood.

"I see," he replied, "and are you nervous? Is that why you sound so terrible?"

"No," I replied awkwardly, wondering why I no longer found the adventure I'd be embarking on the next day so thrilling.

"Cheer up, Daryakum, we'll be celebrating my birthday together in a week and a half."

"Yes," I answered.

"Daryakum, you don't sound good to me. What's wrong? Is your sister okay?"

"Yes, my sister's fine, everything's fine, nothing happened, I just miss you, that's all." By this time, I wanted to end the conversation so I wouldn't burst out crying again.

"It doesn't sound like it, Darya. If you don't tell me I'll get right on a plane and come there," he threatened me in a tender and gentle tone, like you talk to a disobedient child refusing to finish her meal. It was enough to bring tears to my eyes, which constricted my throat.

"I…I'm…fine, it's just…I saw my ex today. I'm sorry, Otto, but it made me feel so bad. I had to talk to someone…I'm sorry it fell on you, but—"

"That's okay, my darling, I'm glad you decided to talk to me."

"Really?" I wailed, "Aren't you mad?"

"Angry? Why would I be mad? I can understand you. It's not easy breaking up with someone after twelve years together. It's natural that it can't be easy to see him."

"Tell me, did you also find it hard to see Greta that Saturday, when she came to the picnic with that guy?"

"Not really, why do you ask?" he wondered. "Oh, I understand. Did you see your boyfriend today with another woman? Is that why you're crying?"

"Uhm, yes, not…exactly," I stammered, when I realized I was saying too much and my heart started pounding in panic.

"Daryakum, it's okay, you can tell me the truth. It sounds perfectly natural to me to feel bad in such circumstances."

"Otto, you're an angel," I said, relieved.

"So are you, sweetie, I love you whatever state you're in, even when you're crying. And if you want to continue talking about it until you feel better, then as far as I'm concerned, you can talk all night. I'm listening."

"I'm fine, I feel better," I immediately told him, feeling that I'd caused enough damage for one night. Despite how extremely kind and tender he was, I knew that this was not something I could just move on from. I would have been a little mad, or at least frustrated, if I were in his place.

"Good," he replied, "so are you going to sleep now?"

"No, I'm going to join my ex and his girlfriend," I giggled in irritation. "What do you think I'm going to do? Of course I'm going to sleep."

"Daryakum, you don't have to be so tough on yourself and expect twelve minutes to be enough to forget a man you lived with for twelve years. It takes time. It's natural to mourn your breakup, even if you initiated it, and it's natural for it to be hard seeing him with another woman."

"Tell me, do you moonlight as a psychologist?" I asked, feeling the conversation going in very strange directions. After repeating the word natural so many times, it seemed very unnatural to me that he was showing such understanding of how I was feeling about it. It would have much more natural to demand an explanation as to why I was making such a big deal out of running into Oren and some woman, when I myself am deep in a new relationship with him and claiming that I'm madly in love with him to boot.

"No, I've very happy in my profession," I heard his amused reply.

"Sorry, Otto, you're awesome, and I'm just beating you up for it," I apologized. "I guess it's not my day. I think I really should go to sleep now."

"All right, sweetie, good night and pleasant dreams, and try to keep them about me, okay?"

"Okay," I assured him, determined to expel any hint of Oren from my thoughts. But somehow, much to my distress, that's not what happened. I tossed and turned in bed trying in vain to fall asleep, and all I could think about was Oren and what he was doing with his young babe, and whether I'd ruined something in my relationship with Otto by calling him so foolishly in the middle of the night.

***

Despite the eventful night, I woke up in the morning in eager anticipation of beginning my search for Angelika. I packed a few clothes in a small carry-on, just in case I had to stay there for more than a day, and I left for Orly Airport. The flights took forever, and almost all I could think about was what I'd find out when I arrived at the Saint Florence convent, which was where Angelika had asked Molnar to send the painting, and also where she lived, of course. I hardly gave Oren a thought.

I arrived in Biarritz, a beautiful and picturesque holiday resort, and caught a cab to the convent. Although the driver demanded an exorbitant fee, I decided not to perform market research, because the anticipation was making me more than tense enough.

The beautiful road winding through the mountains was the perfect setting to give me a feel for the place. When the driver stopped at the small, unimpressive gray convent, I felt a little disappointed. My legs were quivering slightly as I walked toward the heavy wooden door that had a real iron bell on the wall beside it. I rang it. The bell clanged a few times but no one came. I made a fist and knocked hard on the door. This time it was opened by a young nun with almost translucent skin, who stood in the doorway and asked me something in French. God! I thought to myself nervously, Please make it that someone here speaks English!

"I'm looking for Angelika," I said to the nun in the broken French I remembered from high school.

"Angelika?!" she looked stunned, but not in a way that made me think she didn't know who I was talking about. She immediately rattled off a long speech but I couldn't understand a word of what she said.

"Do you speak English, perhaps?" I asked pleadingly.

The nun stopped talking and looked at me for a few long moments before motioning me to follow her inside.

It was pleasantly dim in the large prayer hall she led me to, where a few nuns were immersed in their books. None of them looked up at me, and the nun who had taken me there had disappeared. A few minutes later, she returned with another young nun.

"This is Sister Florrie," she whispered, introducing the other nun, who smiled pleasantly and nodded, "she speaks English, come with us."

I followed them. We passed a line of closed doors, until we arrived at another, that was a different size and color. The door was beautiful, made of copper with stunning etchings, and the nun in the lead knocked on the door a few times. She waited a moment before opening it. Sister Florrie and I followed her in. An elderly nun with kind eyes looked up at us and inspected me intently. "Hello, my child," she said slowly in French, "I'm Mother Yvonne, and I understand that you're looking for Angelika."

"Yes," I replied.

And who are you?" she inquired, "Are you a relative of hers?"

"No," I answered and continued in English, "my name is Darya Schwartz and I'm from Israel, but I'm looking for Angelika because she used to be very close to my family. She helped them during the war and saved some of them, and—"

I realized that Flory was translating what I said into French and couldn't keep up. I stopped and waited for her to finish.

"I see," Mother Yvonne said, looking me over again, as if trying to see if I had something hidden in my clothes, "so you're not related?"

"No, but I want to know what happened to her. She was very dear to my family, and they all thought she disappeared in Budapest after the Second World War."

Again, I paused to give Florrie time to translate.

"I see, sit down please," Yvonne said, pointing to the chair on the other side of the table. I sat down. I was utterly confused. I didn't understand why I was being interrogated so thoroughly, and why the mother superior was scrutinizing me with such suspicion, as if she thought I was bin Laden's younger sister.

"A while ago, I found a letter from Angelika," I continued of my own accord, "which she sent from Paris when everyone thought she was no longer alive, and in this letter, she asked for a painting to be sent here, to this convent, so I thought…we all thought that she might have come here without notifying anyone."

"I see," Mother Yvonne said again, after Flory translated what I'd said. I was becoming irritated. If the conversation continued like that, there was no way I'd find out what happened to Angelika before my flight from Paris to New York took off.

"Then could you tell me where she is, or at least what happened to her?" I blurted out the question with an almost compulsive urge. Mother Yvonne nodded slowly, as if mulling over something. Then she opened the drawer on the side of the table and took out a few documents.

"Are you looking for Angelika Lenardi, who was born in Saint-Jean-de-Luz in 1922?" she asked, looking at the documents.

"I think so, that sound's right," I mumbled in desperation. "Do you have a picture of her? I might be able to recognize her."

"Unfortunately, no," Mother Yvonne replied as she browsed through the documents, "but I do have a photograph of her daughter, Andriana, if that's of any use to you."

For a moment I thought I hadn't heard correctly. I stared in complete shock at Sister Flory's lips, after she'd translated what Mother Yvonne had told me. This time I knew I'd heard correctly, that they'd said that Angelika had a daughter.

"Do you want to look at it?" I heard Mother Yvonne ask, seemingly for the second time, because her voice sounded a little impatient.

"Yes…yes," I quickly stood up and went over to her, my legs weak, "but how is that possible? After all, she was a…nun."

"Look," the mother superior pointed at the small passport photo stapled to the document in her hand, "that's Adriana, Angelika's daughter."

I stared at the small picture from which a beautiful, young brunette looked back with bright, mischievous eyes. I froze. Her eyes were just like Grandpa Yoshka's.

"No way…" I heard myself say in Hebrew, my mind running wild with crazy thoughts. No way did Grandpa Yoshka get Angelika pregnant. It's just unthinkable, even for a person like him, with so little restraint.

"You can sit down again," Mother Yvonne said softly. Naturally, she had noticed the turmoil I was in.

I could barely move.

"I understand that finding out about Angelika's daughter could be very disconcerting for you," she continued, her expression frozen, and Flory translated.

"Yes, a little," I stammered, "despite all the stories I've heard about her, this had never occurred to me."

Mother Yvonne motioned to the nun with the translucent skin to leave the room, and she quickly did as she was told.

"Understand, my child," she started speaking again as soon as the door closed, and again, Flory translated for me, "Angelika was very dear to Mother Nadine, my predecessor. She swore us all to keep her secret. At the time of the war, I was a young nun myself, being educated here. One day, Angelika arrived and gave birth here to her baby. After the Nazis invaded France, Angelika joined the French Resistance and entrusted Mother Nadine with her daughter. She told her she'd come back for her when the war ended. I helped with Adriana's birth, so I'm certain she's Angelika's daughter."

"Do you know who the father was?" I asked, choking on the words, still refusing to believe that my grandfather had been involved.

Mother Yvonne nodded silently. I was becoming increasingly distraught. It was obvious that she had no intention of telling me who the father was. Then I recalled something that alleviated my suspicions. Mother Yvonne had said that Angelika's daughter was born after she joined the resistance. If so, it was also before she met Grandpa Yoshka. I breathed a sigh of relief.

"Mother Yvonne, could you at least tell me the precise date that the baby was born?"

"Yes," she looked down at the papers, "on December the eighth, 1940." That really eased my mind. The puzzle was coming together wonderfully. The baby could be Shandor's daughter, since he told me that he slept with Angelika. It also explained the resemblance between Andriana and Grandpa Yoshka, who was his brother.

"Good," I said, "so now I think I know who the father is, even without you telling me. But what happened to them? Are they living somewhere? Can I meet them?"

"Tell me," Yvonne replied, and again scrutinized my face, "of all the stories you heard about Angelika—did you also hear about her life before she came to the convent?"

"Yes," I nodded somberly, "I heard that her father abused her and that her mother ran away, then came back and burned him to death."

Mother Yvonne raised her hand, as if to stop me and protect herself from what I was saying.

"Well," she took a deep breath and continued, "in 1945, when the war was over and Angelika came back for her daughter, she was attacked by her father's relatives, who had always believed it was her who burned down the house, and they murdered her."

"How awful!" I jumped to my feet, horrified. My legs began to tremble and I dropped back into the chair.

"We mourned her for many years," Mother Yvonne continued, the compassion she felt written on her face. "She was a very dear woman, we all loved and admired her despite…what led to her bringing a child into the world. We raised Adriana here, thinking it was the right way to honor her dear memory. Then, when Adriana reached puberty, she started acting in a way that…was not exactly becoming of a nun. Mother Nadine tried to reach her, to explain that with that kind of behavior we wouldn't be able to let her stay with us. Adriana, however, didn't care. On the contrary, she seemed to want to leave the convent. And indeed, when she turned twenty, Mother Nadine realized that she'd been too lenient with the girl, and if she continued that way, she would lose any trace of discipline and the respect of the other nuns. And so, she gave her money and a letter to her father, and sent her to him."

"She sent her to Shandor?! No way!" I exclaimed, astonished. "Why didn't he tell me about her? Why did he hide her from us for all these years?"

"I don't know," Mother Yvonne replied, her face a mask, "Mother Nadine died a short while after Adriana left us, and the father, whose name you mentioned, never contacted us."

"And Adriana? What about her? Did she also never write to you?"

"Never," Yvonne nodded, "we never heard another word from her."

***

Mother Yvonne was generous enough to offer me a bed for the night. She also asked if I wanted to go for a tour of Saint-Jean-de-Luz, which as it turned out, was a very popular tourist destination. I was in no mood to visit the village of Angelika's murderers. I preferred to stay at the convent, have a simple dinner with them of lentil soup and bread, and think about the story I'd heard. It's not fair, I thought to myself as I looked at the expressionless faces of the nuns around me as they sat and ate in silence, "what a stupid, unnecessary death for a woman who had fought with the Resistance, crossed the most dangerous of borders, and saved so many people, just to fall into the hands of hooligan scum! Where was the logic and justice in that?

Once in bed, covered with a rough woolen blanket that scratched me despite the sheet I had under it, I continued to mull over the chilling twists of fate. "Where is the justice?" I mumbled at the picture of Jesus and Mary hanging over the bed. "How did you allow such a thing to happen to Angelika, after all the good deeds she did for others? Did she deserve such a miserable fate because of one silly mistake, just because she got pregnant from Shandor?"

I eventually grew tired of hurling profound questions at the picture, especially since I was receiving no answers, and I tried to fall asleep. But my thoughts were relentless, about Shandor this time and the question of whether he knew about Adriana. If he did, why did he hide her from us? I tried to think up a way of finding out more details without breaking his heart. Mother Yvonne's story didn't paint a pretty picture of Adriana. She probably inherited something else from the unruly Schwartz family other than beautiful eyes. It made sense to assume that a woman with a wild and unruly character wouldn't be thrilled to live under the patronage of a father she never knew, and she simply took the money and used it to live her life as she wished, free in Paris, or even New York.

***

When I woke up in the morning to the brazen rays of sun coming through the window, I was surprised to discover that I'd had a good night's sleep, without any ghosts from the village disrupting my rest. I glanced at my watch and saw that if I didn't rush off, I'd miss my flight from Biarritz to Toulouse, and I'd have to spend another day there.

I got dressed quickly and went to Mother Yvonne's office, where she greeted me with a smile. I thanked her for the wonderful hospitality and asked if she would call me a cab. She did as I asked in the same calm and relaxed manner that so characterized her. I thanked her again and went on my way. Mother Yvonne accompanied me out and asked me to write to her if I found out what happened to Adriana. I promised to do so, even though I had no clue where to even begin.

I found myself deep in thought on the flights to Biarritz to Toulouse and from there to Paris. And yet, when I arrived at the hotel at dusk, I still hadn't decided on a course of action. I had no idea how to start a conversation about Adriana with Shandor Bachi without putting his health at risk.

On the way to New York, I had thought up a way that may encourage Shandor Bachi to tell me what he knew: I decided to show him Angelika's letter to see if he knew that she'd made it to France. I'd see how the conversation developed and take it from there.

It was only when I arrived at a hotel in New York to find a message waiting for me from Otto that I realized: I hadn't given him a second thought since the morning I left Paris for the convent.

Otto had sent me his love and a reminder that his birthday was on the thirtieth of the month. Touched, I smiled to myself, my heart filling with warmth. I hung up the phone and fell into a deep asleep. The next day, I would be embarking on a complex mission requiring a great deal of energy.

CHAPTER 25

There was a surprise waiting for me at the airport in Miami in the form of Angela, who had come to pick me up. It really was beyond my expectations. Although this visit had been prearranged, and I had no intention of stealing the villa in Boca Raton, I still didn't expect such a momentous deed or the warm hug that she gave me when she said, "Hello, Darya, It's good to see you again, and I'm so happy to hear that your sister is well."

"Thanks," I replied, trying not to show how bewildered I was by her behavior toward me. "And what's happening with the movie? How is it coming along?"

I had no idea what she meant. "What movie?" I inquired.

"The movie about Angelika, the nun from San Sebastián," she said, scrutinizing me.

"The movie about Angelika?! What are you talking about?"

"When you came to interview Shandor, you said you were working with a producer who wants to do a movie about Shandor's experiences during the Spanish Civil War," Angela grimaced in disappointment, like a child whose toy had been taken away. Luckily, I finally remembered what she was talking about and quickly added another lie to the pile of sins I'd accrued in my debt.

"Oh, that movie! Yes, I remember, it's just that I'm working on so many things simultaneously," I replied weakly, "well, that's the thing, I need more details, that's why I'm back again. The producer loved the story, but he said he needs me to elaborate on it and I…don't worry, Angela, if he goes ahead with it, you'll be the first to audition."

"Great, thanks," she answered, then fell silent. I, too, said nothing until we arrived at Shandor Bachi's house, now that I knew the reason for the friendly welcome that she'd given me.

Shandor Bachi was delighted to see me. "Hello, Daryakum! How are you? How long are you planning to stay with me?" he asked, much to my surprise.

"Um, I hadn't really planned on staying," I replied. In fact, it all depended on his cooperation. If he opened his mouth and supplied me with answers to all my questions, I would do so willingly until my flight back to Israel.

"I'd love you to, at least until tomorrow," he said, then immediately explained, "Angela wants to go to Key West until tomorrow evening. She's starting marine biology studies this year, and there's some research center there. It would be very nice of you to stay until then and keep me company. I don't need much help, you know, just to push the panic button if something happens to me," he winked, "and naturally, I'm not planning on anything happening to me, it's only for the insurance. They agreed to insure me only if someone is always at home with me, you understand?"

"Yes, yes, Shandor Bachi," I answered quickly, confused, "I'm happy to stick around until tomorrow evening."

"That's wonderful of you! Thank you!" he exclaimed and pointed at the white sofa by the wall. "The panic button is there, by the phone, do you see it?"

"Yes," I answered and looked where he was pointing. Now I understood even better why Angela was being so nice to me. She wanted me to feel at home so I'd agree to look after Shandor for her. Before she left the house, she even laid the table with a ton of food that looked and smelled wonderful.

"Have fun, you guys," she said, hesitating for a moment in the doorway before waving goodbye and leaving, a large travel bag in hand.

"Does she go away often?" I asked Shandor after Angela left.

"No," he answered and piled pasta penne and meatballs onto my plate. "Eat, Daryakum, you must be very hungry."

"Thanks," I replied and started eating. The pasta tasted homemade and was delicious.

"So how are things at home, Daryakum?" Shandor inquired after he tasted the food himself. "I hope everything's okay now after your sister's surprising recovery."

"Everybody's fine," I replied, wondering how to bring up the subject of Angelika. In the end, I decided to begin by telling him how I tracked down the family treasure. Shandor Bachi sat and listened, taking a small bite of food now and then from his plate. His eyes lit up when I got to the part about the paintings.

"You found the painting of Angelika and Adrianus at Molnar's house?" he exclaimed enthusiastically, placing his hand on his heart.

"Yes, and it's not there anymore, I took it home to Israel," I answered, and as I told him about the arguments between Mom and Dad over where to hang it, a thought crossed my mind. For some reason I hadn't thought of it before. "Shandor Bachi, would you like the painting?"

"I would, very much," he answered eagerly, then continued more weakly, "Naturally, I wouldn't want to argue with your parents over it, but if they don't find a place to hang it and decide to sell it, then I'd love to put in my bid for it, although I couldn't offer any more than the museum in Budapest."

"All right, I'll let them know," I mumbled uncomfortably. In my opinion, it was only right that Shandor should have the painting since he was the closest to Angelika and Adrianus but, deep inside, I knew that I'd also find it difficult to give up. Somehow, it put a weird kind of spell on anyone who looked at it.

"Perhaps I'll come to Israel," he blurted out, as if the thought had just occurred to him, "I have a yen to see the painting again before I die."

"How can you say that, Shandor Bachi?" I reproached him, "We'd all love you to visit us in Israel, but only on the condition that you live for many years to come. How can you talk about death now, after convincing me that nothing's going to happen to you and that I have to be here only because of the insurance?"

"Well, Daryakum, I don't plan on dying soon, but it will happen sometime," he winked at me. "Luckily I was never enough of a saint for anyone upstairs to want me by his side."

"That is lucky," I agreed, my thoughts wandering again to Angelika and the horrific way she died. "Listen, Shandor Bachi," I said, taking the letters out of my purse, "I found something else in Molnar's house." I showed him the letter. "Angelika sent it from France in May 1945. Did you know she made it to France?"

"What?" he furrowed his brow and held his hand out for the letter. For some reason, he didn't look as shocked as I'd expected, so I felt more relaxed when I handed it to him.

Shandor took the letter out of the envelope and started reading intently. After a few minutes, he looked up at me and said, his voice catching, "How is this possible? We all thought she disappeared in Budapest after she left your grandparents' place."

"Why didn't you try to look for her? You had a lot of money back then— couldn't you have sent a detective or someone else to look for her in Hungary?"

"No," he replied, his mouth quivering, "while we could still get into Hungary, we wasted precious time because Imre, who as usual had his head in the clouds, remembered only months after Angelika disappeared to write to Yoshka asking after her. He just sat there waiting like an idiot, thinking that nothing bad could happen to her. And then, when we realized that we should try to find her, we could no longer set foot in Hungary. I asked Yoshka to try to trace her steps, but he couldn't find out a thing. No one had seen her or even heard of her, or they were too afraid to talk." I noticed him shiver, even though it was a warm evening, and I decided to stop torturing him with questions. He didn't seem to know anything, and Adriana never came to him. I felt that maybe it was a better idea to look for her myself, although I had no idea where to begin.

***

The next day, I started interviewing Shandor Bachi for my thesis. I wanted to get his personal angle on people back then. He insisted that the only reason the media in the States didn't publish the enormous magnitude of the Jewish Holocaust in Europe, at a time when it was still possible to intervene and stop the genocide, was that they didn't know about it.

"So how do you explain this?" I asked, and showed him two articles I found in the Library of Congress, which included a report regarding survivors who had managed to escape from Auschwitz to the Soviet Union and who described explicitly what was being done there. The two articles were published in 1942 and appeared in a file with the title Holocaust."

Shandor narrowed his eyes, reading the names of the newspapers that had published the original articles. "Well, you see." he looked up eventually, "They were published in newspapers that were considered communist. And who believed anything they said, back then? They thought they were deliberately spreading false propaganda to force the United States to join the war."

"I'm familiar with that excuse," I replied, "but believing the administration's line suits the ordinary man on the street. How did the journalists, media executives, and intellectuals agree to do the same and ignore the truth, without even trying to investigate it? That's what I don't get."

"They were afraid, Daryakum, they were simply afraid to believe such horrific stories," Shandor sighed. "You see, even after the war when the soldiers released the camps and returned to the States, they didn't talk about what they saw there. They were afraid to deal with it themselves. It was the greatest atrocity ever. I personally knew a few journalists who covered the trials, friends of Hugo Scott, and I saw what a hard time they had, dealing with what they heard and saw. They would come back so shocked that they'd burst into tears whenever they tried to talk about it, and you know how journalists are, how cynical and skeptical they are usually. But this was beyond what they could take. I don't believe that any of them had imagined the atrocity beforehand, before witnessing it for themselves. It was incomprehensible!"

Throughout that day, the question, Shandor Bachi, do you know that you had a daughter called Adriana? was on the tip of my tongue, but I couldn't bring myself to say it.

In the evening, when Angela returned, enthused by her trip to Key

West, I thought of talking to her and trying to summon her help somehow in discussing it with Shandor. But in the end, I decided to drop the matter entirely until I could consult Dad. Despite the changes in my uncle's devoted caregiver's behavior, I still couldn't shake the family's suspicion that she was after his money, and as such, I didn't want to give her too many cards to play.

***

When I got back to New York, I had another surprise waiting. This one was certainly not good. There was a message for me at the hotel telling me that my flight back to Israel was currently delayed by twelve hours. This was a real blow, as I knew I wouldn't make it to Budapest for Otto's birthday. Deeply upset, I called him and told him I would probably miss the occasion.

At first, Otto sounded disappointed, but toward the end of the conversation, when he realized that my mood was deteriorating, he snapped out of it and said, "It's fine, Daryakum, we don't need to make a big deal out of it. It's merely an arbitrary date. We'll celebrate when you get here, it doesn't matter when."

"True," I tried to cheer myself up, "I'll catch the first flight to Budapest, as soon as I land in Israel. I won't even go home!"

"Don't overdo it," he laughed, "you have my permission to go home, shower, and change your clothes. But then come right here, okay? I really miss you!"

"I miss you too!" I said in response. Otto laughed, sending me kisses over the phone before saying that he had to get back to work.

New York was rainy and gray for the next two days, so I spent most of my time in museums. I went to the Museum of Modern Art, the Metropolitan, and the Guggenheim, looking mainly at the classic, impressionist, and post-impressionist paintings, and every evening, I'd find myself coming to the same conclusion: None of the paintings I saw came close to Imre's depiction of Angelika and Adrianus when it came to beauty and deep emotion. Maybe I was a little biased, but that's how I felt, and that made me proudly exhilarated.

My anticipations were high when I woke up to catch my flight back to Israel. I was finally setting off in the right direction, with Otto waiting for me at the end. Nothing could darken my mood that morning, not even the fact that the steward was the grumpy type who sent me to work in the back kitchen. Even when I was told about a delay due to a malfunction in one of the engines, I didn't consider it reason for concern. Even the passengers, who were irritable when they boarded the plane, only made me smile more, and I handled them with understanding, since they, too, may have a loved one who'd been forced to miss them for longer than foreseen.

The Buddhist theory, which claims that what you put out there comes back to you twofold was fully confirmed on that flight. The passengers calmed down, and it was really nice to work with them while they were still awake, and naturally, even more so after they fell asleep. That is until we were somewhere over Europe and the plane suddenly began to shake. After the shaking stopped, the captain announced that an engine had broken down again and that we would have to land at the first airport to give us permission. This had a severe impact on my mood. I wasn't worried about the plane because I knew that it had another three engines and we'd be able to land without a problem. But I couldn't take in this extra, unexpected delay. I was dying to see Otto. In fact, I almost burst into tears from the frustration, but then the captain announced that we would be landing at Budapest Airport.

My delight knew no limit. I thought that fate itself had intervened so that I could arrive in time for Otto's birthday. It was almost midnight in Hungary, which meant that I couldn't get there precisely on the date, but it would be nice to surprise him just a few hours later, if only to give him a quick kiss and congratulate him. I couldn't wait to land.

***

The passengers were tense and confused, and we needed all our mental strength to calm them down. However, when the captain announced we'd be spending a day in Budapest and that they'd be put up in a hotel, I almost danced with joy.

It took forever to get off the plane, and everyone was tired and nerve-wracked. Then we wasted at least another hour on the drive to the hotel. When I finally walked into my room, I debated whether to call Otto and let him know about the unexpected developments or whether to surprise him. In the end, I decided to call, but Otto didn't pick up his cell phone or his landline. I assumed he was already asleep. Since I had a key to the apartment, I thought it would be an even better surprise for him to wake up in my arms.

I showered and changed my clothes, called a cab, and set off. By the time I got to Andrassy Avenue, it was two-thirty. I climbed the stairs, my heart expanding with longing and expectation, and I held my breath as the key turned easily in the lock. The entrance hall was utterly dark. The curtains we'd hung over the large windows were doing a good job, allowing no light to penetrate the room. As I fumbled for the light switch, I noticed a sharp smell of alcohol and cigarettes. I was beginning to feel apprehensive, even before I felt myself tread on something—or someone. I screamed in fear and tried to move back toward the door. Someone, I guess the person I'd stepped on, cursed in Hungarian, and a moment later I was looking at Latsi and Diana's panicky eyes. They were lying right by the door. Then all at once, everyone started shouting, and by the light of the night lamp that one of the blonde twins switched on, I was able to make out a few faces in the crowd. They were all sprawled out in weird positions, half-dressed, lying among the beer bottles and cups. When I saw that Otto wasn't there, I didn't know whether to be relieved or concerned, but before I could regain my senses and decide what I thought about the decadent scene I had disrupted, he burst out of the bedroom covering himself with a sheet and walked toward me.

"Daryakum?!" he exclaimed, and a moment later he was hugging me with one hand while holding the sheet with the other. I almost closed my eyes and allowed myself to fall willingly into his arms and ignore the mess all around us, but a moment before I did, I caught a glimpse of Greta and the other twin following him out of the bedroom and diving into the bathroom. This time, I didn't need time to understand what was going on or how I felt about it.

"Let me go!" I screamed at Otto, trying to wiggle out of his arms, but he continued to hold me tight. Without thinking twice, I scratched his back. He yelled and loosened his grip on me.

Within two seconds, I was on the street, desperately trying to find a cab through the tears that were blinding me. I could hear Otto panting behind me, running and shouting, "Darya, wait a minute, I'll drive you!"

What was left of my brain was insisting: Don't you dare let him anywhere near you. I thought I could see a car approaching, and I prayed it was a cab as I stepped off the sidewalk to stop it. The car drove toward me without slowing down. Overwhelmed and distraught, I tried to step back onto the sidewalk, but I stumbled on the curb. The screech of brakes burst in my head with insane intensity, paralyzing my body, which prepared itself for the blow that was coming. Petrified, I waited for it, when suddenly I felt two strong hands wrap themselves around my body and pull me back. A moment later, I opened my eyes but all I saw was the black sky above me. I was splayed out on top of Otto, who was lying on the sidewalk, holding me by the hips and breathing heavily.

"Darya, are you okay?" I heard him grunt. Against my will, I burst out laughing from hysteria and relief, which mixed with the tears that were choking me. I tried to get up, but my legs were still weak. Otto sat up and cradled me in his arms.

"Daryakum, calm down," he whispered. I looked at his face, which was showing a mixture of pain, fear, relief, and acceptance.

"I don't want to calm down!" I barked and tried again to stand up. "I don't want to ever see you again! Let me get up!"

Still holding my hips, Otto somehow managed to bring us both to our feet. "I do understand," he said weakly, but he didn't let go of me. "You have every right to be mad at me, but for God's sake, let me at least take you to a hotel!"

Loud voices were coming from the entrance to Otto's apartment building, which I had almost started to think of as my second home. A group from the party I'd ruined were standing there, calling to us in Hungarian. Otto barked apparently daunting answers at them, because they were too afraid to come near us. Instead, they just stood there awkwardly. I tried again to get away, guessing what mocking looks Greta, the queen of darkness, was shooting at my back. All I wanted was to disappear and never see them again. But my legs were trembling, and I couldn't take a single normal step. The last thing I wanted to happen was to stumble in front of her.

"Come," Otto whispered to me, supporting me by the waist, "I'm getting you out of here!"

This time, I didn't argue. I allowed him to lead me to his car, and only after we got in, did I glare helplessly at him. "All you will do is drive me to my hotel and drop me off!"

Otto nodded and started the car. His expression was still so hurt, I was afraid that if he spoke, he would also burst into tears. The whole way there, I battled against the insane urge to reach out and squeeze his arm to comfort him. If it hadn't been so sad, I would have burst out laughing: Here I was, sitting in a car with the man who had just caused me the worst humiliation of my life, and I wanted to offer him my support, to comfort him, and wipe his face free of pain, which for all in knew, was all for show.

"Which hotel are we going to?" he mumbled through tight lips, and when I turned to answer, I saw two, huge tears rolling down his cheeks. This time I couldn't resist and I reached out to touch them. "Stop it," Otto pulled away from me, "stop it, Daryakum." His broken voice drove me to tears. All the way to the hotel, we drove in heavy silence and wet with tears. Otto stopped the car, gave a heartbreaking sigh, and leaned his head back on the headrest.

"Could you say something?!" I snapped at him, when I realized that I couldn't bring myself to get quietly and calmly out of his car. My heart was broken, because of me, and because of him, and I was hoping he'd have something to say that would mend it. The odds of that were definitely slim.

"What can I say?" he muttered and stared at me with such a pained and final expression that I couldn't help but burst into tears again. "That I love you? That I made a stupid mistake that has ruined the greatest love I ever had or that I will ever have? That I don't know what I'm going to do with myself once you get out of the car? Those are all overused clichés. There is nothing I can say that will make clear the hell that I'm in. But it's my own fault, and I have to pay the price like a man—"

"Stop it, Otto," I crushed his hand in mine and scratched him again. His face twitched in pain but he said nothing. "Stop feeling sorry for yourself! You should have thought of that before…and not…how?! How could you do this to me?! To me and you? To us both? What the hell was going through your mind when you got into bed with Greta and that…stupid blonde?!"

"Darya, I told you…I have no excuse, I was an idiot. I wasn't thinking at all, but, just so you know, I didn't go to bed with them…and if I'd had time to think about it before, it wouldn't have happened."

"What are you trying to say?!" I attacked him venomously, shocked that he was trying to soften me up with silly excuses, "That you couldn't see well? That they didn't come out of your room naked with just a sheet?! Or that it was rape and those two feather-weight girls managed to pin you to the bed despite all your sexy muscles?"

"I told you that anything I have to say would sound bad," he responded, his face frozen as he tried in vain to control his facial muscles, which couldn't hide his anguish. "What's that saying? A picture's worth a thousand words, and unfortunately you saw a picture, and all that I can say now won't help to erase it from your mind—"

"Otto, stop trying to wiggle your way out of it, I want to hear exactly what happened in there!"

"Really?" he stared at me hesitantly, but I could detect a spark of hope in his eyes.

"Yes," I replied firmly, even though I knew that it would hurt even more.

"And do you promise to believe me?"

"I promise, if it makes sense," I replied, venomously, to hide my fear of what I was about to hear. "If you tell me that a spaceship dropped those two witches in your bed, then…I'm not sure I'll be able to believe you, as much as I may want to."

"Fine, then I don't know. It wasn't exactly a spaceship, but…Darya, the truth is—and you have to believe me—I didn't know that Greta was coming. They, the gang, came over at about nine in the evening without telling me. They wanted to surprise me. Before that, after you called and told me that you wouldn't be able to make it, I spoke to Latsi on the phone. He asked what my plans were for my birthday, and I told him that you wouldn't be able to get here in time. I was terribly disappointed and in a bad mood, and I guess he thought it would be a good idea to surprise me. They arrived in the evening with loads of food and drink and tried to cheer me up. Greta wasn't with them, and no one told me that she was meant to be coming. At some point, I felt tired and I wanted to go to sleep. I thought you'd be arriving the next day and I wanted to have the energy to celebrate all day with you. I went to sleep at about one, and then—I don't even know what time it was, shortly before you arrived—they woke me up, Greta and one of the twins. I don't even know which one of them it was. They got into bed with me, naked, and woke me up—"

"I don't believe you!" I interrupted him, stunned, "And all your nice friends allowed it to happen? Why didn't they stop them?"

"I don't know, Darya," he sighed in defeat, "but it wouldn't be fair to blame them now. They…the bottom line is that it's my fault."

"Don't play the martyr with me," I said. "You were asleep, and I'm sure you were confused when you woke up, until you realized what was happening, what had already happened. But they, they were outside and saw it before it happened. Why didn't they do anything?"

Otto didn't reply. My heart sank at the look on his face. He looked so agonized that I couldn't stop myself and said, "Do you want to continue this conversation in my room?"

"What?!" he looked at me, stunned. "Are you asking me to come up to your room? Really?"

"Yes," I replied and held out my hand. He took it and squeezed it, as if trying to check if my intentions were sincere. "I'm willing to forgive you precisely because you took responsibility and didn't try to blame the entire world for what happened. It's touching, it makes me think that maybe you do deserve another chance, but we'll talk about that later. Let's go to sleep now."

***

Although Otto was surprised and moved by my willingness to forgive him, it didn't stop him from falling asleep three minutes after we got into bed. I, on the other hand, tossed and turned, even though I really wanted to sleep and have more energy to talk the next day. I felt that I could stay with him only on the condition that he cut all ties with his friends from Baja. I knew that I wouldn't be able to look them in the eye without the humiliation and anger from that night suffocating me again. Apart from all that, I also saw them as the main culprit for what had happened. Clearly, I also realized it he'd find it very difficult to agree to. After all, they were his childhood friends whom he'd spent most of his life with.

I tossed and turned for hours, thanking God and the hotel manager for making the bed wide enough not to wake Otto up. Dad's words kept running through my mind, blending with the images from that damned party and of Oren and that stupid attendant hanging on his arm. Oren would never have done such a thing to me, I thought I had finally found something to give him credit for. No one would have treated an outburst resulting from running into an ex with more understanding and respect. I must have fallen asleep in the end, because when the phone rang, I pounced on it, startled and surprised by the bright morning light that was blinding me. Otto also woke up and looked at me in surprise, as if I was the last person he'd have expected to find in his bed. I'd love to know what he dreamed about in the night, I thought for a moment before picking up the phone and trying to push the thought out of my mind.

"Darya Schwartz?" I heard a woman say in English, "I'm speaking from the reception desk, we've been asked to inform you that the plane will be ready at six-thirty this evening. Pick-up will be at precisely four o'clock. You also have a coupon for breakfast, which you can pick it up here, at reception."

"Thank you," I replied and hung up. Otto rolled toward me and leaned on his elbow facing me.

"How did you sleep?" he asked, removing a strand of hair from my forehead.

"Fine," I answered and tried to smile. "Do you want breakfast?"

"Only if you do," his eyes said clearly that he'd rather stay in bed with me, but he was careful enough not to show it physically.

"I'd like to at least have a cup of coffee after I shower," I answered and got out of bed. Otto rolled onto his back and put his hands under his head.

"I can go down to get you coffee and something to eat while you're in the shower."

"Okay," I replied, "here's the key. There's a coupon for breakfast at reception, if you want to try to use it instead of me. Tell them that you represent Darya Schwartz from the El Al staff."

Otto smiled and got out of bed. The sight of his smile made me rush into the bathroom. I knew full well that any physical contact between us would weaken my determination to confront him.

By the time I'd finished showering, he was sitting at the table, on which there was a tray bearing two cups of coffee, a glass of orange juice, a croissant, and a red rose, which he handed to me with theatrical cheerfulness.

"This is for you, as a symbol my gratitude to you for being willing to forgive me," he said.

"That's very kind of you," I replied awkwardly and sat down in the chair in front of him.

"And Daryakum, again—I want to say how sorry I am for what happened yesterday."

"I know you're sorry, Otto, but that's not enough. We have to think about what to do so that nothing like this ever happens again."

"It won't happen again, Darya, I promise you. I'm not prepared to feel again what I felt last night when I saw your face. It was as if…I'd been stabbed in the heart, I could barely breathe, Daryakum, I love you so much that just the thought that I may hurt you paralyzes me."

"And yet, it did happen," I replied, the pain in my voice apparent. "Otto, I think that I won't be able to get over it, over the fear that it'll happen again, not unless you have nothing to do with your friends from Baja anymore."

For a moment, Otto said nothing. The shock on his face was clear. "I see," he said finally. He sounded despondent.

"It's not a punishment, Otto. I'm not trying to punish you for what happened, it's just that…I'll never be able to relax when I'm not with you if I know that those friends of yours and Greta are in the vicinity. The fact that they watched her going into your room when they knew full well what her intentions were and they didn't try to stop her or warn you, to me that sounds very bad. I wouldn't call them good friends after something like that."

"They are good friends, Darya, they really are. They just didn't think that it was…such a big deal. You know that their mentality is different. I told you that they've all had flings with everyone else, and none of them thought of making a big deal when couples switched."

"Or threesomes," I answered in painful cynicism, "even I forgot about the twin for a moment. I guess I'm beginning to get used to your mentality, and that, I really don't like."

"Daryakum, understand, that's the mentality everyone has here in Hungary. Even if I cut myself off from my old friends, I'll meet new ones here, and they too will think the same about those…hookups. I also think that it's nonsense and that they aren't a big deal, but only because it may hurt you so much, I'll do all I can so that it won't happen again…because you're more important to me than anything."

A familiar sharp pain hit me, as if I'd known all along that I was going to hear precisely that, and I'd been too afraid to think about it about what it meant.

"Otto, it won't work," I whispered. It was all I could do I was in such agony.

He stared at me questioningly. "What won't work, Daryakum?"

"I don't see it working," my throat constricted and I felt the tears coming again, "you and I, we perceive the world so differently, it'll never work…"

"Darya, what are you talking about?" his eyes looked startled and he came up and gripped my hand tightly, "Sure it'll work. You don't find a love like ours every day, we'll protect it, Darya, it'll only get stronger."

"It'll get stronger on my part, but not on yours…" I choked, bursting into uncontrollable tears. "I know myself, Otto, it'll become an obsession for me, I'll constantly be suspicious, and I'll worry about who you're with and what you're doing…and you'll grow distant…that's how it is."

"But you won't have to worry, I promise you won't!"

"Otto, the fact that you'll still be surrounded by people who see it as a normal way of life, that's what frightens me. Especially when all that'll prevent you from hooking up will be the knowledge that it would hurt me. And what will happen if, say, one day we have some stupid argument, and suddenly you feel like hurting me? It's not normal to live that way. It's impossible."

"It really isn't normal to live the way you want," he squeezed my hands, which were beginning to sweat, "jumping between two worlds. That's why I suggested you come and live here."

"I can't, I have a family in Israel, I can't cut myself off from them."

"Then I'll come and live there," he put his arms around my neck and held his head to mine, "I have no problem with it, Darya, I'm prepared to try for you. I'll ask at IBM if they can transfer me to Israel after I've been working there for a while."

I didn't respond. My head was resting on his shoulder, and for a while I managed to imagine the two of us living together, near the shore in Tel Aviv. But immediately the cracks began to appear in the idyllic image. Otto would never be able to live there, I thought, the country is tough to handle even for the people it was founded for. No one can live there just because of their partner and be happy. With time, he'll become disgruntled and turn all his anger toward me.

"Well, what do you say?" I heard him whisper in my ear.

"That it would be hard, Otto," I whispered back, "you'd have to convert, and they'll give you a really hard time until you do. You'd have to give up your beliefs, and you'd always feel alienated, disconnected from your natural place, from your own beliefs and culture. You wouldn't find it easy."

"I'm willing to work hard. I'll do whatever's necessary for us to be happy together."

I pulled away. I wanted to look into his eyes and draw strength from them. But when I saw him looking enthusiastically at me, like a kid becoming excited before a new adventure, I realized that it wouldn't work. It hurt like crazy when I thought about how he had waited for someone from our family to appear, so he could return our property to us. Most people in Israel would laugh at him, think that he was a sucker, that he was stupid for not taking the money for himself. He would never survive there; it just wasn't the place for him. Living in Israel would at best make him hard, irritable, and bitter. At worst, he would simply run away and leave me with broken dreams. If I loved him less, maybe I would be prepared to give it a shot. But I loved him too much, and I didn't want anything to ruin that love. I preferred to end it so that at least I'd have the memories of a great and beautiful love, which unfortunately had no real chance of being realized.

CHAPTER 26

When I tearfully told Dad all about how it ended between me and Otto, he said he was proud of me. He thought I had no reason to cry. "You had an interesting adventure," he said, "and you managed to learn something about yourself, too," he tried to help me understand the situation and put it into perspective. "Now you know that you're much stronger than you thought."

"Yes," I grumbled, "I'm strong enough to live my life all on my own."

"You aren't alone, Daryakum, you'll always have us. And I'm certain that if you want to rekindle your relationship with Oren, he'll be over the moon."

"Dad, stop it, I don't want to hear about Oren now. Having you all is really the most important thing right now, but no nagging, give me time to recover."

"Take your time, my child, just know that I'm incredibly proud of you."

Knowing that he was proud somehow helped get back on my feet again, even though I didn't think it would happen when I first got home to Israel. I found myself constantly haunted by the memory of Otto's face as he sat there looking at me through his pain, refusing to believe that it was truly over. I kept asking myself if I'd done the right thing, and it weighed heavily on me, threatening to steal every drop of air from my lungs at the most inopportune moments. I even found myself sobbing when I sat with my thesis supervisor and he explained that I didn't have enough material and that I'd have to look for more old documents.

Later that week, when my parents took me to see the new place that

Mom had set her heart on buying, I could feel the walls closing in on me as she proudly showed us around the spacious living room, the lower part of which would be transformed into a gallery in which we could proudly hang the two paintings I'd brought from Baja. Dad noticed the change in my mood, and as soon as we got home, he followed me into his office and asked me how I was feeling. To be honest, I didn't want to tell him everything. I was afraid to look into his eyes and see them say "I told you so." But when I saw the compassion in his face as I started talking, I felt encouraged to continue and told him the whole story.

Then, when he said how proud he was of me, I went on to tell him about my visit to the convent and about what Mother Yvonne had told me. This time, he was stunned into silence for quite some time.

"I don't understand it," he mumbled when he recovered, "so this Adriana, did she go to Shandor or not?"

"Well, that's the thing, I have no idea," I replied, "the nuns said they sent her to him with a letter, but…maybe she couldn't track him down. They didn't know exactly where he lived. I wouldn't be surprised if Adriana did try to find him, but while she was looking for him, she was drawn into the vibrant life of some big city, perhaps New York or Florida. She may have even become caught up in something in Paris and not even made it to the States. I think we should look for her, she could be alive!"

"Why didn't you ask him about her? How did you hold back?"

"I was afraid to. I thought he may have a heart attack from the shock. I didn't want to be the one to tell him about Angelika's horrifying death and that he had a daughter who disappeared thirty-two years ago."

"Assuming that he didn't already know," Dad replied, glancing at the photo, "I don't know, Darya, it sounds very strange to me that in all those years he never found out the truth. He had plenty of money and very little to keep him busy. Anyone else in his situation would have turned the world upside down to find out what happened to the only woman he ever loved."

"He said that he tried, but he could no longer get into Hungary, and everyone thought that Angelika had disappeared there," I explained to him.

"Still, it's weird…" Dad sunk into thought, then straightened up and said, "Well then, you said that he's planning to come here for a visit."

"Yes, to see the painting."

"Fine, then when he's looking at the painting, we'll use it as an opening to start reminiscing," he said. "Maybe then we'll be able to get him talking a little."

"Do you really think he's hiding something from us?" I asked in surprise.

"Yes," Dad replied, "when I think about how long it's been since he was here last…thirty something…how long ago is it…let me think…thirty-two years, Darya, he was here precisely when they sent his daughter away from the convent!"

"Do you think the two are connected?!" I tensed.

"I'm sure of it, I just have no idea how," Dad replied. "Do you have his phone number?"

"Yup," I answered and immediately added with concern, "you don't intend to interrogate him over the phone, do you?"

"Not at all, are you crazy?" Dad smiled and began to dial. "Is that what you think of me, that I'm so insensitive? I'm going to say that I heard he wants to visit and that I'll invite him to our housewarming party when we move, that's all."

Dad and Shandor spoke in Hungarian, so I could barely understand a word of what they were saying. When Dad hung up, however, he smiled at me and said, "That's it, we've set a date. He said it'll take him some time to organize the trip and that he'll be here in about a month and a half, right on my birthday."

"That's wonderful!" I cheered. "Your birthday's going to be interesting!"

"Yes, very!" Dad replied. Neither of us thought we were being overly optimistic.

***

Happily, I didn't see Oren at all for a while. After that one-way sighting in Paris, I asked Dana, my friend from the schedule planning team, to try not to schedule us for the same flights, and she took her job seriously. I believed that at some point, he'd get tired of that silly flight attendant who had her claws in him. I hadn't even bothered to find out her name, I just waited for time to do its thing. I tried to suppress the feeling I was having now and then that I had ruined things, usually when I found myself brooding over him and our relationship. Noa, who had moved onto a spiritual path after her illness, persuaded me that what needed to would happen sooner or later no matter what. Meanwhile, I tried to get used to the fact that I was alone, at least as much as one was when surrounded by a warm and noisy family, and I tried to enjoy it.

An intense month went by, during which we moved into our spacious new home with its small lawn, and I was assigned half of the basement. During the move, Mom worked us like dogs, and thirty days after we settled into our new home, we all gathered to celebrate her birthday and the other happy events that our family had recently been blessed with. The first surprise came from Vered and Gilad, who arrived exhilarated and arm in arm to tell us that they were pregnant. Noa jumped up to be the first to hug them, but then immediately started moaning that she'd no longer get to be the pampered baby of the family. With an amused tinge to her voice, Mom accused Dad of spoiling her too much and making her selfish, self-centered, and incapable of letting anyone else be the center of attention. Dad laughed and said she was right, and that from now on he'd be spoiling only himself. That's when he dropped the bombshell and said that for his birthday, which would be two weeks later, he wanted to buy a motorbike. This time, he added with a wink, he had waited to buy the house first, and now he could use the money they had left. Mom's smile evaporated instantaneously and she asked, her voice filled with concern and astonishment, "Are you serious?!"

"Absolutely!" Dad grinned and marched over to the new sideboard in the living room. He came back with a shiny brochure of motorbikes. He quickly paged through it and showed us the new bike he wanted to buy. It was a black-and-silver Kawasaki Z1300, with a comfortable backrest for an old person such as himself, Dad added, and it cost the modest sum of 100,000 shekels in easy payments.

"Peter, you have completely lost your mind," Mom declared, "that's just what you need at your age. A motorbike!"

"What's the problem," Dad said happily, "we can take trips around the country, the kind you enjoy, and visit all our old haunts. Finally, you'll be able to show me exactly where the truck got stuck the day you didn't arrive for our date at the Moghrabi."

"I got there in the end," Mom blushed like a teenager, but her eyes showed awkward willingness.

"Mom, that's an awesome idea," Noa said, as if to prove she was capable of wanting what's best for others, "you and Dad can take trips, visit the places Dad lived when he arrived in Israel, the kibbutz, and…"

"The falafel stand by Tel Hashomer, what was it called before? Sarafand?" I added with a wink, when suddenly the doorbell rang. Mickey started barking and ran to the door with Noa behind him. I guessed it was her current boyfriend and turned my attention back to our lively family banter, which had taken an unexpected turn in support of Dad's idea. Mom was becoming more enthusiastic about the crazy idea of taking a bike trip at their ripe old age and had even pulled out a map of Israel to plan the trip. We were all thrilled by her metamorphosis, and so we didn't notice Oren enter the room with Noa until he was standing in the middle.

"Hello, dear Schwartzs. Congratulations!" he said and kissed Mom on both cheeks. By the time I got my breath back, she had already opened his gift: a string of pink pearls and a pair of matching earrings. Mom, who was mad about pearls, beamed with joy. "Thank you, Oren, honey," she hugged him. I noticed Dad looking at me in amusement. That's when I realized he was behind it, and I pulled a face at him. Dad stopped smiling and nodded, as if he didn't deny inviting Oren, and that he thought I should grab the opportunity to straighten things out with him. I would have done so gladly if I'd known what to say, but unfortunately, I hadn't yet prepared a repentance speech, possibly because I didn't want to think of myself as a sinner. Oren wasn't showing any sign of noticing I was wavering, and he behaved naturally. After completing his gift-giving ceremony, he went over to Vered and kissed her on the cheek, then to Gilad and patted him on the back. After that, he kissed me too, casually on the cheek and then asked why we had a motorbike catalog and map of Israel on the table. Mom and Dad enthusiastically started telling him about their plans, and he happily added his bit. Overwhelmed by mixed feelings, I cringed in the corner of the sofa. I could have tried to pretend that nothing had happened, that it was just another fun evening in the Schwartz family home, but I just couldn't do it. I felt a bitter taste of loss as I watched Oren fitting in so easily with my beloved family. The fact that he was no nonchalant when it came to me made me all the more frustrated. But there was something else there, something that made me freeze: For the first time ever, I realized how much I loved him, and not only in the painful way, which I had felt to my core when I saw him walk into the hotel in Paris with that annoying attendant hanging off his arm. No, I loved him in every way possible. I missed his serenity, the way he calmed me down when I thought that the world had come to an end, I missed the innate integrity with which he conducted himself and treated others, the steady path he charted for himself, cutting no corners, playing no games with anyone. I used to find him boring, but now I realized that the boredom stemmed from within me, from the constant restlessness that gnawed at me as I looked for exciting ways out. When I was a kid, whenever I complained about being bored, Dad would suggest I stick my butt out of the window so a crowd of people could come and look at it, and that would be interesting. Only now, I realized how much wisdom there was in that silly Hungarian joke, which made it clear that boredom stemmed from within. The fact was, in the last few months of imposing a life of loneliness and supposed boredom on myself, I had managed to make progress on the thesis I'd been battling with for five years.

 I had realized that only with one particular man by my side could I develop in whatever direction I chose and create an interesting life for myself, discover the interests that stem from within and not be stimulated by exciting blonds who look like models and jump into bed with every one of them.

 I came to this realization the first time I managed to think in an orderly way about things, but I was incapable of talking about it. I was afraid that it was too late, I was scared of being rejected. I was terrified that, after giving a long speech, after saying that I'd finally seen the light, Oren would look at me with amused compassion, like Rhett Butler in Gone with the

Wind, raise his chin and say, "Frankly, my dear, I don't give a damn about you and your plans," to quote very freely.

***

"Now it's time for the cake, I made it myself!" I heard Dad announce through the fog in my mind. He stood up and took my hand, pulling me after him into the kitchen. "Darya, come and help me cut it," he added.

"Dad, we can only cut the cake after Mom's blown out the candles," I informed him in the kitchen.

"Then help me put the candles on," he insisted, his smile amused.

"Fine," I sighed and placed seven small candles on the edge of the chocolate cake, a candle for each decade, "but you know you aren't fooling anyone. They could all tell that you wanted to talk to me in private."

"Good, then it'll be quick," he retorted and lit the candles with the lighter he took out of his pocket, conclusive evidence that he was still smoking behind our backs, despite the warnings of his doctors and Mom's protests. "I think that you should talk to Oren today. You're procrastinating and it's not making anyone feel any better, certainly not yourself."

"Dad, I don't know what to say to him," I confessed, "anything I think of sounds idiotic to me."

"You know what to say, you're just scared that he'll turn his back on you. So be brave and strong, like some people think you are, and tell him what you feel. Whatever he chooses to do with it, that's his problem."

"I don't know," I hesitated, "if he rejects me now, I'll never be able to bring myself to talk to him again."

"Daryakum, do me a favor, I wouldn't ask you to do this if I didn't believe that you're both about to miss a wonderful opportunity. It would be a real shame. Oren is that rare kind of person who lets me sleep well when I know he's by your side."

"Dad, since when have you been such a Jewish mother?" I smiled forgivingly.

"Since your Mom agreed to take a bike trip with me. I think someone has to be the responsible adult in this family," he smiled back at me. "Now, let's go out with the cake before the candles melt."

"Okay," I followed him out, still trying to decide when and how to talk to Oren. I was still thinking about it when Oren got up, said his goodbyes, and promised Dad to come with him to buy the bike. When he moved toward the door with Mickey on his heels, I decided that now was the time. No one had stood up to see him to the door, proving to me that they were all expecting me to.

"Oren, wait a sec," I called after him. He stopped by the door and looked at me questioningly.

"We have to talk," I said, and when he didn't respond I continued, "I mean, I have to talk to you. You have every right to be silent if you want."

"Are you arresting me or something?" he joked, breaking the ice. I breathed a sigh of relief.

"No, heaven forbid, just don't go calling a lawyer now."

"Fine," he studied me, his eyes thoughtful, "let's go to my place."

***

I climbed on the back of his motorbike, the butterflies in my stomach fluttering between hope and despair. Oren obviously knew what I wanted to say to him, and he was inviting back to the home that was once mine, which meant he probably wasn't planning to reject me. Unless, that is, he wanted to humiliate me so badly that, as I'd told Dad, I would never dare to go anywhere near him again.

As we climbed the stairs to the apartment, I tried to read his face for a sign of what was to come, but it was expressionless. When we finally entered the apartment, I was relieved to see that nothing had changed. Except that it wasn't messy, as one might expect from Oren after months of living on his own.

"Okay," I said, leaning on the wall, refusing to feel at home, at least until I'd spoken my mind, "so this is it. I'll just dive right in, then. Basically, I must have been having some kind of crisis, turning thirty and all, because I just don't understand how I could have broken up with you. But I want you to know, Oren, that a moment hasn't passed that I haven't thought about you, even when I was—"

"Darya," he interrupted me sharply, "please, save me the romantic bits with your Hungarian, all right?"

"But, Oren…it's important. I'm not going to go into details, but I really want you to know that I was thinking about you all the time, because… because you have become a part of me, and it's not just out of habit, it's mainly because I truly and honestly love you. I love your serenity and your stability, the fact that you're not a fake, that you know what you want from yourself and from your life, without putting on an act for other people. You are a complete human being, Oren, you're at peace with yourself and with the reality that you've created for yourself, and that's quite something, even admirable, and it's also very…sexy to me—"

"Oh, there's the word I was waiting for," a familiar smile appeared on his face, and he stretched his arms out to me. "Does that mean that from now on, you won't push me away every time I try to touch you?"

"No, not ever, Oren," I fell gratefully into his arms, "on the contrary, you'll have to pull yourself out of my arms whenever you want to get out of bed."

"Those are just words," he gave me a long kiss, and I inhaled the wonderfully familiar scent of his aftershave, "Are we going to get married? Have children?"

"We sure will," my heart expanded as I imagined Oren playing with our kids in the yard, "we'll have wall-to-wall children, and my parents will babysit them whenever we go abroad. Can you guess what my Dad said to me this evening? That when he knows I'm with you, he can sleep peacefully."

"Wow, now that's something to say before we get into bed," he smiled sardonically, letting me go and heading for the bar. "Let's have a glass of good wine first, to save the evening."

"Okay, but not the best you have, save it for the wedding," I said, looking at the muscles of his back, which I could see through his T-shirt when he bent over to pour the wine. I had never longed to touch anyone so badly before. And that was precisely why I remained leaning against the wall, deliberately drawing out the moment, intensifying the feeling of being swept away.

How could I have left him? I wondered as he handed me a glass of wine and devoured me with his loving eyes. The only time I ever felt like the most perfect woman in the world was when I was with him.

When we finished our drinks and he took me in his arms, I fell into them with a sense of wellbeing and expectation, realizing that everything had gone just as I'd hoped. We had owed it to ourselves to have different experiences, to take an adventure to prove that we weren't missing anything outside our relationship. I certainly needed it. It seemed that I had inherited the adventurous, wild side of my family and it had been looking for a way to express itself.

"I love you," I whispered, when Oren picked me up in his arms and carried me to the bed.

"I know," he whispered, leaning over me and kissing me long on my lips, neck and below it, until any trace of organized thought evaporated in the cloud of hormones flooding my brain.

***

In the morning, I woke up sweaty, sticky, and filled with happiness. Even the fact that Oren hadn't closed the blinds and turned on the air conditioner during the night had no impact on my mood. He lay beside me holding me in his arms, and when I opened my eyes, he immediately said, "That's it, that's what I missed the most—seeing you wake up in the morning and griping straight away."

"But I didn't say a word," I protested with a laugh.

"Yes, but I could read your eyes when you opened them, and the first thing you thought was damn, he didn't close the blinds!"

"Not true," I indulged myself and kissed him, "the first thing I thought was damn, why the hell didn't you make me breakfast…"

"Chop chop, you poor starved woman," he covered my face and neck with kisses, "the cook only wants to draw some positive energy from you…"

My phone rang, interrupting him, and we both looked at it lazily. "Who could it be at this hour?" he wondered, "Are you on standby today?"

"No," I said, for a moment considering not answering, but I glanced at the screen just to see who was calling. It was Vered, so I decided to answer.

"Darya," her voice sounded strange, broken, fragmented. My heart constricted in panic.

"Yes, Vered, it's me…what's the matter? Did something happen to Noa?"

'It's Dad,' she tried to choke back the tears, then burst out crying, "Darya, Dad…passed away."

"What???!!" My scream seemed to echo through the room, refusing to end. I could hear it breaking in my ears like the waves of a stormy sea.

Oren sat down on the bed, looking at me in horror. "What happened?" he seemed to be asking, but I couldn't hear a word, I just saw his lips moving through the veil of black dots covering my eyes.

"Darya, come here quickly, Mom and Noa are completely broken. I need you here," I heard Vered say. She sounded far away.

"But Vered, how…how did it happen…"

"His heart…he had a heart attack, Darya. Come quickly, I'm waiting for you…" Vered hung up and I was left lying paralyzed on the bed. I couldn't even cry. Dad was dead…it was incomprehensible…I hoped that I was sleeping and it was all just a nightmare, but the distress and nausea that had spread so quickly inside of me were entirely palpable.

"Darya," Oren took me in his arms and shook me lightly, "what happened? Talk to me!"

"It's Dad," I whispered, my voice breaking, "My dad…is dead."

Oren hugged me tight, he didn't say a word. I saw the enormous pain in his eyes, and I couldn't bear it. I buried my head in his chest, then started sobbing harder than I imagined possible. Everything was now dwarfed by this loss. Nothing else seemed important. This pain, burning in my chest, threatened to turn my heart into ashes.

I cried and cried in Oren's arms, which this time, were unable to protect me from the horror. It can't be true, I kept thinking, he was so happy last night…he was planning to buy a bike…how can someone die like that while they're making plans?

My cell phone rang again. Oren answered. After he put it down, he took me in his arms again and whispered, "Darya, we have to go, they need us there. Come, take a shower, wash your face…"

"I don't want to!!!" I screamed, my voice hoarse, terrified of having to deal with the harsh facts, "I'm not going there, Oren! I don't want to see my father…dead…I…let me stay here…and die quietly in bed…" My voice faded away as a crazy thought passed through my mind. Dad had known! He could feel that he was going to die, that's why he urged me to talk to Oren, he said himself that he would only be able to sleep peacefully once I was with Oren…

He had felt that he was going to die…he probably felt unwell and… Why didn't he take care of himself, damn it?! Why didn't he go to the doctor? And why was I in such a hurry to do as he asked? If I hadn't run after Oren, he would have lived until he was certain he had no reason to worry about me.

CHAPTER 27

The new house that my parents bought, optimistically assuming that they'd be living there happily ever after, was silent when we got there. Even Mickey was lying on the grass, a forlorn expression in his eyes. I was really hoping that no one had printed the death announcements yet and that I wouldn't encounter one as we entered. It was more than I could bear, seeing Dad's name printed in black and white. When we walked in, Gilad greeted us with pure relief. He told us that Mom and Noa had been given shots to sedate them, and they were both resting now in the main bedroom under the supervision of a doctor, Mom's second cousin, whom they'd called in the morning and who had come right over.

"Vered went to the Ministry of Interior to have the death certificate issued," he continued, "and she asked me to join her as soon as you arrived so that we could go to the chevra kadisha together to arrange the burial. Please can you stay here and deal with the stream of people drifting in."

Only then did I notice that the house was full of people, some of them utter strangers to me. They looked uncomfortable, standing there and talking quietly. I noticed Mr. Klein from the bank sitting in the corner, and he looked sadly at me.

"Where's Dad? I want to see him!" I said quietly, my voice catching. I knew that the void inside me would never be filled if I didn't prove to myself with my own two eyes that Dad was no longer with us. Deep in my heart I was hoping that Noa's weird theories were right and that his soul was still floating beside him and that, somehow, I'd be able to convince it to return to his body.

"He's at the hospital," Gilad answered weakly, looking down at the floor. "Yael called an ambulance as soon as she found him like that...in the bathroom. She was hoping they could still save him...and—"

"How did it happen?" I kept pushing him, even though I could feel he was already on edge. "Yesterday he looked perfectly healthy, and happy and excited for his own birthday, and the motorbike he wanted to buy... how? How does a person in his condition suddenly...die?"

Oren held me tightly, as if afraid I would collapse. But I had no such plans. I stood steadily and stared demandingly at poor Gilad as if he could provide me with the answers that would make some sense of the chaos in my head and heart.

"He...I don't know precisely what happened, but from what Yael told me, I understand that he was absolutely fine when he got up in the morning, and he said that he wanted to try out the new hot tub, and that's it. He went into the bathroom, and after a while, she wanted to see what he was up to. She opened the door and saw him lying there...in the hot tub.

"The hot tub...it was the hot tub that killed him," my blood was pounding so loudly in my temples, I was afraid my head would explode any moment. I forced myself out of Oren's arms and ran to Dad's office to his toolbox; I wanted to take the biggest hammer he had and smash that goddamn hot tub. Dad had teased Mom about wanting one in the new house. He said it was so nouveau riche, that all the yuppies have them installed just to show off, but they didn't have any time to take a bath, since they worked all the time to have the money to buy a hot tub in the first place. But Mom insisted that it wasn't at all expensive and that it cost almost the same as a regular bathtub, and since they were improving their standard of living, why not have one installed. Naturally, Dad gave in, as he usually did when it came down to his ideology versus her practicality. And now the hot tub had killed him. For God's sake! What a curse I've brought on us all, with that damn money I got from Otto! I'll never be able to forgive myself, ever!

Oren caught up with me in the office and grabbed my hand. "Darya, that's enough, leave the hot tub alone, stop looking for someone or something to blame, you don't need it, no one is to blame for what happened.

Peter was feeling healthy and happy when he died in that hot tub. Many people wish to die that way. What did you want? For him to reach the ripe old age of ninety, sick and exhausted, miserable and dependent on other people?"

"He wouldn't have been sick and tired when he reached ninety. Look how old Grandpa Yoshka was when he died, and if he hadn't been injured in that accident, he'd still be alive today," I cried.

"Peter wasn't like Grandpa Yoshka," Oren sat me down on the sofa, and gently stroked my head. "Listen to me, Darya, your father was all heart and soul, and Grandpa Yoshka—with all due respect—had no heart at all. Can you imagine your father letting you go abroad without money like your grandfather did to him?"

"No," I mumbled, "but Grandpa didn't know he was planning on leaving…"

"He knew, he told me himself that he knew. He said that he had sensed that Peter was going to run away, but he hoped that if he had no money, he'd drop the idea. And that night, when your grandmother ran after him, he realized that it was happening, and he decided that if Peter was such a hero, then he could manage on his own, that would show him. He allowed his anger at Peter for going against his will to overcome any other feeling. Is that the kind of father you wish you had?"

"No! I replied immediately, realizing that I wouldn't give up my father for any other and certainly not for Grandpa Yoshka, who although was very amusing and nice as a grandfather, had caused so much pain to those who loved him, especially Dad and Grandma.

***

Vered and Gilad got back around noon and told us that the funeral would be at five that afternoon. I asked Oren to take me to the hospital to say goodbye to Dad. When we stood in the entrance to the room where his body was, an icy wave ran through my body and I started trembling. Oren held my shoulder, "You don't have to do this if it's too hard for you," he said tenderly.

"No, I have to," I answered firmly and used all my strength to find my inner balance, "I want to be alone with him for a few minutes."

"Okay, I'll be right outside," he let go and went outside. I walked into the room, teetering on faltering legs, until I was standing by the man who, until yesterday, was the father who I loved more than life itself. He was covered with a white sheet, and I quivered again as I thought about how I was about to see his face. My hand shaking, I lifted the sheet and forced myself to look at him. Dad looked like he was sleeping, like he would wake up any moment and laugh and explain that it was all just a practical joke. I took his hand, it was cold and hard, just like my heart. Nevertheless, I didn't let it go, and I found myself talking to him. "Dad," I said, my voice shaky, "you can't do this to us now, you have to come back…I know that your soul is here in this room! Return it to your body and let's go home." Dad's face didn't even twitch, and the silence in the room was unbearable. I started sobbing again, my body shaking. "Dad," I cried, "it's not fair, Mom's waiting for you, you promised to take her on a biking trip, and… Vered is going to have a baby soon, you were supposed to be the coolest grandfather on Earth, how can you give that up? Dad, I'm not leaving until you recover…I…how am I supposed to survive without you? It's just not fair…"

Suddenly, a gust of wind swept across my neck. Surprised, I lifted my eyes and looked around the room. It had no windows. My legs quivering, I scrambled to my feet and tried to find the source but the room was still again. Dad was still lying there in front of me, not moving, but for a moment he seemed to smile. The room spun around me and black spots hid Dad's face. I hoped I would faint, but I didn't. instead, I dropped to the chair beside him and the dizziness passed. "Are you messing with me, Dad?" I accused him. "What are you trying to prove? That I'm stronger than I think? That even at such a terrible time, I can survive and not die myself, despite the awful pain that…is almost paralyzing me?"

Again, the room was filled with silence. Dad continued to lie there motionless.

"All right, Dad," I finally whispered, "I see that, as usual, you're being more stubborn than me. I…if you're so insistent, I'll leave you alone.

Maybe you really have grown tired of this life, which didn't give you a dull moment…and you want to rest, I hope that you really will rest…at least there, in the heavens. Take care of yourself…and I just want you to know that…there never was, is, or will be anyone I love more than you…that I couldn't imagine a more wonderful father than you…and I only hope that…I can be as good a mother as you were a father…that I'll be able to pass on to my children something…of your wonderful spirit…that…I… love you so much, Dad…"

✳✳✳

Dad's funeral passed like a bad dream. The only memory I took away from it was the vast number of people who gathered at the cemetery. There were so many shocked and pained faces that I couldn't help but take some comfort in that so many people loved my dad. Vered made a speech, the details of which I couldn't fully grasp, but its basic message was that Dad came to Israel with nothing other than a gold chain and a Star of David, which he sold to buy falafel and a bus ticket to Jerusalem, and now he's left Israel and the world as a whole with so much more: with the love of all these people who would always keep him in their hearts and remember him as a charming, wise, and warm person who wisely never misused his incredible charm; as a man whose infectious love of life radiated from him. And that is more than anyone can ask for in either life or death—to be remembered just like that.

✳✳✳

By the time we got home from the cemetery, the house was full of people, and it remained that way all week. Mom, who had recovered, sat surrounded by a large group of friends and family. She was paging through old albums with them and sharing amusing stories about Dad, because there were no sad stories about him. I looked around for Noa. I was worried more about her than about the others. But she too was sitting with a large group of friends, Mickey on her lap, and she too looked better.

I turned to Oren, who was sitting next to me and scrutinizing me every few minutes with a worried look in his eye, and I asked him to get me a sleeping pill. Oren did as I asked without arguing. He seemed to think I hadn't yet made it through the entire nightmarish day without falling apart, and he was still expecting the worst. After I took the pill, I went down to the basement with him, half of which was mine. "Listen," I mumbled to him, when I was already lying on the bed covered in a thick down comforter, which had no impact on my frozen heart, "I think I'm going to have to move in here, at least for a few months, until Mom recovers."

We'll do whatever you want," Oren answered tenderly, stroking my head, "Vered also told me she would move in and that Gilad will join her on the semester break."

"That's good," I smiled sadly and waited for sleep to come and wrap me in its kind arms, and maybe, just maybe, when I woke up in the morning, I'd discover that it was all just a bad dream, that Dad was playing with Mickey outside in the yard and Mom was complaining that he was even spoiling the dog too much, and they would argue and everything would be utterly normal and as usual.

***

The next day, I woke up at noon to the sound of excited exclamations in English and Hungarian. I felt the anxiety growing in me as I remembered what had happened the day before. Dad's dead, I thought in horror, he's not here, I'm just imagining that I can hear him. I pulled the blanket over my head. I wanted to carry on sleeping, to avoid coping with the awful fact that I was alone in the world, defenseless without his compassionate smile to help me through all the crises I had waiting for me, the kind that always arrive when you're least prepared for them.

"Darya," I heard Oren's voice through the blanket, "wake up, sweetie, you're wanted upstairs, Shandor Bachi from Florida is here."

"Really?!" I threw the blanket off my face and looked at his, which was leaning over me. I could see the love and tenderness in his eyes. "How? Who informed him?"

"I have no idea, probably Vered told him as soon as it happened if he could make it here so quickly."

"What a mensch," I muttered, sitting up in bed. "Look at that, Oren! He came here immediately to be with us, even though he's almost a hundred years old. What a good man he is…look what a big heart he has, and it hasn't stopped him from reaching the ripe old age of a hundred and—"

"Are you kidding?" Oren said, astounded, who seemed to have forgotten the conversation we'd had the day before, about the inverse relationship between being good and living long. "Are you getting up? He can't wait to see you…and nor can Angela…"

"Angela is really important, she mustn't be kept waiting," I said sardonically, which he didn't really get either. He hugged me and whispered in my ear, "Darya, sweetie, get out of bed already, you've slept half the day away, people are waiting for you…Shandor Bachi…and also many of your childhood friends who were here yesterday, but I told them that you're sleeping, so they'll probably come back later today. Do us a favor and get out there. I can't keep that whole lot entertained on my own…"

"That's great," I complained, "my father has died, and I have to entertain friends from my childhood…"

Oren glared at me until I finally sighed and put on the clothes that he'd handed to me. I really wanted to see Shandor Bachi and that helped to ease the pain I'd been feeling since the day before. It was as if the old man, who had known Dad since the day he was born and loved him dearly, could somehow make me feel as if Dad was with us again.

"Daryakum, I'm so sorry," Shandor burst into tears when he saw me in the living room. He staggered to his feet and hugged me, putting all his weight on me. I was about to collapse myself, so I helped him sit back down on the sofa. "I'm so sorry," he continued mumbling, "I should have come sooner. How did I miss the opportunity to see Peter when he was still alive? How? How? I can't forgive myself…"

Angela, who looked like she was about to start crying herself, quickly handed him a bottle of mineral water. Mom sat down beside him and put her hand on his arm, "Shandor, don't cry," she said, "at your age…it can't be good…Peter knew that you loved him. He always told me about the letters you used to send him. He admired you…and all the stories that you told him about the bears…and here, look," she pointed at the painting of Angelika and Adrianus, "he even insisted on hanging that painting here, even though I didn't really like the idea at first."

Shandor stopped crying, turned around, and looked at the painting. His eyes widened. "Angelika," he said softly, "my Angelika…do you see, Angela? That's Angelika…" and again, he burst into heartbreaking tears. Angela walked over to the painting and stared at it as if having a revelation.

"I have…something to tell you all," Shandor's voice choked as he looked around at us, "something important, very important…I wanted Peter to hear this too, but…I was too late. I'm so sorry that…it turned out this way…who would have believed it, that the progeny of the Schwartz family would die of natural causes at such a young age."

"Shandor, don't cry over Peter," Mom said, surprising me, as she stroked his hand softly, "although he died relatively young," her voice broke for a moment as the tears poured down her cheeks, still she continued, "he had a better life than any of the other Schwartzs. He had a marvelous family," she pointed at us and tried to smile, "he received a lot of love and warmth from us…"

At that point, we all burst out crying. Noa ran over to me and buried her head in my shoulder, and Oren leaned over us from behind and stroked her head.

"You're right," Shandor agreed, "Peter did have a good life."

"Would you like something to drink?" Mom asked, who, as usual, thought that dealing with practical matters would help her regain her composure.

"No, no, I want to tell you something, something important…Angela, come sit next to me."

Angela, who was stroking the painting with her fingers, looked tearfully at him and dutifully sat down beside him.

"I want to tell you that…Angela is my granddaughter," Shandor Bachi said and was met with stunned looks from veiled eyes. The room was silent. We all looked at the wrinkled old man and the beautiful woman beside him, who was looking down at her knees.

"Shandor Bachi," I managed to find my voice, "it's okay, you don't have to make up excuses for leaving your money to her. You're entitled to do whatever you want with it…and we'll support you. After all, she has been taking such good care of you for years, now."

"No, Daryakum, you don't understand, I'm not making excuses," Shandor insisted. "I know what you think about me and Angela, and I'm so sorry that I didn't refute the rumors a long time ago. I was old and stubborn…and I was angry with you—so angry that I continued the joke for too long. What a shame, a shame that Peter never had the chance to meet the granddaughter of the woman who saved his life…"

"You're the granddaughter of the woman who saved his life?!" I repeated after him, and all at once, the pieces fell into place. Angela was Adriana's daughter, and Dad had almost guessed the story on his own.

"What are you talking about, Shandor Bachi?" Mom inquired, thinking that the old man must have lost him mind. "Who is the woman who saved Peter's life?"

"Angelika," Shandor Bachi answered, pointing at the painting, "Peter caught scarlet fever when he was fifteen, at the end of the war, and he almost died, didn't you know?"

"I knew," I found my voice again, "Dad told me that Angelika cured him with mold from old bread. So then, Adriana found you after all, Shandor Bachi? Why did you hide it from us?"

"Dad almost died at fifteen?" Noa said, "then…he didn't just die now, he counted backward, starting after his forty-fifth birthday…and now he just got to year zero…"

"Noa, what are you going on about?" I stopped her, afraid that Shandor Bachi would think we were even stranger than he'd imagined and run off before we heard the whole of Adriana's story. But Mom had already added her bit to the strange conversation by declaring, "I told him not to play such stupid games with fate! If only I hadn't gone along with it…" she sobbed.

"Mom, stop it!" I begged. "Let Shandor speak. Getting angry at Dad or at ourselves won't bring him back to life. That was part of Dad's charm, his crazy sense of humor, and we should remember it fondly instead of being angry at him now."

"Thanks, Daryakum," Shandor said softly, silencing them again, "that's quite right. We all have a slightly crazy sense of humor, the Schwartz family…and I also played my fair share of…jokes, which later turned out to be tasteless. Look how I decided not to tell you about my true relationship with Angela when I realized you all thought I was a foolish old man and that she was twisting me around her baby finger just so I'd leave her all my money. Today I can only regret denying my granddaughter the warmth of her family, of you lot, and first and foremost, the love that Peter would have given her."

Angela began to cry softly, and Shandor put his hand on her knee and continued, "But I decided to put an end to this silly game after Darya came to visit me and I realized that she'd already found out part of the story. But firstly, I wanted to tell Angela herself."

"What?" I interrupted him again, dumbstruck. "Angela didn't know she was your granddaughter until a few months ago? How could you hide such a thing from her?"

"I was afraid, Daryakum," Shandor answered, looking directly at me, "and I had good reason to be afraid. You see, I never knew that Angelika had given birth to a daughter, my daughter. She didn't tell me anything. After I left France, she must have hidden her pregnancy from Imre somehow—he always was blind to what was happening around him. When it was time to have the baby, she went to the convent where she was raised, had the baby there, and handed her over to the mother superior to look after. She planned on taking her back after the war. That's what the mother superior told me in the letter she sent with Adriana, our daughter…she was named after Adrianus, the bear. But as you know, she never returned, and to this day, no one knows what happened to her. Adriana stayed at the convent, where she was brought up to be a nun, just like her mother. I guess the over-developed Schwartz family's wild gene, the same one that my brother Yoshka had, was flowing in my daughter's blood too. She wasn't meant to be a nun, and at twenty, the mother superior, who was the only person who knew I was her father, sent her to me in the States. She gave her money and a letter for me. Adriana, however, who was a very beautiful woman, may she rest in peace, decided to stop in New York and try her luck as an actress and dancer and told me nothing. She appeared on my doorstep in Florida only ten years later, after she got herself pregnant by accident and was unable to make a living from dancing. She told me she was my daughter. Naturally, I was over the moon. I took her in and gave her all I could to make up for those years we'd lost. I spoiled her, I wouldn't let her work, and I hoped that she'd grow to see me as her father, despite the tragic circumstances that had kept us from knowing about each other for so many years. That was when I came to visit you in Israel and asked you to move to Florida to live near me. I wanted to enfold my Adriana in a warm and loving family, to compensate her for the lonely years she'd spent at the convent. But you refused to come. Yoshka, who for years after the terrible war stubbornly refused to leave Hungary, suddenly decided that Israel was the only place for the Jews. I was furious and hurt, and for a while, I even cut off all ties with the family. Today I know I was wrong, that I should have come to live near you, here in Israel. But I was too stubborn and angry, and I thought that Yoshka, who was the reason I even went on that adventure, should have agreed to the only request I ever made of him, without asking too many questions. In any case, I made a mistake, which we both paid a heavy price for, both me and Adriana. As soon as Angela was born, she went back to her old, wild way of life, hanging out with dubious characters and using drugs, which eventually led to her death. I found myself left with a broken heart and a one-year-old baby who was my granddaughter and I loved more than anyone. But I didn't know what to do with her. In the end, I decided to raise her myself, to take care of all her needs, but not to tell her that she was my granddaughter."

"But why?!" I heard Oren's voice from behind me. He sounded shaken to the depths of his soul.

"Why? Why? Because I was afraid; afraid that if Angela knew that she was my granddaughter and grew up with all I wanted to pamper her with, it would ruin her. I was afraid that she also had that wild gene, which her mother and other members of the family had. I was afraid that she'd become a brat and land up a wreck like my Adriana, who I hadn't been able to save. When she grew up a little, I told her that she was the daughter of my beloved carer who had died from a serious illness and that I promised to raise her as my own. But in return, she would have to be my housekeeper and take care of me."

"How could you do that?" I asked, looking at Angela, who was still crying, although she wasn't making a sound. "How could you raise her, knowing she was your granddaughter, and stay so distant from her? Didn't it break your heart?"

"I did what I thought was best for the child," Shandor Bachi replied sternly and stroked Angela's head, "and as you can see, she has turned into a charming, intelligent, learned, hardworking woman who can take care of herself even when I die. And what I wanted to ask of you, as the only family we have left, is to open your hearts to her, embrace her as one of your own, treat her like family, because…she is worthy of it. She is such a good girl…"

Oren was right, the thought flashed through my mind when I saw my mother hugging Angela, Dad really was the only Schwartz with a heart.

EPILOGUE

Three months after Dad passed away, Shandor Bachi returned his own soul to the Creator. Angela called to let us know, adding that he'd asked to be buried in Israel, close to Dad and his parents. She arrived with his coffin two days later, and we gathered our few remaining Hungarian relatives and held a modest funeral for him.

After the funeral, Mom invited Angela to stay with us for a while. Angela was thrilled and agreed, and stayed for six months until Vered and Gilad had a beautiful, cute blond baby boy, whose sweet face reminded us of snowy mountain peaks and green forests. Naturally, we made the unanimous decision to call him Peter. Mom wasn't thrilled by the idea and claimed that it was bad luck to name the baby after someone who had died. In the end, we reached a compromise and added the name Sa'ar, but a few days after the newborn arrived, I caught Mom leaning over him and murmuring, "Peter, Peter, smile for Grandma." When she heard me behind her she added, "What can I do? He looks so much like the photos of Dad as a baby."

Naturally, Vered wanted to go right back to work after she gave birth. Angela offered to take care of the baby, but Mom adamantly refused. She said that looking after him was the only thing that put a smile on her face. And that's the way it was. Mom devoted herself to taking care of Peter, and we—we fussed over him and vied for his attention. At that point, Angela decided to move to Eilat to continue her marine biology studies, which she'd started in Key West.

She has kept in touch with us over the phone and online ever since and often comes to visit.

Although life went on, Oren and I found it hard to plan a big, joyful wedding. The shock and sadness over Dad's death were still too present in our lives, too horribly tangible. As such, we decided to postpone the wedding indefinitely. Meanwhile, we moved into the new house with Mom, Noa, and Mickey. Vered and Gilad rented an apartment nearby, and little Peter spent most of his day with us, to the delight of everyone.

After Shandor Bachi told us his story, Oren suggested I put our family saga down on paper, and that's precisely what I did, while still working on my thesis. It took me a year and a half to write this book, and the day I wrote the words "The End" at the bottom of the page, I emerged from the basement into the living room. I wanted to breathe the smell of the new grass Oren had planted outside after Mickey had destroyed the previous lawn.

That's when I saw little Peter standing on his own looking at the painting of Angelika and Adrianus and talking to it, "Bear, bear," he chattered and added, "Peter loves the bear, the bear is Peter's friend, right, Darya?"

"Yes, sweetie," tears filled my eyes and I bent down to hug him. Peter tried to wiggle out of my arms and get closer to the picture. "Peter wants to give honey to the bear, and the bear will be Peter's friend, bears love honey, right Darya?"

"Right, my little prince," I said and took his hand in mine, and together we went to the kitchen. "I'll give you honey, but you can give it to your toy bear, you hear? Not to the bear in the picture, okay, sweetie?"

"No," Peter insisted, standing his ground, "I want to go to the zoo and get a little bear, a real one, to be my friend."

Again, I found my face covered in tears, as I remembered the letter that Dad had written to Shandor. He'd also wanted a bear friend.

"It's not nice to put bears in the zoo in cages," Peter said and put his hand back in mine, "they must be sad there. Come, let's go get a little bear from there and let it go."

"We will, but another time," I said tenderly, glancing around for a toy that could distract him from the bears. When Mom got home, she picked him up and said, "Peter, come and eat."

"I don't want to eat, I want to go to the zoo to get a little bear to be my friend," Peter responded, trying to wiggle out of her arms. She looked up at me and noticed the tears in my eyes. "What's the matter, Darya? Why are you crying?" she asked.

"It's nothing," I answered and fled to the garden to tell Oren it was time we got married, that it was time for another adorable child to join the family, one with a face that resembles green forests and snowcapped mountains, just like little Peter, and the big one too, of course.

Yoshka and Yanka Krauss on their wedding day

THANKS

To Dr. Naftali Brezniak for reading this so quickly and for your enlightening comments and encouragement.

To David Pishto (Yosef) and Yafa Weiss, thank you for your stories and the tape and the time you devoted to me. To Shimon Gal and to Avi Shpitzer, thank you for your stories and for the atmosphere and memories you shared with me. To Dana Izkowitz for the inspiration. To Koby Maimon for your advice.

To Eli, who read the book and liked it, thank you for your support. To Pessia Tzur—thank you for everything. To Mom, Miriam Krauss, thank you for your stories, support, and patience. To Limor and Agat Krauss, my wonderful sisters – thank you for our childhood memories.

Thanks to all of my friends and relatives who wanted to read the drafts and who showed their disappointment when I couldn't print them up quickly enough. I'm sorry, I ask for your forgiveness and, naturally, I truly appreciate your willingness and patience. I promise to make it up to you with official copies.

A special thanks to all the wonderful people at Kinneret Zmora-Bitan Dvir, to Amnon Jackont and Noa Manheim – my amazing editors, to Dov Alfon, Eran Zmora, Yoram Roz, Sefi Bar, Sara Barhom, and Ido Peretz, to Meirav and Rachel, who supported and helped me, who lent me an ear and showed great patience, but most of all, who encouraged me and cared.

MORE FROM THIS SERIES

Surviving the Forest *by Adiva Geffen*

Shurka, her husband and their two children lived a fairytale life in their idyllic village in Poland. Or so they thought… When WWII breaks out, they are forced to flee their home and escape into the dark forest. There, surrounded by animals, they know that this is their only hope of hiding from the real beasts. They have no idea what awaits them, but they know that doing nothing is not an option if they want to survive.

Escaping on the Danube River *by Shmuel David*

Europe, 1939: As the Nazi threat becomes a terrifying reality, Hanne and Inge know that their only option to survive is a daring escape down the Danube river. But their journey becomes increasingly perilous as time goes by. On board a ship, they fall in love, but their desire to build a new life together is in serious danger…

My Name is Vittoria *by Dafna Vitale Ben Bassat*

Vittoria is a noble Jewish woman living in northern Italy. When the Nazis invade her quiet town, She and her family are forced to flee and cross the border under fake identities. But not everything goes according to plan. One of her children is not allowed to cross the border with the rest of the family and must be left behind. Now, Vittoria must make a critical decision that could scar her and her family forever.

The Jewish Spy *by Hayuta Katzenelson*

Poland 1938. Rivka sends her husband and three beloved children to the United States, where they will find safe shelter from the war. She tells everyone that she is staying behind to care for her aging parents, but in reality her motive for remaining in Poland is entirely different. Beyond her work as librarian, Rivka serves as a spy for the Jewish underground. Rivka's brave choice may come at a painful price - losing her own family.

YOU MIGHT ALSO BE INTERESTED IN:
BEST SELLING WORLD WAR II HOLOCAUST MEMOIRS

I Only Wanted to Live *by Arie Tamir*

For 6 long torturous years the only thing that kept Leosz safe in the whirlwind of the Holocaust was his unwavering will to live. This is the incredible and inspiring story of a 6-year-old boy who managed to survive all possible levels of hell by clinging on to life.

Lalechka *By Amira Keidar*

A little girl, smuggled out of a Ghetto by her parents. Two brave women, willing to risk their lives. An inspirational story of survival based on the unique journal written by the girl's mother during the annihilation of the ghetto.

The Strange Ways of Providence in My Life *by Krystyna Carmi*

Krystyna Carmi's childhood in 1930's Poland was full of happy moments. But her happy childhood did not last long. The second world war brought disasters upon her and the Jewish community. The death of her parents and sisters, hiding, hunger, thirst and fear for life. It might be easier to part with the world, but the strange ways of providence of her life have chosen for her to live. A remarkable true story of survival against all odds.

Raking Light from Ashes *by Relli Robinson*

When Relli was just a baby, the Nazis occupied Poland and she, together with her parents, was imprisoned in the Warsaw Ghetto, a final station before death. This is the amazing story of a young Jewish girl holding a false identity, who was able to overcome the most difficult times in the history of humankind thanks to kindhearted, courageous people and a tenacious capacity for survival.

Courage and Grace *by Yoseph Komem*

Joseph and Yitzhak are two young brothers hiding under fake Christian identities in the Aryan section of a city in Poland during the Holocaust. The two brothers know that their lives are in constant danger and that any mistake may expose their true identities, leading them to a horrific death. They are lucky to receive assistance from their courageous gentile friends, but their lives outside the ghetto become increasingly difficult and complex with every passing day…